Language in Thought and Action

THIRD EDITION

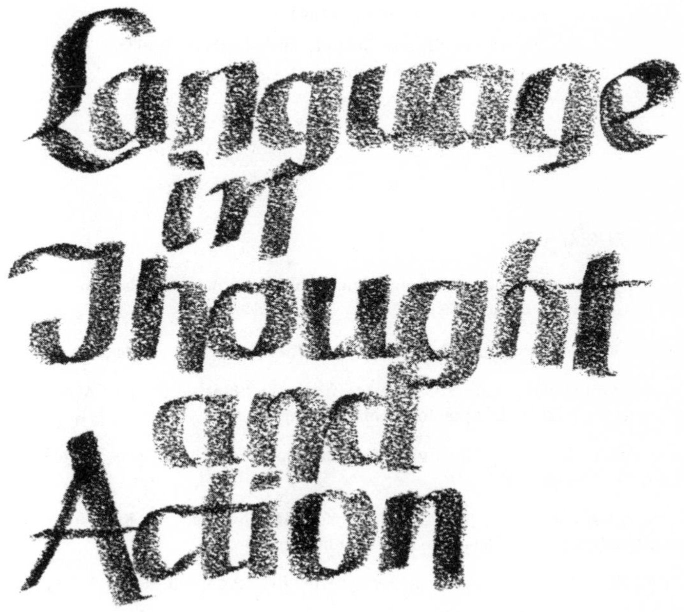

S. I. HAYAKAWA

In consultation with
Arthur Asa Berger and Arthur Chandler
San Francisco State College

HARCOURT BRACE JOVANOVICH, INC.
New York / Chicago / San Francisco / Atlanta

Cover photo by Lynn Karlin

Paperbound ISBN: 0-15-550118-6
Hardbound ISBN: 0-15-148097-4
Library of Congress Catalog Card Number: 75-182338
Printed in the United States of America

ACKNOWLEDGMENTS

The author wishes to thank the following publishers and copyright holders for their permission to reprint the material listed below:

Anderson & Ritchie: For excerpt from *Words and Their Meaning* by Aldous Huxley.

Appleton-Century-Crofts, Inc.: For excerpts from the *Illiteracy of the Literate* by H. R. Huse, copyright, 1933 by D. Appleton-Century Company, Inc.

Barrie & Jenkins Ltd.: For "The Guitarist Tunes Up" from *On a Calm Shore* by Frances Cornford, The Cresset Press.

Delacorte Press: For excerpt from *God Bless You, Mr. Rosewater* by Kurt Vonnegut, Jr., A Seymour Lawrence book, Delacorte Press, Publisher.

ETC.: A Review of General Semantics: For excerpts from the writings of S. I. Hayakawa.

Faber and Faber Ltd.: For "A Study of Reading Habits" from *The Whitsun Weddings* by Philip Larkin. Reprinted by permission of Faber and Faber Ltd.

Fawcett Publications, Inc.: For excerpts from *True Confessions*, August 1948. Courtesy of *True Confessions*. Copyright 1948 Fawcett Publications, Inc.

Grove Press, Inc.: For *Jealousy* from *Two Novels* by Alain Robbe-Grillet. Reprinted by permission of Grove Press, Inc. Translated by Richard Howard. Copyright © 1965 by Grove Press, Inc. *Jealousy* copyright © 1959 by Grove Press, Inc.

Harcourt Brace Jovanovich, Inc.: For excerpts from T. S. Eliot; from *The Meaning of Meaning*, 3rd Edition, by C. K. Ogden and I. A. Richards; and from *The Child's Conception of the World* by Jean Piaget.

Harper & Row, Publishers, Incorporated: For excerpts from *The Mind in the Making* by James Harvey Robinson; and for "Commuter" from *The Lady Is Cold* by E. B. White, copyright 1929 by Harper & Row, Publishers, Incorporated, reprinted with their permission.

Holt, Rinehart and Winston, Inc.: For "Fire and Ice" by Robert Frost. From *The Poetry of Robert Frost*, edited by Edward Connery Lathem. Copyright 1923 by Holt, Rinehart and Winston, Inc., copyright 1951 by Robert Frost, reprinted by permission of Holt, Rinehart and Winston, Inc.; and for "Happiness" from *Chicago Poems* by Carl Sandburg, copyright 1916 by Holt, Rinehart and Winston, Inc., copyright renewed 1944 by Carl Sandburg, reprinted by permission of Holt, Rinehart and Winston, Inc.

Houghton Mifflin Company: For excerpt from *The Human Use of Human Beings* by N. Wiener, Houghton Mifflin Company, Publisher.

Little, Brown and Company: For "Curiosity." Copyright © 1959 by Alastair Reid. This poem originally appeared in *The New Yorker*. From *Passwords* by Alastair Reid, by permission of Atlantic-Little, Brown and Co.

Masses & Mainstream: For excerpt from "The Cult of the Proper Word" by Margaret Schlauch, *New Masses*, April 15, 1947.

McGraw-Hill Book Company: For excerpt from *Understanding Media* by Marshall McLuhan. Copyright 1964 by Marshall McLuhan. Used with permission of McGraw-Hill Book Company.

Hughes Mearns: For "The Man Who Wasn't There." Reprinted by permission of the author.

Oxford University Press: For excerpt from *Problems of Philosophy* by Bertrand Russell, Oxford University Press, Publisher.

Laurence Pollinger Limited: For excerpt from "Morality and the Novel" (in *Phoenix*) by D. H. Lawrence, published in England by William Heinemann Ltd., used by permission of Laurence Pollinger Limited and the estate of the late Mrs. Frieda Lawrence; and for "Happiness" from *Chicago Poems* by Carl Sandburg, published in England by Jonathan Cape Limited.

Princeton University Press: For excerpt from "Has History Any Meaning," in Karl R. Popper, *The Open Society and Its Enemies*, Vol. II, 5th revised edition, 1966, Princeton University Press and Routledge and Kegan Paul, 5th edition, 1966, Princeton Paperback, 1971, p. 270. Reprinted by permission.

Random House, Inc.: Alfred A. Knopf, Inc.: For excerpt from *Culture Against Man* by Jules Henry, p. 59; for "Buick" by Karl Shapiro. Copyright 1941 by Karl Shapiro. Reprinted from *Poems 1940–1953* by Karl Shapiro, by permission of Random House, Inc.; for "Dream Deferred," copyright 1951 by Langston Hughes. Reprinted from *The Panther and the Lash*, by Langston Hughes, by permission of Alfred A. Knopf, Inc.; and for "A Study of Reading Habits" from *The Whitsun Weddings* by Philip Larkin. Copyright © 1964 by Philip Larkin. Reprinted by permission of Random House. Inc.

William H. Schneider. For cartoons from *Danger: Men Talking*, Random House, Inc. Copyright 1954, © 1955, 1963, 1965 by William H. Schneider. Reprinted by permission of William H. Schneider.

Charles Scribner's Sons: For "Invictus" by W. E. Henley, and for excerpt from *A Farewell to Arms* by Ernest Hemingway.

Simon & Schuster, Inc.: For excerpts from *The Story of Civilization*: Vol. IV, by Will Durant, copyright 1950; and from *The Lessons of History*, by Will and Ariel Durant, copyright 1968, Simon & Schuster, Inc., Publisher.

The Viking Press, Inc.: For excerpt from "Morality and the Novel" (in *Phoenix*) by D. H. Lawrence.

E. B. White: For "Commuter" from *The Lady Is Cold* by E. B. White.

preface

To learn to think more clearly, to speak and write more effectively, and to listen and read with greater understanding—these have been the goals of the study of language from the days of the medieval trivium to present-day high school and college English. This book tries to approach these traditional goals by the methods of modern semantics, that is, through an understanding in biological and functional terms of the role of language in human life, and through an understanding of the different uses of language: language to persuade and control behavior, language to transmit information, language to create and express social cohesion, and the language of poetry and the imagination. Words that convey no information may nevertheless move carloads of shaving soap or cake-mix, as we all know from television commercials. Words can start people marching in the streets—and can stir others to stoning the marchers. Words that make no sense as prose can make a great deal of sense as poetry. Words that seem simple and clear to some may be puzzling and obscure to others. With words we sugarcoat our nastiest motives and our worst behavior, but with words we also formulate our highest ideals and aspirations. (Do the words we utter arise as a result of our thoughts, or are our thoughts determined by the linguistic systems we happen to have been taught?) To understand how language works, what pitfalls it conceals, what its possibilities are, is to understand what is central to the complicated business of living the life of a human being. To be concerned with the relation between language and reality, between words and what they stand for in the speaker's or the hearer's thoughts and emotions, is to approach the study of language as both an intellectual and a moral discipline.

Perhaps an illustration will clarify my position. What is the teacher's duty when a child says in class, "Taters ain't doin' good this year"? Traditionally, teachers of English and speech have seen their first duty as that of correcting the child's grammar, pronunciation, and diction in order to bring these up to literate standards. The teacher with a semantic orientation will give priority to a different task. He will ask the student such questions as "What potatoes do you mean? Those on your father's farm, or those throughout the county? How do you know? From personal observation? From reports from credible sources?" In short, the teacher of semantics will concern himself, and teach his students to concern themselves, first of all with the truth, the adequacy, and the degree of trustworthiness of statements. Often, when students who are bored with studying grammar and diagraming sentences become interested in the content and purposes of communication, their hostility to linguistic instruction vanishes, and problems of grammatical and syntactical propriety are solved in passing.

Today the public is aware, perhaps to an unprecedented degree, of the role of communication in human affairs. This awareness arises in large part out of the urgency of the tensions existing everywhere between nation and nation, class and class, individual and individual, in a world that is undergoing rapid change and reorganization. It arises too out of the enormous powers for good and evil—powers apparent to even the least reflective members of society—that lie in the media of mass communication: the press, motion pictures, radio, and television.

The vacuum tube and transistor produced in the twentieth century a revolution in communication, a revolution probably more far-reaching in its effects than the invention of printing, which ushered in the Renaissance. The rising expectations of the people of Asia, Africa, and Latin America are due to advances in transportation and communication: the airplane, the jeep, the helicopter, bringing newspapers, magazines, motion pictures, and especially the radio. In thousands of remote villages, my African students tell me, people who formerly had no cultural contacts beyond the next village gather today around transistor radios to hear the news from London, New York, Tokyo, and Moscow—and start wanting to become citizens of a larger world than they have ever known before.

Television, too, is helping to change the world. In the United States, for example, commercial television invites everyone to participate fully in the benefits of an industrial and democratic culture by buying toothpastes and detergents and automobiles, by taking an interest in national and international affairs, by sharing the emotions and dreams and aspirations and values that are depicted in the entertainment. What television communicates to whites, it also communicates to Negroes, who constitute one-tenth of the nation. There is nothing to be surprised at, therefore, in the increased urgency of Negro demands, not only for better job opportunities, but for full rights as consumers to eat, drink, wear, and enjoy what all other Americans are daily urged to eat, drink, wear, and enjoy. A revolution in the patterns and techniques of communication always has more consequences than are dreamed of at the time the innovations are introduced. The increased density of the communication network in the nation and in the world resulting from technological advances means an increased tempo of social change—and therefore an increased need for semantic sophistication on the part of everyone.

The original version of this book, *Language in Action*, published in 1941, was in many respects a response to the dangers of propaganda, especially as exemplified in Adolf Hitler's success in persuading millions to share his maniacal and destructive views. It was my conviction then, as it remains now, that everyone needs to have a habitually critical attitude toward language—his own as well as that of others—both for the sake of his personal well-being and for his adequate functioning as a citizen. Hitler is gone, but if the majority of our fellow citizens are more susceptible to the slogans of fear and race hatred than to those of peaceful accommodation and mutual respect among human beings, our political liberties remain at the mercy of any eloquent and unscrupulous demagogue.

Semantics is the study of human interaction through communication. Communication leads sometimes to cooperation and sometimes to conflict. The basic ethical assumption of semantics, analogous to the medical assumption that health is preferable to illness, is that cooperation is preferable to conflict. This assumption, implicit in *Language in Action*, was made explicit as a central and unifying theme in *Language in Thought and Action*, an expansion of the earlier work, published in 1949. (Second Edition, 1964.) It remains the central theme of the third edition.

The principal change in the third edition is the new material in the "Applications" at the end of each chapter. A book on semantics is not something simply to be read and put aside. Its principles, to be meaningful, must be tried out in one's own thinking and speaking and writing and behavior; they must be tested against one's own observations and experience. The "Applications" therefore have a double purpose; they offer a means whereby the reader may, in addition to reading about semantics, absorb the semanticist's point of view by undertaking actual semantic investigations and exercises. They are also a way of urging the reader not to take my word for anything that is in this book. (It is further hoped that the reader will find the "Applications" amusing. The world is fortunately full of people who say and write wonderfully preposterous things for the semanticist's notebook.)

In addition to new Applications, examples and references throughout the text have been brought up-to-date; recent books have been added to the lists found in several of the Applications and to the end-of-the-book bibliography. And the new book is enlivened by the addition of semantic cartoons by my friend William H. Schneider, reprinted from his book *Danger: Men Talking*.

My deepest debt in this book is to the General Semantics ("non-Aristotelian system") of Alfred Korzybski. I have also drawn heavily upon the works of other contributors to semantic thought: especially C. K. Ogden and I. A. Richards, Thorstein Veblen, Edward Sapir, Susanne Langer, Leonard Bloomfield, Karl R. Popper, Thurman Arnold, Jerome Frank, Jean Piaget, Charles Morris, Wendell Johnson, Irving J. Lee, Ernst Cassirer, Anatol Rapoport, Stuart Chase. I am also deeply indebted to the writings of numerous psychologists and psychiatrists with one or another of the dynamic points of view inspired by Sigmund Freud: Karl Menninger, Carl Rogers, Kurt Lewin, Abraham Maslow, Prescott Lecky,

Rudolph Dreikurs, Milton Rokeach. I have also found extremely helpful the writings of cultural anthropologists, especially those of Benjamin Lee Whorf, Ruth Benedict, Clyde Kluckhohn, Leslie A. White, Margaret Mead, Dorothy Lee, Weston La Barre.

Insight into human symbolic behavior and into human interaction through symbolic mechanisms comes from all sorts of disciplines: not only from linguistics, philosophy, psychology, and cultural anthropology, but from attitude research and public opinion study, from new techniques in psychotherapy, from physiology and neurology, from mathematical biology and cybernetics. How are all these separate insights to be brought together and synthesized? This is a task which I cannot claim to have performed here, but I have examined the problem long enough to believe that it cannot be done without some set of broad and informing principles such as is to be found in the General Semantics of Korzybski.

Since anything approaching a full citation of sources would have made these pages unduly formidable in appearance, I have appended, in lieu of detailed documentation, a list of books (pp. 275–78) which I have found especially useful. However, none of the authors whose works I have profited by is to be held accountable for the errors or shortcomings of this book or for the liberties I have taken in the restatement, application, and modification of existing theories.

Professors Berger and Chandler of San Francisco State College have suggested revisions and provided new "Applications." Professor Richard Herrnstadt, Iowa State University, and Professor Roger A. Richards, North Shore Community College, Beverly, Massachusetts, reviewed the Second Edition and made many helpful suggestions for the revision. I am indebted also to many students; to innumerable colleagues in the teaching profession including those who have provided "Applications" and help with earlier editions; to business executives, training directors, and advertising men; to friends in medicine, law, labor relations, and government (especially in the diplomatic service) whose criticisms and discussions have helped to clarify and enlarge my views.

S. I. H.

President,
San Francisco State College

contents

Language in Thought and Action

BOOK ONE

the functions of language

"A great deal of attention has been paid . . . to the technical languages in which men of science do their specialized thinking. . . . But the colloquial usages of everyday speech, the literary and philosophical dialects in which men do their thinking about the problems of morals, politics, religion and psychology—these have been strangely neglected. We talk about "mere matters of words" in a tone which implies that we regard words as things beneath the notice of a serious-minded person.

This is a most unfortunate attitude. For the fact is that words play an enormous part in our lives and are therefore deserving of the closest study. The old idea that words possess magical powers is false; but its falsity is the distortion of a very important truth. Words *do* have a magical effect—but not in the way that the magicians supposed, and not on the objects they were trying to influence. Words are magical in the way they affect the minds of those who use them. "A mere matter of words," we say contemptuously, forgetting that words have power to mould men's thinking, to canalize their feeling, to direct their willing and acting. Conduct and character are largely determined by the nature of the words we currently use to discuss ourselves and the world around us."

Aldous Huxley
Words and Their Meanings

Whenever agreement or assent is arrived at in human affairs, . . . THIS AGREEMENT IS REACHED BY LINGUISTIC PROCESSES, OR ELSE IT IS NOT REACHED.

Benjamin Lee Whorf

foreword

Red-Eye and the Woman Problem: A Semantic Parable

Once, long ago, tens of thousands of years before history began, people were worried, as they have often been since, about the chaotic condition of their lives. For in those days men took by force the women they desired. There was no way of stopping them.

If you wanted a woman but found that she was already the partner of another man, all you needed to do was to kill him and drag her home. Naturally, someone else might slug you a little later to get her away from you, but that was the chance you took if you wanted a woman at all.

Consequently, there wasn't much of what you could call family life. The men were too busy suspiciously watching each other. And time that might have been spent fishing or hunting or otherwise raising the general standard of living was wasted in constant and anxious measures to defend one's woman.

Many people saw that this was no way for human beings to live. As they said among themselves: "Truly we are strange creatures. In some ways we are highly civilized. We no longer eat raw flesh, as did our savage ancestors. Our technical men have perfected stone arrowheads and powerful bows so that we can slay the fastest deer that runs. Our medicine men can foretell the running of the fish in the streams, and our sorcerers drive away illnesses. At the Institute for Advanced Studies at Notecnirp, a group of bright young men are said to be working out a dance that will make the rain fall. Little by little, we are mastering the secrets of nature, so that we are able to live like civilized men and not like beasts.

"Yet," they continued, "we have not mastered ourselves. There are those among us who continue to snatch women away from each other by force, so that every man of necessity lives in fear of his fellows. People agree, of course, that all this killing ought to be stopped. But no one is stopping it. The most fundamental of human problems, that of securing a mate and bringing up one's children under some kind of decent, orderly system, remains unsolved. Unless we can find some way of placing the man-woman relationship on a decent and human basis, our pretensions to civilization are hollow."

For many generations the thoughtful men of the tribe pondered this problem. How could men and women, living peacefully together with their children, be protected from the lusts of the few, who went around killing other men in order to possess their women?

Slowly, and only after centuries of groping discussion, they evolved an answer. They proposed that men and women who have decided to live together permanently be bound by a "contract," by which they meant the uttering, before the priests of the tribe, of solemn promises binding on their future behavior. This contract was to be known as marriage. The man in the marriage was to be known as a husband, the woman as a wife.

They further proposed that this contract be observed and honored by all the people of the tribe. In other words, if a given woman, Slendershanks, was known to be the wife of a given man, Beetlebrow, everyone in the tribe was to agree not to molest their domestic arrangements. Furthermore, they proposed that if anyone failed to respect this contract and killed another man to possess that man's wife, he was to be punished by the collective force of tribal authority.

In order to put these proposals into effect, a great conference was called, and delegates arrived from all branches of the tribe. Some came with glad hearts, filled with the hope that humanity was about to enter a new era. Some came with faint hearts, not expecting much to come out of the conference, but feeling that it was at least worth a try. Some came simply because they had been elected delegates and were getting their expenses paid; they were willing to go along with whoever proved to be in the majority.

All the time the conference was going on, however, a big, backward savage called Red-Eye the Atavism, who was so loud-mouthed that he always had a following in spite of his unprepossessing personality, kept shouting scornful remarks from the sidelines. He called the delegates "visionaries," "eggheads," "impractical theorists," "starry-eyed dreamers," "crackpots," and "pantywaists." He gleefully pointed out that many of the delegates had themselves been, at an earlier date, women-snatchers. (This, unfortunately, was true.)

He shouted to Hairy Hands, who was one of the delegates, "You don't think Brawny Legs is going to leave your woman alone just because he makes an agreement, do you?" And he shouted to Brawny Legs, "You don't think Hairy Hands is going to leave your woman alone just because he makes an agreement, do you?" And he poured derision on all the delegates, referring to their discussion as "striped-pants kind of talk, like who ever heard of 'husband,' and 'wife,' and 'marriage' and all that double-dome Choctaw!"

Then Red-Eye the Atavism turned to his following, the crowd of timid and tiny-minded people who always found their self-assurance in the loudness of his voice, and he yelled, "Look at those fool delegates, will you? They think they can change human nature!"

Thereupon the crowd rolled over with laughter and repeated after him, "Haw, haw! They think they can change human nature!"

That broke up the conference. It was another two thousand years, therefore, before marriage was finally instituted in that tribe—two thousand years during which innumerable men were killed defending their women, two thousand years during which men who had no designs on their neighbors' women killed each other as a precaution against being killed themselves, two thousand years during which the arts of peace languished, two thousand years during which people despaired as they dreamed of a distant future time when a man might live with the woman of his choice without arming himself to the teeth and watching over her day and night.

What this illustrates is, of course, that all basic agreements by means of which human beings learn to live together amicably and harmoniously have grown out of prolonged thought, discussion, argumentation, and persuasion. Human institutions such as marriage, law, and government do not just happen somehow. They are social inventions, devised and developed in response to an urgently felt need for order in our lives.

Today many such institutions exist to make life orderly and livable. But as the world changes, new problems of social adjustment arise, and there seems constantly to be much more to do. Blacks and whites, Protestants and Catholics, Arabs and Israelis, French-speaking and Flemish-speaking Belgians, East and West Pakistanis, capitalists and communists, must somehow or other learn to live together.

As for instituting the social agreements to prevent international violence in a world of hydrogen bombs and guided missiles, we don't have two thousand years to find the solution. Indeed, we don't have two hundred years. Nor even twenty. Perhaps not even two.

And *that's* our problem.

One cannot but wonder at this constantly recurring phrase "getting something for nothing," as if it were the peculiar and perverse ambition of disturbers of society. Except for our animal outfit, practically all we have is handed to us gratis. Can the most complacent reactionary flatter himself that he invented the art of writing or the printing press, or discovered his religious, economic, and moral convictions, or any of the devices which supply him with meat and raiment or any of the sources of such pleasures as he may derive from literature or the fine arts? In short, civilization is little else than getting something for nothing.

James Harvey Robinson

language and survival

What Animals Shall We Imitate?

People who think of themselves as tough-minded and realistic, among them influential political leaders and businessmen as well as go-getters and small-time hustlers, tend to take it for granted that human nature is selfish and that life is a struggle in which only the fittest may survive. According to this philosophy, the basic law by which man must live, in spite of his surface veneer of civilization, is the law of the jungle. The "fittest" are those who can bring to the struggle superior force, superior cunning, and superior ruthlessness.

The wide currency of this philosophy of the "survival of the fittest" enables people who act ruthlessly and selfishly, whether in personal rivalries, business competition, or international relations, to allay their consciences by telling themselves that they are only obeying a law of nature. But a disinterested observer is entitled to ask whether the ruthlessness of the tiger, the cunning of the fox, and obedience to the law of the jungle are, in their *human* applications, actually evidences of *human* fitness to survive. If human beings are to pick up pointers on behavior from the lower animals, are there not animals other than beasts of prey from which we might learn lessons in survival?

We might, for example, point to the rabbit or the deer and define fitness to survive as superior rapidity in running away from our enemies. We might point to the earthworm or the mole and define it as the ability to keep out of sight and out of the way. We might point to the oyster or the housefly and define it as the ability to propagate our kind faster than our enemies can eat us up. In Aldous Huxley's *Brave New World*, we see a world designed by those who would model human beings after the social ants. The world, under the management of a super-brain trust, might be made as well integrated, smooth, and efficient as an ant colony and, as Huxley shows, just about as meaningless. If we simply look to animals in order to define what we mean by "fitness to survive," there is no limit to the subhuman systems of behavior that can be devised: we may emulate lobsters, dogs, sparrows, parakeets, giraffes, skunks, or the parasitical worms, because they have all obviously survived in one way or another. We are still entitled to ask, however, if *human* survival does not revolve around a different kind of fitness from that of the lower animals.[1]

Because of the wide prevalence of the dog-eat-dog, survival-of-the-fittest philosophy in our world (although the H-bomb has awakened *some* people to the need for a change in philosophy), it is worthwhile to look into the present scientific standing of the phrase "survival of the fittest." Biologists distinguish between two kinds of struggle for survival. First, there is the *interspecific* struggle, warfare between different species of animals, as between wolves and deer or men and bacteria. Second, there is the *intraspecific* struggle, warfare among members of a single species, as when rats fight other rats or men fight other men. A great deal of evidence in modern biology indicates that those species which have developed elaborate means of intraspecific competition often unfit themselves for interspecific competition, so that such species are either already extinct or are threatened with extinction at any time. The peacock's tail, although useful in sexual competition against other peacocks, is only a hindrance in coping with the environment or competing against other species. The peacock could therefore be wiped out overnight by a sudden change in ecological balance. There is evidence, too, that strength and fierceness in fighting and killing other animals, whether in interspecific or intraspecific competition, have never been enough in themselves to guarantee the survival of a species. Many a mammoth reptile, equipped

[1]For an analysis of the social implications of this question, see Richard Hofstadter's *Social Darwinism in American Thought* (1944).

with magnificent offensive and defensive armaments, ceased millions of years ago to walk the earth.[2]

If we are going to talk about human survival, one of the first things to do, even if we grant that men must fight to live, is to distinguish between those qualities that are useful to men in fighting the environment and other species (for example, floods, storms, wild animals, insects, or bacteria) and those qualities (such as aggressiveness) that are useful in fighting other men.

The principle that if we don't hang together we shall all hang separately was discovered by nature long before it was put into words by man. Cooperation within a species (and sometimes with other species) is essential to the survival of most living creatures. Man, moreover, is the *talking* animal—and any theory of human survival that leaves this fact out of account is no more scientific than would be a theory of beaver survival that failed to consider the interesting uses a beaver makes of its teeth and flat tail. Let us see what talking—human communication—means.

Cooperation

When someone shouts at you, "Look out!" and you jump just in time to avoid being hit by an automobile, you owe your escape from injury to the fundamental cooperative act by which most of the higher animals survive, namely, communication by means of noises. You did not see the car coming; nevertheless, someone did, and he made certain noises to communicate his alarm to you. In other words, although your nervous system did not record the danger, you were unharmed because another nervous system did. You had, for the time being, the advantage of someone else's nervous system in addition to your own.

Indeed, most of the time when we are listening to the noises people make or looking at the black marks on paper that stand for these noises, we are drawing upon the experiences of others in order to make up for what we ourselves have missed. Obviously, the more an individual can make use of the nervous systems of others to supplement his own, the easier it is for him to survive. And, of course, the more individuals there are in a group cooperating by making helpful noises at each other, the better it is for all—within the limits, naturally, of the group's talents for social organization. Birds and animals congregate with their own kind and make

[2]For example, the brain of the massive [about two tons] stegosaur weighed only about 70 grams, or 2½ ounces. . . . By contrast, even the brain of the sheep—which is not a particularly brilliant animal—weighs 130 grams, greater both in absolute size and even more so relatively to body size. . . . So far as strength is concerned, nothing could stop one of the great dinosaurs when it was on its way; but while it is all very well to be able to go where you are going, the reasons for going and what is seen and understood on the way are even more important." Weston La Barre, *The Human Animal* (1954), pp. 24–25.

noises when they find food or become alarmed. In fact, gregariousness as an aid to survival and self-defense is forced upon animals as well as upon men by the necessity of uniting nervous systems even more than by the necessity of uniting physical strength. Societies, both animal and human, might almost be regarded as huge cooperative nervous systems.

While animals use only a few limited cries, however, human beings use extremely complicated systems of sputtering, hissing, gurgling, clucking, cooing noises called *language*, with which they express and report what goes on in their nervous systems. Language is, in addition to being more complicated, immeasurably more flexible than the animal cries from which it was developed—so flexible indeed that it can be used not only to report the tremendous variety of things that go on in the human nervous system but also *to report those reports*. That is, when an animal yelps, he may cause a second animal to yelp in imitation or alarm; the second yelp, however, is not *about* the first yelp. But when a man says, "I see a river," a second man can say, "He says he sees a river"—which is a statement about a statement. About this statement-about-a-statement further statements can be made—and about these, still more. *Language, in short, can be about language*. This is a fundamental way in which human noise-making systems differ from the cries of animals.

The Pooling of Knowledge

In addition to having developed language, man has also developed means of making, on clay tablets, bits of wood or stone, skins of animals, and paper, more or less permanent marks and scratches which *stand for* language. These marks enable him to communicate with people who are beyond the reach of his voice, both in space and in time. There is a long course of evolution from the marked trees that indicated Indian trails to metropolitan daily newspapers, but they have this in common: they pass on what one individual has known to other individuals, for their convenience or, in the broadest sense, instruction. Many of the lobstick trails in the Canadian woods, marked by Indians long since dead, can be followed to this day. Archimedes is dead, but we still have his reports on what he observed in his experiments in physics. Keats is dead, but he can still tell us how he felt on first reading Chapman's Homer. From newspapers, radio, and television we learn with great rapidity facts about the world we live in. From books and magazines we learn how hundreds of people whom we shall never be able to see have felt and thought. All this information is helpful to us at one time or another in throwing light on our own problems.

A human being, then, is never dependent on his own experience alone for his information. Even in a primitive culture he can make use of the experience of his neighbors, friends, and relatives, which they communicate to him by means of language. Therefore, instead of remaining helpless because of the limitations of his own experience and knowledge, instead of having to discover what others have already discovered, instead of exploring the false trails they explored and repeating their errors, he can *go on from where they left off*. Language, that is to say, makes progress possible.

Indeed, most of what we call the human characteristics of our species are expressed and developed through our ability to cooperate by means of our systems of making meaningful noises and meaningful scratches on paper. Even people who belong to backward cultures in which writing has not been invented are able to exchange information and to hand down from generation to generation considerable stores of traditional knowledge. There seems, however, to be a limit both to the amount and to the trustworthiness of knowledge that can be transmitted orally.[3] But when writing is invented, a tremendous step forward is taken. The accuracy of reports can be checked and rechecked by successive generations of observers. The amount of knowledge accumulated ceases to be limited by people's ability to remember what has been told them. The result is that in any literate culture of a few centuries' standing, human beings accumulate vast stores of knowledge—far more than any individual in that culture can read in his lifetime, let alone remember. These stores of knowledge, which are being added to constantly, are made widely available to all who want them through such mechanical processes as printing and computerized information storing and through such distributive agencies as the book trade, the newspaper and magazine trade, and library systems. The result is that all of us who can read any of the major European or Asiatic languages are potentially in touch with the intellectual resources of centuries of human endeavor in all parts of the civilized world.

A physician, for example, who does not know how to treat a patient suffering from a rare disease can look up the disease in the *Index Medicus*, which will send him in turn to medical journals published in all parts of the world. In these he may find records of similar cases as reported and described by a physician in Rotterdam, Holland, in 1913, by another physician in Bangkok, Siam, in 1935, and by still other physicians in Kansas City in 1954. With such records before him, he can better handle his own case. Again, if a person is worried about ethics, he is not limited to the advice of the pastor of the Elm Street Baptist Church; he may go to Confucius, Aristotle, Jesus, Spinoza, and many others whose reflections on ethical problems are on record. If he is worried about love, he can get insights not only from his mother or best friend but from Sappho, Ovid,

[3]This is so despite the fact that preliterate people often exhibit remarkable feats of memory, such as the ability to remember every landmark and detail of a journey that may extend for hundreds of miles or the ability to recall verbatim folk tales and sagas that may take days to recite. Literate people, who rely on notebooks and reference books, have relatively very poor memories.

Propertius, Shakespeare, Donne, Havelock Ellis, or any of a thousand others who knew something about it and wrote down what they knew.

Language, that is to say, is the indispensable mechanism of human life—of life such as ours that is molded, guided, enriched, and made possible by the accumulation of the *past* experience of members of our own species. Dogs and cats and chimpanzees do not, so far as we can tell, increase their wisdom, their information, or their control over their environment from one generation to the next. But human beings do. The cultural accomplishments of the ages, the invention of cooking, of weapons, of writing, of printing, of methods of building, of games and amusements, of means of transportation, and the discoveries of all the arts and sciences come to us as *free gifts from the dead.* These gifts, which none of us has done anything to earn, offer us not only the opportunity for a richer life than our forebears enjoyed but also the opportunity to add to the sum total of human achievement by our own contributions, however small they may be.

To be able to read and write, therefore, is to learn to profit by and take part in the greatest of human achievements—that which makes all other achievements possible—namely, the pooling of our experiences in great cooperative stores of knowledge, available (except where special privilege, censorship, or suppression stand in the way) to all. From the warning cry of primitive man to the latest newsflash or scientific monograph, language is social. Cultural and intellectual cooperation is the great principle of *human* life.

This is by no means an easy principle to accept or to understand—except as a kind of pious truism that we should like, because we are well-meaning people, to believe. We live in a highly competitive society, each of us trying to outdo the other in wealth, in popularity or social prestige, in dress, in scholastic grades or golf scores. As we read our daily papers, there is always news of conflict rather than of cooperation—conflict between labor and management, between rival corporations or movie stars, between rival political parties and nations. Over us all hangs the perpetual fear of another war even more unthinkably horrible than the last. One is often tempted to say that conflict, rather than cooperation, is the great governing principle of human life.

But what such a philosophy overlooks is that, despite all the competition at the surface, there is a huge substratum of cooperation *taken for granted* that keeps the world going. The coordination of the efforts of engineers, actors, musicians, cameramen, utilities companies, typists, program directors, advertising agencies, writers, and hundreds of others is required to put on a single television program. Hundreds of thousands of persons cooperate in the production of motor cars, including suppliers and shippers of raw materials from different parts of the earth. Any organized business activity whatsoever is an elaborate act of cooperation, in which every individual worker contributes his share. A lockout or a strike is a *withdrawal of cooperation:* things are regarded as "back to normal" when cooperation is restored. We may indeed as individuals compete for jobs, but our function in the job, once we get it, is to contribute at the right time and place to that innumerable series of cooperative acts that eventually result in automobiles being manufactured, in cakes appearing in pastry shops, in department stores being able to serve their customers, in the trains and airlines running as scheduled.

This network of cooperation we have created is intricate and complex, and it has been relatively effective. But because it rests so profoundly upon human agreement, it is also fragile and vulnerable. Small groups of dissidents, using such tactics as intimidation and violence, can disrupt society and create chaos, leading to a breakdown in the network of cooperation. What is important for our purposes here is that all this coordination of effort necessary for the functioning of society is *of necessity achieved by language or else it is not achieved at all.*

The Niagara of Words

And how does all this affect Mr. T. C. Mits?[4] From the moment he switches on an early-morning news broadcast until he falls asleep at night over a novel or magazine, or in front of his television, he is, like all other people living in modern, civilized conditions, swimming in words. Newspaper editors, politicians, salesmen, disc jockeys, columnists, luncheon-club speakers, and clergymen; colleagues at work, friends, relatives, wife and children; market reports, direct-mail advertising, books, and billboards—all are assailing him with words all day long. And Mr. Mits himself is constantly contributing to that verbal Niagara every time he puts on an advertising campaign, delivers a speech, writes a letter, or even chats with his friends.

When things go wrong in Mr. Mits's life—when he is worried, perplexed, or nervous, when family, business, or national affairs are not going as he thinks they should, when he finds himself making blunder after blunder in personal or financial matters—he blames a number of things for his difficulties. Sometimes he blames the weather, sometimes his health or the state of his nerves, sometimes his glands; if the problem is a larger one, he may blame his environment, the economic system he lives under, a foreign nation, or the cultural pattern of his society. When he is pondering the difficulties of other people, he may attribute their troubles too to causes such as these, and he may add still another, namely, "human nature." (He doesn't blame his own "human nature" unless he is in a very bad way indeed.) It rarely, if ever, occurs to him to investigate,

[4]Lillian and Hugh Lieber, of Long Island University, are responsible for christening this gentleman The Celebrated Man In The Street. Mits's wife's name is, of course, Wits. See *The Education of T. C. Mits* (1944) and *Mits, Wits, and Logic* (1960).

among other things, the nature and constituents of that daily verbal Niagara as a possible source of trouble.

Indeed, there are few occasions on which Mr. Mits thinks about language as such. He pauses from time to time over a grammatical point. Sometimes he feels an uneasiness about his own verbal accomplishments, and so begins to consider improving his vocabulary. Occasionally he runs into advertisements on "how to increase your word power" and wonders if he shouldn't take steps to become a more effective persuader—and he may buy a book or take a course, which may make him feel better for a while. Confronted by the Niagara of words—the magazines he hasn't time to keep up with and the books he knows he should read—he wonders if it wouldn't help to take a course in speed reading.

Once in a while he is struck by the fact that some people (although he never includes himself among these) twist the meanings of words, especially during the course of arguments, so that words are often very tricky. Occasionally, too, he notices, usually with irritation, that words sometimes mean different things to different people. This condition, he feels, could be corrected if people would only consult their dictionaries oftener and learn the "true meanings" of words. He knows, however, that they will not—at least, not any oftener than he does, which is not very often—so that he puts this failure down as another instance of the weakness of human nature.

This, unfortunately, is about the limit of Mr. Mits's linguistic speculations. And here Mr. Mits is representative not only of the general public, but also of many scientific workers, publicists, and writers. Like most people, he takes words as much for granted as the air he breathes, and he gives them about as much thought. (After all, he has been talking ever since he can remember.) Mr. Mits's body automatically adjusts itself, within certain limits, to changes in climate or atmosphere, to shifts from cold to warm, from dry to moist, from fresh to foul; no conscious effort on his part is required to make these adjustments. Nevertheless, he is ready to acknowledge the effect that climate and air have upon his physical well-being, and he may even take measures to protect himself from unhealthy air, either by getting away from it, or by installing air-conditioning systems to purify it. But Mr. Mits, like the rest of us, also adjusts himself automatically to changes in the verbal climate, from one type of discourse to another, from one set of terms to another, from the listening habits of one kind of social occasion to those of another kind of social occasion, without conscious effort. However, he rarely, if ever, acknowledges the effect of his verbal climate on his mental health and well-being.

Nevertheless, Mr. Mits is profoundly involved in the words he absorbs daily and in the words he uses daily. Words in the newspaper make him pound his fist on the breakfast table. Words his superiors speak to him puff him out with pride or send him scurrying to work harder. Words about himself that he has overheard being spoken behind his back worry him sick. Words that he spoke before a clergyman some years ago have tied him to one woman for life. Words written down on pieces of paper keep him at his job or bring bills in his mail every month that keep him paying and paying. Words written down by other people, on the other hand, keep them paying him month after month. With words woven into almost every detail of his life, it seems amazing that Mr. Mits's thinking on the subject of language should be so limited.

Mr. Mits has also noticed that when large masses of people, for example those under totalitarian regimes, are permitted by their governments to hear and read only carefully selected words, their conduct becomes so strange that he can only regard it as mad. Yet, he has observed that some individuals who have the same educational attainments and the same access to varied sources of information as he has are nevertheless just as mad. He listens to the views of some of his neighbors and he cannot help wondering, "How can they think such things? Don't they see the same things happening that I see? They must be crazy!" "Does such madness," he asks, "illustrate again the 'inevitable frailty of human nature'?" Mr. Mits, who, as an American, likes to regard all things as possible, does not like the conclusion that "nothing can be done about it," but often he can hardly see how he can escape it. Occasionally, timidly, Mr. Mits approaches one more possibility: "Maybe I'm crazy myself. Maybe we're all nuts!" Such a conclusion leads to so complete an impasse, however, that he quickly drops the notion.

One reason for Mr. Mits's failure to get any further in his thinking about language is that he believes, as most people do, that words are not really important; what is important is the "ideas" they stand for. But what is an idea if it is not the *verbalization* of a cerebral itch? This, however, is something that has rarely, if ever, occurred to Mr. Mits. The fact that the implications of one set of terms may lead inevitably into blind alleys, while the implications of another set of terms may not; the fact that the historical or sentimental associations that some words have make calm discussion impossible so long as those words are employed; the fact that language has a multitude of different kinds of use and that great confusion arises from mistaking one kind of use for another; the fact that a person speaking a language of a structure entirely different from that of English, such as Japanese, Chinese, or Turkish, may not even think the same thoughts as an English-speaking person—these are unfamiliar notions to Mr. Mits, who has always assumed that the important thing is always to get one's ideas straight first, after which the words would take care of themselves.

Whether he realizes it or not, however, Mr. Mits is affected every hour of his life not only by the words he hears and uses, *but also by his unconscious assumptions about language.* If, for example, he likes the name Albert and would like to christen his child by that name but super-

Disarmament conference

stitiously avoids doing so because he once knew an Albert who committed suicide, he is operating, whether he realizes it or not, under certain assumptions about the relationship of language to reality. Such unconscious assumptions determine the effect that words have on him—which in turn determines the way he acts, whether wisely or foolishly. Words—the way he uses them and the way he takes them when spoken by others—largely shape his beliefs, his prejudices, his ideals, his aspirations. They constitute the moral and intellectual atmosphere in which he lives—in short, his *semantic environment.*

This book is devoted, then, to the study of the relationships among language, thought, and behavior. We shall examine language and people's linguistic habits as they reveal themselves in thinking (at least nine-tenths of which is talking to oneself), speaking, listening, reading, and writing. *It will be the basic assumption of this book that widespread intraspecific cooperation through the use of language is the fundamental mechanism of human survival. A parallel assumption will be that when the use of language results, as it so often does, in the creation or aggravation of disagreements and conflicts, there is something linguistically wrong with the speaker, the listener, or both.* Human fitness to survive means the ability to talk and write and listen and read in ways that increase the chances for you *and fellow-members of your species* to survive *together.*

APPLICATIONS

Since one of the goals of *Language in Thought and Action* is to give you not only an understanding of the workings of language, but also a sense of what language actually does in the course of our lives, each chapter in this book will conclude with a section entitled "Applications." Here you will be invited to apply the ideas just discussed. All the applications are designed either to test or to exercise your grasp of the chapter you have just read. Some applications will invite you to challenge the author's ideas; many have no "right answer" or "wrong answer." All should be used to explore the potential of language in action and in thought.

I. We all tend to assume that because our eyes have covered all the words of a chapter or a book, we can confidently assert that we have understood what we have read. One helpful way of checking our reading comprehension would be to follow the method Benjamin Franklin used. After reading an essay, he would close the book and attempt to reproduce the essay in writing as accurately as he could, both in form and content. Since most modern readers' stamina falls short of Franklin's, the following list is provided to gauge accuracy of comprehension. Indicate which of the following statements (a) are consistent with, (b) contradict, or (c) deal with concepts extraneous to those discussed in this chapter.

1. "Survival of the fittest" is the universal law governing the health or the extinction of all species.
2. The Civil War is an example of *intraspecific* struggle.
3. Rat poison is a weapon in an *interspecific* struggle.
4. Man's ability to use language is irrelevant to any theory of human survival.
5. We must attempt to find out how animals communicate before we can discover how man communicates.
6. Many species of animals accumulate knowledge from one generation to the next.
7. Cultural and intellectual cooperation is the great principle of human life.
8. We often take for granted the huge substratum of cooperation that underlies the daily operations of life.
9. Competition, even in economic enterprise, should be avoided.
10. The coordination of effort necessary for the functioning of society is achieved by language, or it is not achieved at all.
11. The faulty state of human nature is the source of man's shortcomings.
12. Words are not really important; what is important is the ideas they stand for.
13. Our semantic environment has been decaying in quality for several generations.
14. Talking to oneself is a symptom of insanity.
15. When the use of language creates or aggravates disagreements and conflicts, there is something linguistically wrong with the speaker, the listener, or both.

II. Discuss the following quotations in relation to this chapter:

1. Language has two interconnected merits: first, that it is social, and second, that it supplies public expression for thoughts which would otherwise remain private. Without language, or some prelinguistic analogue, our knowledge of the environment is confined to what our own senses have shown us, together with such inferences as our congenital constitution may prompt; but by the help of speech we are able to know what others can relate, and to relate what is no longer sensibly present but only remembered.

BERTRAND RUSSELL, *Human Knowledge: Its Scope and Limits*

2. No more talk! Revolution now!

Political Leaflet

3. Two young girls were introduced to each other at a party. Their host gave their names as Carol and Patricia. Carol immediately replied, "Oh, she doesn't look like a Patricia at all; she looks just like a Mary."

4. It would be difficult to exaggerate the degree to which we are influenced by those we influence.

ERIC HOFFER, *The Passionate State of Mind*

III. Further topics for discussion.

1. Sports are often considered citadels of competitiveness, since in most cases the goal is simply to win. But are there any areas of cooperation in sports? Is more or less cooperation required as the number of participants increases? Do all sports have rules—and if they do, why not disregard those rules if a loss seems imminent? What is the value, in terms of language, of having cheerleaders and a crowd of vocal supporters for a team? Can they actually affect the actions in which they take no direct part?

2. Do you adjust your listening habits to your surroundings? For example, do you listen to children with the same attention you give to adults? What about the way you listen to people of different nationalities, races, or political persuasions—do you listen with a view toward *understanding* the speaker, or toward *refuting* him?

3. Are words always necessary for communication? Examine some television commercials with the volume turned down and see what messages you receive. Is television merely illustrated radio, or is it more than that? What images of man do we get from its advertisements?

4. Ask yourself the question, "What constitutes my daily Niagara of words?" Then try to estimate, roughly, the number of words that come flooding in upon you from radio, television, conversations, newspapers, magazines, and other sources. Aside from conversations, it should be obvious that the Niagara of words comes largely from the mass media. What kind of messages and information do you get from the media? If they are part of your "education," are you getting a good or bad education?

5. We are exposed, it is estimated, to thousands of advertisements every day. What kinds of effects would you guess they have on us? What model do they offer us as far as solving personal and, by extension, social problems?

6. Until recently there have been few Negroes in advertisements. What other elements of society tend to be left out or ignored in advertisements? Why?

IV. The study of language has been one of man's most fascinating preoccupations. The following books are recommended for students who wish to investigate language more extensively.

Some books on various aspects of language are: Edward T. Hall, *The Silent Language* (1959); T. P. Brockway, *Language and Politics* (1965); Irving and Harriet Deer, *Languages of the Mass Media* (1965); Weston La Barre, *The Human Animal* (1954), especially Chapters 10, 11, and 12; Noah Jonathan Jacobs, *Naming Day in Eden* (1959); Margaret Schlauch, *The Gift of Tongues* (1942).

The relations between language and thought are discussed in Stuart Chase's *Power of Words* (1954), especially Chapter 10. The important source books in this area are: Alfred Korzybski, *Science and Sanity: An Introduction to Non-Aristotelian Systems and General Semantics*, fourth edition (1958); and John B. Carroll, editor, *Language, Thought, and Reality: Selected Writings of Benjamin Lee Whorf* (1956).

Language in Thought and Action argues that cooperation is more fundamental than conflict in man and his societies. Some books that deal with this subject are: Peter Kropotkin, *Mutual Aid: A Factor in Evolution* (1955); Walter B. Cannon, *The Wisdom of the Body* (1963); Lewis Coser, *The Functions of Social Conflict* (1956); Robert Ardrey, *The Territorial Imperative* (1966); Konrad Lorenz, *On Aggression* (1966); Ralph Dahrendorf, *Class and Conflict in Industrial Society* (1959). There is also a journal devoted to the subject: *The Journal of Conflict Resolution.*

This basic need, which certainly is obvious only in man, is the need of symbolization. The symbol-making function is one of man's primary activities, like eating, looking, or moving about. It is the fundamental process of the mind, and goes on all the time.

Susanne K. Langer

Man's achievements rest upon the use of symbols.

Alfred Korzybski

symbols

The Symbolic Process

Animals struggle with each other for food or for leadership, but they do not, like human beings, struggle with each other for things that *stand for* food or leadership: such things as our paper symbols of wealth (money, bonds, titles), badges of rank to wear on our clothes, or low-number license plates, supposed by some people to stand for social precedence. For animals, the relationship in which one thing *stands for* something else does not appear to exist except in very rudimentary form.[1]

The process by means of which human beings can arbitrarily make certain things *stand for* other things may be called the *symbolic process*. Whenever two or more human beings can communicate with each other,

[1]One investigator, J. B. Wolfe, trained chimpanzees to put poker chips into an especially constructed vending machine ("chimpomat") which supplied grapes, bananas, and other food. The chimpanzees proved to be able to distinguish chips of different "values" (one grape, two grapes, zero, and so on) and also proved to be willing to work for them if the rewards were fairly immediate. They tended, however, to stop work as they accumulated more chips. Their "money system" was definitely limited to rudimentary and immediate transactions. See Robert M. Yerkes' *Chimpanzees: A Laboratory Colony* (1943).

they can, by agreement, make anything stand for anything. For example, here are two symbols:

X *Y*

We can agree to let *X* stand for buttons and *Y* stand for bows; then we can freely change our agreement and let *X* stand for the Chicago White Sox and *Y* for the Cincinnati Reds; or let *X* stand for Chaucer and *Y* for Shakespeare, *X* for North Vietnam and *Y* for South Vietnam. *We are, as human beings, uniquely free to manufacture and manipulate and assign values to our symbols as we please.* Indeed, we can go further by making symbols that stand for symbols. If necessary we can, for instance, let the symbol *M* stand for all the *X*'s in the above example (buttons, White Sox, Chaucer, North Vietnam) and let *N* stand for all the *Y*'s (bows, Cincinnati Reds, Shakespeare, South Vietnam). Then we can make another symbol, *T*, stand for *M* and *N*, which would be an instance of a symbol of symbols of symbols. This freedom to create symbols of *any* assigned value and to create *symbols that stand for symbols* is essential to what we call the symbolic process.

Everywhere we turn, we see the symbolic process at work. Feathers worn on the head or stripes on the sleeve can be made to stand for military rank; cowrie shells or rings of brass or pieces of paper can stand for wealth; crossed sticks can stand for a set of religious beliefs; buttons, elks' teeth, ribbons, special styles of ornamental haircutting or tattooing, can stand for social affiliations. The symbolic process permeates human life at the most primitive and the most civilized levels alike. Warriors, medicine men, policemen, doormen, nurses, cardinals, and kings wear costumes that symbolize their occupations. Vikings collected their victims' armor and college students collect membership keys in honorary societies to symbolize victories in their respective fields. There are few things that men do or want to do, possess or want to possess, that have not, in addition to their mechanical or biological value, a symbolic value.

All fashionable clothes, as Thorsten Veblen has pointed out in his *Theory of the Leisure Class* (1899), are highly symbolic: materials, cut, and ornament are dictated only to a slight degree by considerations of warmth, comfort, or practicability. The more we dress up in fine clothes, the more we restrict our freedom of action. But by means of delicate embroideries, easily soiled fabrics, starched shirts, high heels, long and pointed fingernails, and other such sacrifices of comfort, the wealthy classes manage to symbolize, among other things, the fact that they don't have to work for a living. On the other hand, the not-so-wealthy, by imitating these symbols of wealth, symbolize their conviction that, even if they do work for a living, they are just as good as anybody else.

With the changes in American life since Veblen's time, many changes have taken place in our ways of symbolizing social status. There have been major changes in the fashion world, and flamboyant styles and striking colors are now popular, inspired in part by the hippies, pop art, and new sexual codes.[2]

In Veblen's time a deeply tanned skin was indicative of a life spent in farming and other outdoor labor, and women in those days went to a great deal of trouble shielding themselves from the sun with parasols, wide hats, and long sleeves. Today, however, a pale skin is indicative of confinement in offices and factories, while a deeply tanned skin suggests a life of leisure—of trips to Florida, Sun Valley, and Hawaii. Hence, a sun-blackened skin, once considered ugly because it symbolized work, is now considered beautiful because it symbolizes leisure. "The idea is," as Stanton Delaplane said in the San Francisco *Chronicle*, "to turn a color which, if you were born with it, would make it extremely difficult to get into major hotels." And pallid people in New York, Chicago, and Toronto who cannot afford midwinter trips to the West Indies find comfort in browning themselves with drugstore tanning solutions.

Food, too, is highly symbolic. Religious dietary regulations, such as those of the Catholics, Jews, and Mohammedans, are observed in order to symbolize adherence to one's religion. Specific foods are used to symbolize specific festivals and observances in almost every country—for example, cherry pie on George Washington's birthday and haggis on Burns' Nicht. And eating together has been a highly symbolic act throughout all of man's known history: "companion" means one with whom you share your bread.

People from outside the American South often find it difficult to understand how many white southerners accept close physical contact with Negro servants and yet become extremely upset at the idea of sitting beside Negroes in restaurants or buses. The attitude of the southerner rests on the fact that the ministrations of a Negro servant—even personal care, such as nursing—have the symbolic implication of social inequality, while admission of Negroes to buses, restaurants, and nonsegregated schools has the symbolic implication of social equality.[3]

We select our furniture to serve as visible symbols of our taste, wealth, and social position. We often choose our residences on the basis of a feeling that it "looks well" to have a "good address." We trade in

[2]J. Huizinga, in *The Waning of the Middle Ages* (1924), has an interesting chapter on "Pessimism and the Ideal of the Sublime Life," which deals with symbolism in medieval clothing styles and life.

[3]Today the word "Negro" has fallen into disfavor and is being supplanted by "black," although the latter term was found so offensive only a few years ago that most people used "colored" instead. The shifting nomenclature reflects changes in the situation of Negroes as well as changes in their view of themselves, from "black" as something to be ashamed of to "black is beautiful."

In spite of current fashion, in this book I shall continue to use the term "Negro," which has been dignified by centuries of struggle, suffering, cultural achievement, and a heroic will to live. The movement for the incorporation of Black Studies into high school and college curriculums is to be welcomed, since the understanding of America can never be complete without an understanding of the Negro's part in shaping American history and American experience.

perfectly good cars for later models, not always to get better transportation, but to give evidence to the community that we can afford it.[4]

Such complicated and apparently unnecessary behavior leads philosophers, both amateur and professional, to ask over and over again, "Why can't human beings live simply and naturally?" Often the complexity of human life makes us look enviously at the relative simplicity of lives such as those that dogs and cats lead. But the symbolic process, which makes possible the absurdities of human conduct, also makes possible language and therefore all the human achievements dependent on language. The fact that more things can go wrong with motorcars than with wheelbarrows is no reason for going back to wheelbarrows. Similarly, the fact that the symbolic process makes complicated follies possible is no reason for wanting to return to a cat-and-dog existence. A better solution is to understand the symbolic process, so that instead of being its victims we become, to some degree at least, its masters.

Language as Symbolism

Of all forms of symbolism, language is the most highly developed, most subtle, and most complicated. It has been pointed out that human beings, by agreement, can make anything stand for anything. Now, human beings have agreed, in the course of centuries of mutual dependency, to let the various noises that they can produce with their lungs, throats, tongues, teeth, and lips systematically stand for specified happenings in their nervous systems. We call that system of agreements *language*. For example, we who speak English have been so trained that, when our nervous systems register the presence of a certain kind of animal, we may make the following noise: "There's a cat." Anyone hearing us expects to find that, by looking in the same direction, he will experience a similar event in his nervous system—one that will lead him to make an almost identical noise. Again, we have been so trained that when we are conscious of wanting food, we make the noise "I'm hungry."

There is, as has been said, *no necessary connection between the symbol and that which is symbolized.* Just as men can wear yachting costumes without ever having been near a yacht, so they can make the noise "I'm hungry" without being hungry. Furthermore, just as social rank can be symbolized by feathers in the hair, by tattooing on the breast,

[4]I once had an eight-year-old car in good running condition. A friend of mine, a repairman who knew the condition of the car, kept urging me to trade it for a new model. "But why?" I asked. "The old car's in fine shape still." The repairman answered scornfully, "Yeah, but what the hell. All you've got is transportation."

The term "transportation car" often appears in advertisements; for example, "'63 Dodge—Runs good; transportation car. Must sell. $100." Apparently it means a car that has no symbolic or prestige value and is good only for getting you there and bringing you back—a miserable kind of vehicle indeed!

by gold ornaments on the watch chain, or by a thousand different devices according to the culture we live in, so the fact of being hungry can be symbolized by a thousand different noises according to the culture we live in: *J'ai faim*, or *Es hungert mich*, or *Ho appetito*, or *Hara ga hetta*, and so on.

However obvious these facts may appear at first glance, they are actually not so obvious as they seem except when we take special pains to think about the subject. Symbols and things symbolized are independent of each other; nevertheless, we all have a way of feeling as if, and sometimes acting as if, there were necessary connections. For example, there is the vague sense we all have that foreign languages are inherently absurd: foreigners have such funny names for things, and why can't they call things by their right names? This feeling exhibits itself most strongly in those tourists who seem to believe that they can make the natives of any country understand English if they shout loud enough. Like the little boy who was reported to have said, "Pigs are called pigs because they are such dirty animals," they feel that the symbol is inherently connected in some way with the thing symbolized. Then there are the people who feel that since snakes are "nasty, slimy creatures" (incidentally, snakes are *not* slimy), the word "snake" is a *nasty, slimy word*.

The Pitfalls of Drama

Naiveté regarding the symbolic process extends to symbols other than words, of course. In the case of drama (stage, movies, television), there appear to be people in almost every audience who never quite fully realize that a play is a set of fictional, symbolic representations. An actor is one who symbolizes other people, real or imagined. In a movie some years ago, Fredric March enacted with great skill the role of a drunkard. Florence Eldridge (Mrs. March) reports that for a long time thereafter she got letters of advice and sympathy from women who said that they too were married to alcoholics. Also some years ago it was reported that when Edward G. Robinson, who used to play gangster roles with extraordinary vividness, visited Chicago, local hoodlums would telephone him at his hotel to pay their professional respects.

One is reminded of the actor, playing the role of a villain in a traveling theatrical troupe, who, at a particularly tense moment in the play, was shot by an excited cowpuncher in the audience. But this kind of confusion does not seem to be confined to unsophisticated theatergoers. Paul Muni, after playing the part of Clarence Darrow in *Inherit the Wind*, was invited to address the American Bar Association; Ralph Bellamy, after playing the role of Franklin D. Roosevelt in *Sunrise at Campobello*, was invited by several colleges to speak on Roosevelt. Also, there are those astonishing patriots who rushed to the recruiting offices to help defend the nation when, on October 30, 1938, the United States was "invaded" by an "army from Mars" in a radio dramatization.[5]

The Word Is Not the Thing

The above, however, are only the more striking examples of confused attitudes toward words and symbols. There would be little point in mentioning them if we were *uniformly and permanently aware* of the independence of symbols from things symbolized, as all human beings, in the writer's opinion, *can be* and *should be*. But we are not. Most of us have, in some area or other of our thinking, improper habits of evaluation. For this, society itself is often to blame: most societies systematically encourage, concerning certain topics, the habitual confusion of symbols with things symbolized. For example, if a Japanese schoolhouse caught fire, it used to be obligatory in the days of emperor-worship to try to rescue the emperor's *picture* (there was one in every schoolhouse), even at the risk of one's life. (If you got burned to death, you were posthumously ennobled.) In our society, we are encouraged to go into debt in order that we may display, as symbols of prosperity, shiny, new automobiles. Strangely enough, the possession of shiny automobiles even under these conditions makes their "owners" *feel* prosperous. In all civilized societies (and probably in many primitive ones as well), the symbols of piety, of civic virtue, or of patriotism are often prized above actual piety, civic virtue, or patriotism. In one way or another, we are all like the student who cheats on his exams in order to make Phi Beta Kappa: it is so much more important to have the symbol than the things it stands for.

The habitual confusion of symbols with things symbolized, whether on the part of individuals or societies, is serious enough at all levels of culture to provide a perennial human problem.[6] But with the rise of modern communications systems, the problem of confusing verbal symbols with realities assumes peculiar urgency. We are constantly being talked at, by teachers, preachers, salesmen, public-relations counsels, governmental agencies, and moving-picture sound tracks. The cries of the hawkers of soft drinks, detergents, and laxatives pursue us into our homes, thanks to radio and television—and in some houses the sets are never turned off from morning to night. The mailman brings direct-mail advertising. Billboards confront us on the highway, and we even take transistor radios with us to the seashore.

We live in an environment shaped and largely created by hitherto

[5] See Hadley Cantril's *The Invasion from Mars* (1940) and John Houseman's "The Men from Mars," *Harper's* (December 1948).

[6] The charge against the Pharisees, it will be remembered, was that they were obsessively concerned with the symbols of piety at the expense of an adequate concern with its spirit.

unparalleled semantic influences: mass-circulation newspapers and magazines which are given to reflecting, in a shocking number of cases, the weird prejudices and obsessions of their publishers and owners; radio and television programs, both local and network, almost completely dominated by commercial motives; public-relations counsels who are simply highly paid craftsmen in the art of manipulating and reshaping our semantic environment in ways favorable to their clients. It is an exciting environment, but fraught with danger: it is only a slight exaggeration to say that Hitler conquered Austria by radio. Today the full resources of advertising agencies, public-relations counsels, radio, television, and slanted news stories are brought to bear in order to influence our decisions in election campaigns, especially in years of presidential elections.

Citizens of a modern society need, therefore, more than that ordinary "common sense" which was defined by Stuart Chase as that which tells you that the world is flat. They need to be systematically aware of the powers and limitations of symbols, especially words, if they are to guard against being driven into complete bewilderment by the complexity of their semantic environment. The first of the principles governing symbols is this: The symbol is *not* the thing symbolized; the word is *not* the thing; the map is *not* the territory it stands for.

The symbol	**IS NOT**	the thing symbolized
The map		the territory
The word		the thing

Maps and Territories

There is a sense in which we all live in two worlds. First, we live in the world of happenings which we know at first hand. This is an extremely small world, consisting only of that continuum of the things that we have actually seen, felt, or heard—the flow of events constantly passing before our senses. So far as this world of personal experience is concerned, Africa, South America, Asia, Washington, New York, or Los Angeles do not exist if we have never been to these places. Jomo Kenyetta is only a name if we have never seen him. When we ask ourselves how much we know at first hand, we discover that we know very little indeed.

Most of our knowledge, acquired from parents, friends, schools, newspapers, books, conversation, speeches, and television, is received *verbally*. All our knowledge of history, for example, comes to us only in words. The only proof we have that the Battle of Waterloo ever took place is that we have had reports to that effect. These reports are not given us by people who saw it happen, but are based on other reports:

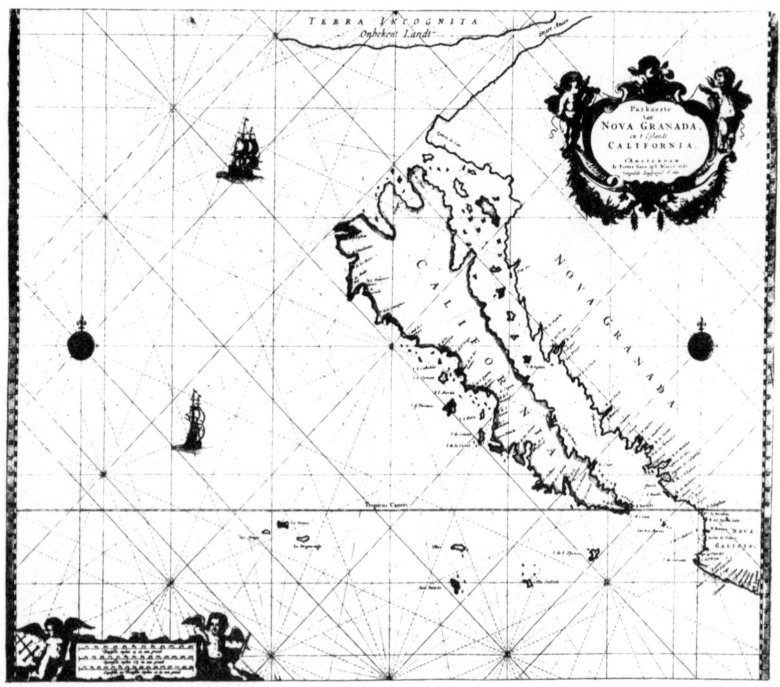

reports of reports of reports, which go back ultimately to the first-hand reports given by people who did see it happening. It is through reports, then, and through reports of reports, that we receive most knowledge: about government, about what is happening in the Middle East, about what picture is showing at the downtown theater—in fact, about anything that we do not know through direct experience.

Let us call this world that comes to us through words the *verbal world,* as opposed to the world we know or are capable of knowing through our own experience, which we shall call the *extensional world.* (The reason for the choice of the word "extensional" will become clear later.) The human being, like any other creature, begins to make his acquaintance with the extensional world from infancy. Unlike other creatures, however, he begins to receive, as soon as he can learn to understand, reports, reports of reports, reports of reports of reports. In addition, he receives inferences made from reports, inferences made from other inferences, and so on. By the time a child is a few years old, has gone to school and to Sunday school, and has made a few friends, he has accumulated a considerable amount of second-hand and third-hand information about morals, geography, history, nature, people, games—all of which information together constitutes his verbal world.

Now, to use the famous metaphor introduced by Alfred Korzybski in his *Science and Sanity* (1933), this verbal world ought to stand in relation to the extensional world as a *map* does to the *territory* it is supposed to represent. If a child grows to adulthood with a verbal world in his head which corresponds fairly closely to the extensional world that he finds around him in his widening experience, he is in relatively small danger of being shocked or hurt by what he finds, because his verbal world has told him what, more or less, to expect. He is prepared for life. If, however, he grows up with a false map in his head—that is, with a head crammed with error and superstition—he will constantly be running into trouble, wasting his efforts, and acting like a fool. He will not be adjusted to the world as it is; he may, if the lack of adjustment is serious, end up in a mental hospital.

Verbal World	Reports	Map
Extensional World	Experience	Territory

Some of the follies we commit because of false maps in our heads are so commonplace that we do not even think of them as remarkable. There are those who protect themselves from accidents by carrying a rabbit's foot. Some refuse to sleep on the thirteenth floor of hotels—a situation so common that most big hotels, even in the capitals of our scientific culture, skip "13" in numbering their floors. Some plan their lives on the basis of astrological predictions. Some play fifty-to-one shots on the basis of dream books. Some hope to make their teeth whiter by changing their brand of toothpaste. All such people are living in verbal worlds that bear little, if any, resemblance to the extensional world.

Now, no matter how beautiful a map may be, it is useless to a traveler unless it accurately shows the relationship of places to each other, the structure of the territory. If we draw, for example, a big dent in the outline of a lake for, let us say, artistic reasons, the map is worthless. But if we are just drawing maps for fun, without paying any attention to the structure of the region, there is nothing in the world to prevent us from putting in all the extra curlicues and twists we want in the lakes, rivers, and roads. No harm will be done *unless someone tries to plan a trip by such a map.*

Similarly, by means of imaginary or false reports or by false inferences from good reports or by mere rhetorical exercises, we can manufacture at will, with language, "maps" which have no reference to the extensional world. Here again no harm will be done unless someone makes the mistake of regarding such "maps" as representing real territories.

We all inherit a great deal of useless knowledge, and a great deal of misinformation and error (maps that were formerly thought to be accurate), so that there is always a portion of what we have been told

The symbol		the thing symbolized
The map	**IS NOT**	the territory
The word		the thing

that must be discarded. But the cultural heritage of our civilization that is transmitted to us—our socially pooled knowledge, both scientific and humane—has been valued principally because we have believed that it gives us accurate maps of experience. The analogy of verbal worlds to maps is an important one and will be referred to frequently throughout this book. It should be noticed at this point, however, that there are two ways of getting false maps of the world into our heads: first, by having them given to us; second, by creating them ourselves when we misread the true maps given to us.

APPLICATIONS

The reader who wants to put to work the ideas that are presented in this book would do well to start keeping a scrapbook or a filing folder or a set of 5 × 7 filing cards. Start a collection of quotations, newspaper clippings, editorials, anecdotes, and so forth that illustrate in one way or another the confusion of symbols with things symbolized. The ensuing chapters of this book will suggest other kinds of confusion to look for. Look for those instances in which people seem to think that there are *necessary* connections between symbols and things symbolized—between words and what words stand for.

After a few such examples are collected and studied, the reader will be able to recognize readily similar patterns of thought in his contemporaries and friends and, perhaps, even in himself.

I. In the following examples the symbol plays an unusually strong, sometimes exaggerated role with respect to the thing symbolized. Can you discern the assumptions, explicit or implicit, that govern the writer's use of symbols? If you discover that the writer is consciously distorting his map, can you tell whether he is trying to give you a false impression of the territory or whether he is simply trying to get you to "see" the territory in a new light?

1. The gates of the 1933 Century of Progress Exposition at Chicago were opened, through the use of the photoelectric cell, by the light of the star Arcturus. It is reported that a woman, on being told this, remarked, "Isn't it wonderful how those scientists know the names of all those stars."

SAMPLE ANALYSIS: Apparently this woman, on the basis of an unconscious assumption that there are necessary connections between names and things, believes that scientists discover a star's name by observing it very carefully. Come to think of it, how *do* stars get their names? Obviously, every star that has a name was *given* its name by somebody at some time. Apparently in ancient times people named stars after gods and goddesses and star-clusters on the basis of accidental resemblances to known objects, like the Dipper and the Scales. Query: Do scientists have any more systematic ways of naming stars today? Surely they must. Check and find out. *Webster's New International Dictionary* or the *Encyclopædia Britannica* will help.

2. A rose by any other name would smell as sweet.

WILLIAM SHAKESPEARE, *Romeo and Juliet*

3. My foreign-aid program will mainly consist of sending money and food to needy people in foreign lands—like Mississippi and Alabama.

DICK GREGORY, *Write Me In!*

4. No title of Nobility shall be granted by the United States. And no Person holding any Office or Profit under them shall, without Consent from Congress, accept any . . . Title of any kind whatever, from any King, Prince, or foreign State.

Constitution of the United States, Article I

5. If you spell it backwards, it spells Nature's!

Patent medicine advertisement

6. "I despise any flag, not just the American flag. It's a symbol of a piece of land that's considered more important than the human lives on it."

JOAN BAEZ, interview in *Playboy*

7. Much have I travelled in the realms of gold,
And many goodly states and kingdoms seen;
Round many western islands have I been
Which bards in fealty to Apollo hold.
Oft of one wide expanse have I been told
That deep-browed Homer ruled as his demesne
Yet did I never breathe its pure serene
Till I heard Chapman speak out loud and bold:
Then felt I like some watcher of the skies
When a new planet swims into his ken;
Or like stout Cortez when with eagle eyes
He stared at the Pacific—and all his men
Looked at each other with a mild surmise—
Silent, upon a peak in Darien.

JOHN KEATS, "On First Looking into Chapman's Homer"

8. "Looky here, Jim; does a cat talk like we do?"
"No, a cat don't."
"Well, does a cow?"
"No, a cow don't, nuther."
"Does a cat talk like a cow, or a cow talk like a cat?"
"No, dey don't."
"It's natural and right for 'em to talk different from each other, ain't it?"

"Course."

"And ain't it natural and right for a cat and a cow to talk different from *us?*"

"Why, mos' sholy it is."

"Well, then why ain't it natural and right for a *Frenchman* to talk different from *us?* You answer me that."

"Is a cat a man, Huck?"

"No."

"Well, den, dey ain't no sense in a cat talkin' like a man. Is a cow a man?—er is a cow a cat?"

"No, she ain't neither of them."

"Well, den, she ain' got no business to talk like either one er the yuther of 'em. Is a Frenchman a man?"

"Yes."

'*Well,* den! Dad blame it, why doan' he *talk* like a man? You answer me *dat!*

SAMUEL L. CLEMENS, *Huckleberry Finn*

9. Dear Abby:

Have you heard about the new doll they are going to put on the market? It is called the Mama Doll, and this is how it is described in an advertisement:

"When the doctor lifts the mama doll's skirt, a baby doll will slide out. On the baby doll's chest is written, 'I am the result of LOVE.'"

It says in the ad that a child psychologist approves of the doll.

This is about the worst thing I have ever heard of. When they made dolls that walked, talked, and danced, that was fine, because the whole idea of a doll is to give a child something to play with, but I really thought they went a little too far when they made a doll who could wet her pants. And now this! I think the idea of making a doll who can "give birth" is SICK!

I would like your opinion.

Horrified

10. In the comic books, "Shazam!" is a word which transforms Billy Batson, a youth, into Captain Marvel, the "strongest and mightiest" man in the world. What other "magic" words have you come across?

II. Can the map ever be identical with the territory? Is the language in *Language in Thought and Action* a map, a territory, or both?

III. Do the words "Semites," "Jews," "Israelis," and "Hebrews" stand for the same group of people? What elements do these maps have in common, and how are their territories different?

IV. Checking on how closely our maps and territories correspond to one another is an endless task. In fact, when we use the word "true" we are assuming that truth represents a correspondence between what we *say* about reality (the map) and the reality *itself* (the territory). Can you think of any other kinds of truth? Does "thinking make it so"?

V. The word "personality" is derived from the Latin term *persona*, "mask." To what degree is your personality a true map of your self? How do you know the answer to this question? How can you?

VI. The literature of "error" is enormous. A large percentage of nonfiction books actually deal with this matter, either directly—as in exposing errors usually taken as truth—or indirectly, as in attempting to clear up misconceptions. Some books which you might find interesting are:

Ernest Dichter, *The Strategy of Desire* (1960), a fascinating study of motivational research that deals with such matters as the difference between what we think motivates us and what "really" motivates us. Dichter's *Handbook of Consumer Motivation* (1964) is also worth investigating.

W. Lloyd Warner, *American Life: Dream and Reality* (1953), an analysis of the problems and possibilities of American society, from the perspective of social anthropology.

R. D. Laing, *The Divided Self* (1959), a remarkable investigation of the schizophrenic that, in a sense, deals with the same kind of phenomena described in the section on maps and territories.

Daniel Boorstin, *The Image: A Guide to Pseudo-Events* in America (1964), an investigation of the difference between reality and pseudo-reality.

VII. Two excellent books that deal with the nature and manipulation of symbols are : Suzanne Langer, *Philosophy in a New Key* (1942); and C. K. Ogden and I. A. Richards, *The Meaning of Meaning* (1923). The surprising and mischievous workings of words as symbols have been collected in the entertaining little book by C. C. Bombaugh, *Oddities and Curiosities of Words and Literature* (1961).

To put it briefly, in human speech, different sounds have different meanings. To study this co-ordination of certain sounds with certain meanings is to study language. This co-ordination makes it possible for man to interact with great precision. When we tell someone, for instance, the address of a house he has never seen, we are doing something which no animal can do.

Leonard Bloomfield

Vague and insignificant forms of speech, and abuse of language, have so long passed for mysteries of science; and hard or misapplied words with little or no meaning have, by prescription, such a right to be mistaken for deep learning and height of speculation, that it will not be easy to persuade either those who speak or those who hear them, that they are but the covers of ignorance and hindrance of true knowledge.

John Locke

reports, inferences, judgments

For the purposes of the interchange of information, the basic symbolic act is the *report* of what we have seen, heard, or felt: "There is a ditch on each side of the road." "You can get those at Smith's Hardware Store for $2.75." "There aren't any fish on that side of the lake, but there are on this side." Then there are reports of reports: "The longest waterfall in the world is Victoria Falls in Rhodesia." "The Battle of Hastings took place in 1066." "The papers say that there was a smash-up on Highway 41 near Evansville." Reports adhere to the following rules: first, they are *capable of verification;* second, they *exclude,* as far as possible, *inferences* and *judgments.* (These terms will be defined later.)

Verifiability

Reports are verifiable. We may not always be able to verify them ourselves, since we cannot track down the evidence for every piece of history we know, nor can we all go to Evansville to see the remains of the smash-up before they are cleared away. But if we are roughly agreed upon the names of things, upon what constitutes a "foot," "yard," "bushel," "kilogram," "meter," and so on, and upon how to measure time, there is relatively little danger of our misunderstanding each other. Even in a world such as we have today, in which everybody seems to be quarreling with everybody else, *we still to a surprising degree trust each other's reports.* We ask directions of total strangers when we are traveling. We follow directions on road signs without being suspicious of the people who put them up. We read books of information about science, mathematics, automotive engineering, travel, geography, the history of costume, and other such factual matters, and we usually assume that the author is doing his best to tell us as truly as he can what he knows. And we are safe in so assuming most of the time. With the interest given today to the discussion of biased newspapers, propagandists, and the general untrustworthiness of many of the communications we receive, we are likely to forget that we still have an enormous amount of reliable information available and that deliberate misinformation, except in warfare, is still more the exception than the rule. The desire for self-preservation that compelled men to evolve means for the exchange of information also compels them to regard the giving of false information as profoundly reprehensible.

At its highest development, the language of reports is the language of science. By "highest development" we mean greatest general usefulness. Presbyterian and Catholic, workingman and capitalist, East German and West German *agree* on the meanings of such symbols as $2 \times 2 = 4$, $100°$ *C*, HNO_3, *3:35* A.M., *1940* A.D., *1,000 kilowatts, Quercus agrifolia,* and so on. But how, it may be asked, can there be agreement about even this much among people who disagree about political philosophies, ethical ideas, religious beliefs, and the survival of my business versus the survival of yours? The answer is that circumstances *compel men to agree,* whether they wish to or not. If, for example, there were a dozen different religious sects in the United States, each insisting on its own way of naming the time of the day and the days of the year, the mere necessity of having a dozen different calendars, a dozen different kinds of watches, and a dozen sets of schedules for business hours, trains, and television programs, to say nothing of the effort that would be required for translating terms from one nomenclature to another, would make life as we know it impossible.[1]

The language of reports, then, including the more accurate reports of science, is "map" language, and because it gives us reasonably accurate representations of the "territory," it enables us to get work done. Such language may often be dull reading: one does not usually read logarithmic tables or telephone directories for entertainment. But we could not get along without it. There are numberless occasions in the talking and writing we do in everyday life that *require that we state things in such a way that everybody will be able to understand and agree with our formulation.*

Inferences

The reader will find that practice in writing reports is a quick means of increasing his linguistic awareness. It is an exercise which will constantly provide him with his own examples of the principles of language and interpretation under discussion. The reports should be about first-hand experience—scenes the reader has witnessed himself, meetings and social events he has taken part in, people he knows well. They should be of such a nature that they can be verified and agreed upon. For the purpose of this exercise, inferences will be excluded.

Not that inferences are not important—we rely in everyday life and in science as much on *inferences* as on reports—in some areas of thought, for example, geology, paleontology, and nuclear physics, reports are the foundations; but inferences (and inferences upon inferences) are the main body of the science. An inference, as we shall use the term, is *a statement about the unknown made on the basis of the known.* We may *infer* from the material and cut of a woman's clothes her wealth or social position; we may *infer* from the character of the ruins the origin of the fire that destroyed the building; we may *infer* from a man's calloused hands the nature of his occupation; we may *infer* from a senator's vote on an

[1] According to information supplied by the Association of American Railroads, "Before 1883 there were nearly 100 different time zones in the United States. It wasn't until November 18 of that year that . . . a system of standard time was adopted here and in Canada. Before then there was nothing but local or 'solar' time. . . . The Pennsylvania Railroad in the East used Philadelphia time, which was five minutes slower than New York time and five minutes faster than Baltimore time. The Baltimore & Ohio used Baltimore time for trains running out of Baltimore, Columbus time for Ohio, Vincennes (Indiana) time for those going out of Cincinnati. . . . When it was noon in Chicago, it was 12:31 in Pittsburgh, 12:24 in Cleveland, 12:17 in Toledo, 12:13 in Cincinnati, 12:09 in Louisville, 12:07 in Indianapolis, 11:50 in St. Louis, 11:48 in Dubuque, 11:39 in St. Paul, and 11:27 in Omaha. There were 27 local time zones in Michigan alone. . . . A person traveling from Eastport, Maine, to San Francisco, if he wanted always to have the right railroad time and get off at the right place, had to twist the hands of his watch 20 times en route." Chicago *Daily News* (September 29, 1948).

armaments bill his attitude toward Russia; we may *infer* from the structure of the land the path of a prehistoric glacier; we may *infer* from a halo on an unexposed photographic plate its past proximity to radioactive materials; we may *infer* from the sound of an engine the condition of its connecting rods. Inferences may be carefully or carelessly made. They may be made on the basis of a broad background of previous experience with the subject matter or with no experience at all. For example, the inferences a good mechanic can make about the internal condition of a motor by listening to it are often startlingly accurate, while the inferences made by an amateur (if he tries to make any) may be entirely wrong. But the common characteristic of inferences is that they are statements about matters which are not directly known, made on the basis of what has been observed.[2]

The avoidance of inferences in our suggested practice in report-writing requires that we make no guesses as to what is going on in other people's minds. When we say, "He was angry," we are not reporting; we are making an inference from such observable facts as the following: "He pounded his fist on the table; he swore; he threw the telephone directory at his stenographer." In this particular example, the inference appears to be safe; nevertheless, it is important to remember, especially for the purposes of training oneself, that it is an inference. Such expressions as "He thought a lot of himself," "He was scared of girls," "He has an inferiority complex," made on the basis of casual observation, and "What Russia really wants to do is to establish a communist world dictatorship," made on the basis of casual reading, are highly inferential. We should keep in mind their inferential character and, in our suggested exercises, should substitute for them such statements as "He rarely spoke to subordinates in the plant," "I saw him at a party, and he never danced except when one of the girls asked him to," "He wouldn't apply for the scholarship, although I believe he could have won it easily," and "The Russian delegation to the United Nations has asked for *A, B,* and *C.* Last year they voted against *M* and *N* and voted for *X* and *Y.* On the basis of facts such as these, the newspaper I read makes the inference that what Russia really wants is to establish a communist world dictatorship. I agree."

Even when we exercise every caution to avoid inferences and to report only what we see and experience, we all remain prone to error, since the making of inferences is a quick, almost automatic process. We may watch a car weaving as it goes down the road and say, "Look at that *drunken driver,*" although what we *see* is only *the irregular motion of the car.* I once saw a man leave a dollar at a lunch counter and hurry out. Just as I was wondering why anyone should leave so generous a tip in so

[2]The behaviorist school of psychology tries to avoid inferences about what is going on in other people's minds by describing only external behavior. A famous joke about behaviorism goes: Two behaviorists meet on the street. The first says, "You're fine. How am I?"

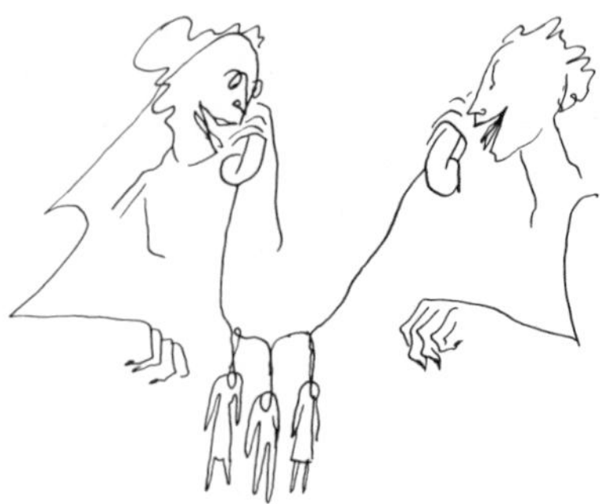

Fun with inferences

modest an establishment, the waitress came, picked up the dollar, put it in the cash register as she punched up ninety cents, and put a dime in her pocket. In other words, my description to myself of the event, "a dollar tip," turned out to be not a report but an inference.

All this is not to say that we should never make inferences. The inability to make inferences is itself a sign of mental disorder. For example, the speech therapist Laura L. Lee writes, "The aphasic [brain-damaged] adult with whom I worked had great difficulty in making inferences about a picture I showed her. She could tell me what was happening at the moment in the picture, but could not tell me what might have happened just before the picture or just afterward."[3] Hence the question is not whether or not we make inferences; the question is whether or not we are aware of the inferences we make.

Report	Can be verified or disproved
Inference	A statement about the unknown made on the basis of the known
Judgment	An expression of the writer's approval or disapproval

Judgments

In our suggested writing exercise, judgments are also to be excluded. By judgments, we shall mean *all expressions of the writer's approval or disapproval of the occurrences, persons, or objects he is describing.* For example, a report cannot say, "It was a wonderful car," but must say something like this: "It has been driven 50,000 miles and has never

[3]"Brain Damage and the Process of Abstracting: A Problem in Language Learning," *ETC.: A Review of General Semantics*, XVI (1959), 154–62.

required any repairs." Again, statements such as "Jack lied to us" must be suppressed in favor of the more verifiable statement, "Jack told us he didn't have the keys to his car with him. However, when he pulled a handkerchief out of his pocket a few minutes later, a bunch of car keys fell out." Also a report may not say, "The senator was stubborn, defiant, and uncooperative," or "The senator courageously stood by his principles"; it must say instead, "The senator's vote was the only one against the bill."

Many people regard statements such as the following as statements of "fact": "Jack *lied* to us," "Jerry is a *thief*," "Tommy is *clever*." As ordinarily employed, however, the word "lied" involves first an inference (that Jack knew otherwise and deliberately misstated the facts) and second a judgment (that the speaker disapproves of what he has inferred that Jack did). In the other two instances, we may substitute such expressions as, "Jerry was convicted of theft and served two years at Waupun," and "Tommy plays the violin, leads his class in school, and is captain of the debating team." After all, to say of a man that he is a "thief" is to say in effect, "He has stolen *and will steal again*"—which is more of a prediction than a report. Even to say, "He has stolen," is to make an inference (and simultaneously to pass a judgment) on an act about which there may be difference of opinion among those who have examined the evidence upon which the conviction was obtained. But to say that he was "convicted of theft" is to make a statement capable of being agreed upon through verification in court and prison records.

Scientific verifiability rests upon the external observation of facts, not upon the heaping up of judgments. If one person says, "Peter is a deadbeat," and another says, "I think so too," the statement has not been verified. In court cases, considerable trouble is sometimes caused by witnesses who cannot distinguish their judgments from the facts upon which those judgments are based. Cross-examinations under these circumstances go something like this:

WITNESS: That dirty double-crosser Jacobs ratted on me.
DEFENSE ATTORNEY: Your honor, I object.
JUDGE: Objection sustained. (Witness's remark is stricken from the record.) Now, try to tell the court exactly what happened.
WITNESS: He double-crossed me, the dirty, lying rat!
DEFENSE ATTORNEY: Your honor, I object!
JUDGE: Objection sustained. (Witness's remark is again stricken from the record.) Will the witness try to stick to the facts.
WITNESS: But I'm telling you the facts, your honor. He did double-cross me.

This can continue indefinitely unless the cross-examiner exercises some ingenuity in order to get at the facts behind the judgment. To the witness it is a "fact" that he was "double-crossed." Often patient questioning is required before the factual bases of the judgment are revealed.

Many words, of course, simultaneously convey a report and a judgment on the fact reported, as will be discussed more fully in a later chapter. For the purposes of a report as here defined, these should be avoided. Instead of "sneaked in," one might say "entered quietly"; instead of "politician," "congressman" or "alderman" or "candidate for office"; instead of "bureaucrat," "public official"; instead of "tramp," "homeless unemployed"; instead of "dictatorial set-up," "centralized authority"; instead of "crackpot," "holder of nonconformist views." A newspaper reporter, for example, is not permitted to write, "A crowd of suckers came to listen to Senator Smith last evening in that rickety firetrap and ex-dive that disfigures the south edge of town." Instead he says, "Between 75 and 100 people heard an address last evening by Senator Smith at the Evergreen Gardens near the South Side city limits."

Snarl-Words and Purr-Words

Throughout this book, it is important to remember that we are not considering language as an isolated phenomenon. Our concern, instead, is with language in action—language in the full context of the nonlinguistic events which are its setting. The making of noises with the vocal organs is a muscular activity and, like other muscular activities, is often involuntary. Our responses to powerful stimuli, such as to things that make us very angry, are a complex of muscular and physiological events: the contracting of fighting muscles, the increase of blood pressure, a change in body chemistry, clutching of our hair, *and* the making of noises, such as growls and snarls. We are a little too dignified, perhaps, to growl like dogs, but we do the next best thing and substitute series of words, such as "You dirty double-crosser!" "The filthy scum!" Similarly, if we are pleasurably agitated, we may, instead of purring or wagging the tail, say things like "She's the sweetest girl in all the world!"

Speeches such as these are, like direct expressions of approval or disapproval, judgments in their simplest form. They may be said to be human equivalents of snarling and purring. "She's the sweetest girl in all the world!" is not a statement about the girl; it is a purr. This seems to be a fairly obvious fact; nevertheless, it is surprising how often, when such a statement is made, both the speaker and the hearer feel that something has been said about the girl. This error is especially common in the interpretation of utterances of orators and editorialists in some of their more excited denunciations of "Reds," "pigs," "Wall Street," "radicals," "foreign ideologies," and in their more fulsome dithyrambs about "our way of life." Constantly, because of the impressive sound of the words, the elaborate structure of the sentences, and the appearance of intellectual progression, we get the feeling that something is being said about something. On closer examination, however, we discover that these utterances

The compliment

merely say, "What I hate ('Reds,' 'Wall Street,' or whatever) I hate very, very much," and "What I like ('our way of life') I like very, very much." We may call such utterances "snarl-words" and "purr-words." They are not reports describing conditions in the extensional world in any way.

To call these judgments "snarl-words" and "purr-words" does not mean that we should simply shrug them off. It means that we should be careful to *allocate the meaning correctly*—placing such a statement as "She's the sweetest girl in the world!" as a revelation of the speaker's state of mind, and not as a revelation of facts about the girl. If the "snarl-words" about "Reds" or "pigs" are accompanied by verifiable reports (which would also mean that we have previously agreed as to who, specifically, is meant by the terms "Reds" or "pigs"), we might find reason to be just as disturbed as the speaker. If the "purr-words" about the sweetest girl in the world are accompanied by verifiable reports about her appearance, manners, character, and so on, we might find reason to admire her too. But "snarl-words" and "purr-words" as such, unaccompanied by reports, offer nothing further to discuss, except possibly the question, "Why do you feel as you do?"

It is usually fruitless to debate such questions as "Is the President a great statesman or merely a skillful politican?" "Is the music of Wagner the greatest music of all time, or is it merely hysterical screeching?" "Which is the finer sport, tennis or baseball?" "Could Joe Louis in his prime have licked Rocky Marciano in his prime?" To take sides on such issues of conflicting judgments is to reduce oneself to the same level of stubborn imbecility as one's opponents. But to ask questions of the form, "Why do you like (or dislike) the President (or Wagner, or tennis, or Joe Louis)?" is to learn something about one's friends and neighbors. After listening to their opinions and their reasons for them, we may leave the discussion slightly wiser, slightly better informed, and perhaps slightly less one-sided than we were before the discussion began.

How Judgments Stop Thought

A judgment ("He is a fine boy," "It was a beautiful service," "Baseball is a healthful sport," "She is an awful bore") is a conclusion, summing up a large number of previously observed facts. The reader is probably familiar with the fact that students almost always have difficulty in writing themes of the required length because their ideas give out after a paragraph or two. The reason for this is that those early paragraphs contain so many judgments that there is little left to be said. When the conclusions are carefully excluded, however, and observed facts are given instead, there is never any trouble about the length of papers; in fact, they tend to become too long, since inexperienced writers, when told to give facts, often give far more than are necessary, because they lack discrimination between the important and the trivial.

Still another consequence of judgments early in the course of a written exercise—and this applies also to hasty judgments in everyday thought—is the temporary blindness they induce. When, for example, a description starts with the words, "He was a real Madison Avenue executive" or "She was a typical hippie," if we continue writing at all, we must make all our later statements consistent with those judgments. The result is that all the individual characteristics of this particular "executive" or this particular "hippie" are lost sight of; and the rest of the account is likely to deal not with observed facts but with stereotypes and the writer's particular notion (based on previously read stories, movies, pictures, and so forth) of what "Madison Avenue executives" or "typical hippies" are like. The premature judgment, that is, often prevents us from seeing what is directly in front of us, so that clichés take the place of fresh description. Therefore, even if the writer feels sure at the beginning of a written account that the man he is describing is a "real leatherneck" or that the scene he is describing is a "beautiful residential suburb," he will conscientiously keep such notions out of his head, lest his vision be obstructed. He is specifically warned against describing *anybody* as a "beatnik"—a term (originally applied to literary and artistic Bohemians) which was blown up by sensational journalism and movies into an almost completely fictional and misleading stereotype. If a writer applies the term to any actual living human being, he will have to expend so much energy thereafter explaining what he does *not* mean by it that he will save himself trouble by not bringing it up at all. The same warning applies to "hippies" and other social classifications that tend to submerge the individual in a category.

Slanting

In the course of writing reports of personal experiences, it will be found that in spite of all endeavors to keep judgments out, some will creep in.

An account of a man, for example, may go like this: "He had apparently not shaved for several days, and his face and hands were covered with grime. His shoes were torn, and his coat, which was several sizes too small for him, was spotted with dried clay." Now, in spite of the fact that no judgment has been stated, a very obvious one is implied. Let us contrast this with another description of the same man. "Although his face was bearded and neglected, his eyes were clear, and he looked straight ahead as he walked rapidly down the road. He seemed very tall; perhaps the fact that his coat was too small for him emphasized that impression. He was carrying a book under his left arm, and a small terrier ran at his heels." In this example, the impression about the same man is considerably changed, simply by the inclusion of new details and the subordination of unfavorable ones. Even if explicit judgments are kept out of one's writing, implied judgments based on selective perception will get in.

How, then, can we ever give an impartial report? The answer is, of course, that we cannot attain complete impartiality while we use the language of everyday life. Even with the very impersonal language of science, the task is sometimes difficult. Nevertheless, we can, by being aware of the favorable or unfavorable feelings that certain words and facts can arouse, attain enough impartiality for practical purposes. Such awareness enables us to balance the implied favorable and unfavorable judgments against each other. To learn to do this, it is a good idea to write two accounts of the same subject, both strict reports, to be read side by side: the first to contain facts and details likely to prejudice the reader in favor of the subject, the second to contain those likely to prejudice the reader against it. For example:

FOR	AGAINST
He had white teeth.	His teeth were uneven.
His eyes were blue, his hair blond and abundant.	He rarely looked people straight in the eye.
He had on a clean, white shirt.	His shirt was frayed at the cuffs.
His speech was courteous.	He had a high-pitched voice.
His employer spoke highly of him.	His landlord said he was slow in paying his rent.
He liked dogs.	He disliked children.

This process of selecting details favorable or unfavorable to the subject being described may be termed *slanting*. Slanting gives no explicit judgments, but it differs from reporting in that it deliberately makes certain judgments inescapable. Let us assume for a moment the truth of the statement "When Clyde was in New York last November he was seen having dinner with a show girl. . . ." The inferences that can be drawn from this statement are changed considerably when the following words are added: ". . . and her husband and their two children." Yet, if Clyde is a married man, his enemies could conceivably do him a great deal of harm by talking about his "dinner-date with a New York show girl." One-sided or biased slanting of this kind, not uncommon in

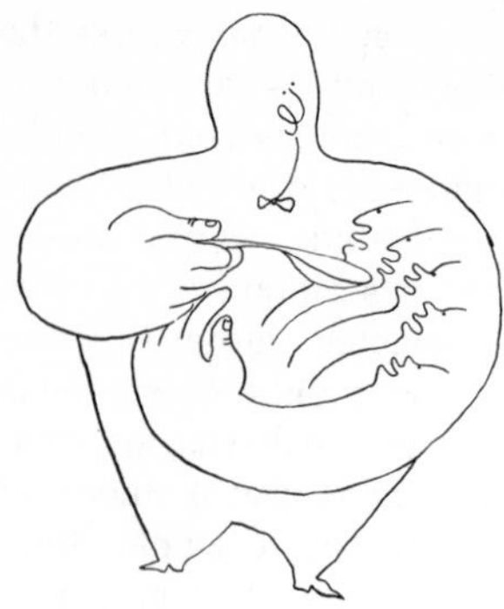

Press secretary spoon-feeding the press

private gossip and backbiting and all too common in the "interpretative reporting" of newspapers and news magazines, can be described as a technique of lying without actually telling any lies.

Discovering One's Bias

Here, however, caution is necessary. When, for example, a newspaper tells a story in a way that we dislike, leaving out facts we think important and playing up important facts in ways that we think unfair, we are tempted to say, "Look how unfairly they've slanted the story!" In making such a statement we are, of course, making an inference about the newspaper's editors. We are assuming that what seems important or unimportant to us seems equally important or unimportant to them, and on the basis of that assumption we infer that the editors "deliberately" gave the story a misleading emphasis. Is this necessarily the case? Can the reader, as an outsider, say whether a story assumes a given form because the editors "deliberately slanted it that way" or because that was the way the events appeared to them?

The point is that, by the process of selection and abstraction imposed on us by our own interests and background, experience comes to all of us (including newspaper editors) already "slanted." If you happen to be prolabor, pro-Catholic, and a stock-car racing fan, your ideas of what is important or unimportant will of necessity be different from those of a man who happens to be indifferent to all three of your favorite interests. If, then, newspapers often side with the big businessman on public issues, the reason is less a matter of "deliberate" slanting than the fact that publishers are often, in enterprises as large as modern urban newspapers, big businessmen themselves, accustomed both in work and in social life to associating with other big businessmen. Nevertheless, the best newspapers, whether owned by "big businessmen" or not, do try to tell us as accurately as possible what is going on in the world, because they are run by newspapermen who conceive it to be part of their professional responsibility to present fairly the conflicting points of view in controversial issues. Such newspapermen are *reporters* indeed.

The writer who is neither an advocate nor an opponent avoids slanting, except when he is seeking special literary effects. The avoidance of slanting is not only a matter of being fair and impartial; it is even more importantly a matter of making good maps of the territory of experience. The profoundly biased individual cannot make good maps because he can see an enemy *only* as an enemy and a friend *only* as a friend. The individual with genuine skill in writing—one who has imagination and insight—can look at the same subject from many points of view. The following examples may illustrate the fullness and solidity of descriptions thus written:

> Adam turned to look at him. It was, in a way, as though this were the first time he had laid eyes on him. He saw the strong, black shoulders under the red-check calico, the long arms lying loose, forward over the knees, the strong hands, seamed and calloused, holding the reins. He looked at the face. The thrust of the jawbone was strong, but the lips were heavy and low, with a piece of chewed straw hanging out one side of the mouth. The eyelids were pendulous, slightly swollen-looking, and the eyes bloodshot. Those eyes, Adam knew, could sharpen to a quick, penetrating, assessing glance. But now, looking at that slack, somnolent face, he could scarcely believe that.
>
> ROBERT PENN WARREN, *Wilderness*

> Soon after the little princess, there walked in a massively built, stout young man in spectacles, with a cropped head, light breeches in the mode of the day, with a high lace ruffle and a ginger-coloured coat. This stout young man [Pierre] was the illegitimate son of a celebrated dandy of the days of Catherine, Count Bezuhov, who was now dying in Moscow. He had not yet entered any branch of the service; he had only just returned from abroad, where he had been educated, and this was his first appearance in society. Anna Pavlovna greeted him with a nod reserved for persons of the very lowest hierarchy in her drawing-room. . . .
>
> Pierre was clumsy, stout and uncommonly tall, with huge, red hands; he did not, as they say, know how to come into a drawing-room and still less how to get out of one, that is, how to say something particularly agreeable on going away. Moreover, he was dreamy. He stood up, and picking up a three-cornered hat with the plume of a general in it instead of his own, he kept hold of it, pulling the feathers until the general asked him to restore it. But all his dreaminess and his inability to enter a drawing-room or talk properly in it were atoned for by his expression of good-nature, simplicity and modesty.
>
> COUNT LEO TOLSTOY, *War and Peace*
> (Translated by Constance Garnett)

APPLICATIONS

I. The following statements represent the mixture of reports, inferences, and judgments we encounter daily. Try to classify each statement. Since some cannot be neatly classified in only one category, a single-word answer might not be sufficient. If any of the statements are inferences or judgments, what kinds of evidence would you seek to support them?

1. She goes to church only in order to show off her clothes.

   SAMPLE ANALYSIS: In usual circumstances under which such a statement would be made, this would be an *inference,* since people ordinarily do not admit that they go to church for that reason. A *judgment* is also strongly implied, since it is assumed that one ought to have better reasons.

2. Stock prices were up slightly today in light trading.

3. Overweight people should not wear stripes, plaids, or excessively bright colors.

4. An apple a day keeps the doctor away.

5. Compared with the persecution of heresy in Europe from 1227 to 1492, the persecution of Christians by the Romans in the first three centuries after Christ was a mild and humane procedure. Making every allowance required of an historian and permitted to a Christian, we must rank the Inquisition, along with the wars and persecutions of our time, as among the darkest blots on the record of mankind, revealing a ferocity unknown in any beast.

   WILL DURANT, *The Story of Civilization,* IV.

6. Commuter—one who spends his life
   In riding to and from his wife;
   A man who shaves and takes a train
   And then rides back to shave again.

   E. B. WHITE

7. The Chinese people do not want war.

8. Many so-called religious people are hypocrites.

9. If you travel via Highway 60, the trip only takes two hours.

10. Beauty is only skin deep.

11. For rent: charming two-bedroom house in woods, easy walk to bus stop, $225 a month plus deposit.

12. And Adam lived an hundred and thirty years, and begat a son in his likeness, after his image; and called his name Seth: And the days of Adam after he had begotten Seth were eight hundred years: and he begat sons and daughters: And all the days that Adam lived were nine hundred and thirty years: and he died.

    Genesis 5:3–5

13. Crisp as Jack Frost, crunchy and crackle-happy . . . redder than a fire sale of long-handle flannels. Your big delicious beauties arrive

so fresh we don't guarantee they won't talk back to folks . . . in a flavor-full language all their own. Shipping weight about 9 pounds.

Advertising material accompanying
a Fruit-of-the-Month Club delivery

14. William Jameson is a skinny, crippled, tuberculosis-ridden little man, weighing only 95 pounds and standing only 5 feet tall. And every ounce and inch of him is criminal—incorrigible, remorseless and vicious.

New York *World-Telegram & Sun*

15. If you will study the history of almost any criminal, you will find he is an inveterate cigarette smoker.

HENRY FORD

16. An intelligent man makes his own opportunities.

II. Once the verifiability of a statement has been ascertained, the task of verifying still remains. If any of the following are reports, how would you verify them?

1. $A^2 + B^2 = C^2$.
2. Families of four with incomes of less than $4,000 per year live in poverty.
3. Hops can grow as much as eight inches in one day.
4. Cigarette smoking can be dangerous to your health.
5. Mixing your drinks leads to terrible hangovers.
6. America has never lost a war.
7. My car gets twenty-two miles to the gallon.

III. In a book called *Ideology and Utopia* the distinguished social-psychologist Karl Mannheim argued that there are certain people, "ideologists," who tend to see only the positive features of the societies in which they live, and other people, "utopians," who only see the negative features of their societies. Mannheim's point is that, whether we recognize it or not, our interests determine the way we see the world, and our knowledge is tied to our interests. Discuss the problems of slanting and bias in terms of Mannheim's concepts. Is it possible to avoid bias, or are we limited to *recognizing* that we do have a particular slant on things?

IV. Take a number of publications dealing with important issues in American society and try to discern the "slant" from which they are written. Compare, for example, the following: *The National Review, The New York Review of Books, The National Rifleman, The Rotarian, American Opinion, The Nation, The Black Panther,* and *Grit.*

V. In addition to trying such exercises in report-writing and in the exclusion of judgments and inferences as are suggested in this chapter, the reader might try writing (a) reports heavily slanted *against* persons or organizations he *likes*, and (b) reports heavily slanted *in favor of* persons or organizations he *dislikes*. For example, imagine that your luncheon club or fraternity or lodge is a subversive organization and report the facts about its activities and members upon which unfavorable inferences could be made; or imagine that one of your most disagreeable neighbors has been offered a job two thousand miles away and write a factual letter of recommendation to help him get the job.

VI. "A youth and a man were killed and three teenagers seriously injured early today in two auto accidents." Write:

1. A *report* of these accidents, inventing names and places.
2. A *slanted report* for a newspaper campaigning for stricter laws against juvenile delinquency. (Be sure to use factual statements only, letting your reader make his own inferences and judgments.)
3. A *slanted report* for a newspaper highly critical of the local city administration. (Again, use factual statements only.)

VII. Discuss the use of inference in the following passage from Sir Arthur Conan Doyle. Are the inferences made by Sherlock Holmes the kind that are described in this chapter? Comment on the validity and verifiability of Holmes's inferences.

With a resigned air and a somewhat weary smile, Holmes begged the beautiful intruder to take a seat, and to inform us what it was that was troubling her.

"At least it cannot be your health," said he, as his keen eyes darted over her; "so ardent a bicyclist must be full of energy."

She glanced down in surprise at her own feet, and I observed the slight roughening of the side of the sole caused by the friction of the edge of the pedal.

"Yes, I bicycle a good deal, Mr. Holmes. . . ."

My friend took the lady's ungloved hand, and examined it with as close an attention and as little sentiment as a scientist would show to a specimen.

"You will excuse me, I am sure. It is my business," said he, as he dropped it. "I nearly fell into the error of supposing you were typewriting. Of course, it is obvious that it is music. You observe the spatulate finger-ends, Watson, which are common to both professions? There is a spirituality about the face, however"—she gently turned it towards the light—"which the typewriter does not generate. This lady is a musician."

"Yes, Mr. Holmes, I teach music."

"In the country, I presume, from your complexion."

"Yes, sir, near Farnham, on the borders of Surrey."

 *[On being asked to define New Orleans jazz]: Man, when you got to ask what it is, you'll never get to know.*

Louis Armstrong

 *Dictionary definitions frequently offer verbal substitutes for an unknown term which only conceal a lack of real understanding. Thus a person might look up a foreign word and be quite satisfied with the meaning "bullfinch" without the slightest ability to identify or describe this bird. Understanding does not come through dealings with words alone, but rather with the things for which they stand. Dictionary definitions permit us to hide from ourselves and others the extent of our ignorance.* 

H. R. Huse*

contexts

How Dictionaries Are Made

It is widely believed that every word has a correct meaning, that we learn these meanings principally from teachers and grammarians (except that most of the time we don't bother to, so that we ordinarily speak "sloppy English"), and that dictionaries and grammars are the supreme authority in matters of meaning and usage. Few people ask by what authority the writers of dictionaries and grammars say what they say. I once got into a dispute with an Englishwoman over the pronunciation of a word and offered to look it up in the dictionary. The Englishwoman said firmly, "What for? I am English. I was born and brought up in England. The way I speak *is* English." Such self-assurance about one's own language is not

* From *The Illiteracy of the Literate* by H. R. Huse, copyright, 1933, by D. Appleton-Century Company, Inc. Reprinted by permission of Appleton-Century-Crofts, Inc.

uncommon among the English. In the United States, however, anyone who is willing to quarrel with the dictionary is regarded as either eccentric or mad.

Let us see how dictionaries are made and how the editors arrive at definitions. What follows applies, incidentally, only to those dictionary offices where first-hand, original research goes on—not those in which editors simply copy existing dictionaries. The task of writing a dictionary begins with reading vast amounts of the literature of the period or subject that the dictionary is to cover. As the editors read, they copy on cards every interesting or rare word, every unusual or peculiar occurrence of a common word, a large number of common words in their ordinary uses, and also the sentences in which each of these words appears, thus:

> pail
> The dairy *pails* bring home increase of milk
> Keats, *Endymion*
> I, 44–45

That is to say, the context of each word is collected, along with the word itself. For a really big job of dictionary-writing, such as the *Oxford English Dictionary* (usually bound in about twenty-five volumes), millions of such cards are collected, and the task of editing occupies decades. As the cards are collected, they are alphabetized and sorted. When the sorting is completed, there will be for each word anywhere from two or three to several hundred illustrative quotations, each on its card.

To define a word, then, the dictionary-editor places before him the stack of cards illustrating that word; each of the cards represents an actual use of the word by a writer of some literary or historical importance. He reads the cards carefully, discards some, rereads the rest, and divides up the stack according to what he thinks are the several senses of the word. Finally, he writes his definitions, following the hard-and-fast rule that each definition *must* be based on what the quotations in front of him reveal about the meaning of the word. The editor cannot be influenced by what *he* thinks a given word *ought* to mean. He must work according to the cards or not at all.

The writing of a dictionary, therefore, is not a task of setting up authoritative statements about the "true meanings" of words, but a task of *recording*, to the best of one's ability, what various words *have meant* to authors in the distant or immediate past. *The writer of a dictionary is a historian, not a lawgiver.* If, for example, we had been writing a dictionary in 1890, or even as late as 1919, we could have said that the word "broadcast" means "to scatter" (seed, for example), but we could not have decreed that from 1921 on, the most common meaning of the word should become "to disseminate audible messages, etc., by radio transmission." To regard the dictionary as an "authority," therefore, is to credit the dictionary-writer with gifts of prophecy which neither he nor anyone else possesses. In choosing our words when we speak or write, we can be *guided* by the historical record afforded us by the dictionary, but we cannot be *bound* by it, because new situations, new experiences, new inventions, new feelings are always compelling us to give new uses to old words. Looking under a "hood," we should ordinarily have found, five hundred years ago, a monk; today, we find a motorcar engine.[1]

Verbal and Physical Contexts

The way in which the dictionary-writer arrives at his definitions merely systematizes the way in which we all learn the meanings of words, beginning at infancy and continuing for the rest of our lives. Let us say that we have never heard the word "oboe" before, and we overhear a conversation in which the following sentences occur:

> He used to be the best *oboe*-player in town. . . . Whenever they came to that *oboe* part in the third movement, he used to get very excited. . . . I saw him one day at the music shop, buying a new reed for his *oboe*. . . . He never liked to play the clarinet after he started playing the *oboe*. . . . He said it wasn't much fun, because it was too easy.

Although the word may be unfamiliar, its meaning becomes clear to us as we listen. After hearing the first sentence, we know that an "oboe" is "played," so that it must be either a game or a musical instrument. With the second sentence the possibility of its being a game is eliminated. With each succeeding sentence the possibilities as to what an "oboe" may be are narrowed down until we get a fairly clear idea of what is meant. This is how we learn by *verbal context.*

But even independently of this, we learn by physical and social context. Let us say that we are playing golf and that we have hit the ball in a certain way with certain unfortunate results, so that our companion says, "That's a bad *slice*." He repeats this remark every time our ball fails to go straight. If we are reasonably bright, we learn in a very short time to say, when it happens again, "That's a bad slice." On one occasion, however, our friend says, "That's not a *slice* this time; that's a *hook*." In this case we consider what has happened, and we wonder what is different about the last stroke from those previous. As soon as we make

[1] *Webster's Third New International Dictionary* lists the word "hood" also as a shortened form of "hoodlum."

The time that elapsed between *Webster's Second Edition* (1934) and the *Third* (1961) indicates the enormous amount of reading and labor entailed in the preparation of a really thorough dictionary of a language as rapidly changing and as rich in vocabulary as English.

the distinction, we have added still another word to our vocabulary. The result is that after nine holes of golf, we can use both these words accurately—and perhaps several others as well, such as "divot," "number-five iron," "approach shot," *without ever having been told what they mean.* Indeed, we may play golf for years without ever being able to give a dictionary definition of "to slice": "To strike (the ball) so that the face of the club draws inward across the face of the ball, causing it to curve toward the right in flight (with a right-handed player)" *(Webster's New International Dictionary, Second Edition).* But even without being able to give such a definition, we should still be able to use the word accurately whenever the occasion demands.

We learn the meanings of practically all our words (which are, it will be remembered, merely complicated noises), not from dictionaries, not from definitions, but from hearing these noises as they accompany actual situations in life and then learning to associate certain noises with certain situations. Even as dogs learn to recognize "words," as for example by hearing "biscuit" at the same time as an actual biscuit is held before their noses, so do we all learn to interpret language by being aware of the happenings that accompany the noises people make at us—by being aware, in short, of contexts.

The definitions given by little children in school show clearly how they associate words with situations; they almost always define in terms of physical and social contexts: "Punishment is when you have been bad and they put you in a closet and don't let you have any supper." "Newspapers are what the paper boy brings and you wrap up the garbage with it." These are good definitions. They cannot be used in dictionaries mainly because they are too specific; it would be impossible to list the myriads of situations in which every word has been used. For this reason, dictionaries give definitions on a high level of abstraction, that is, with particular references left out for the sake of conciseness. (The term "high level of abstraction" is more fully explained in Chapter 10.) This is another reason why it is a great mistake to regard a dictionary definition as telling us all about a word.

Extensional and Intensional Meaning

Dictionaries deal with the world of intensional meanings, but there is another world which a dictionary by its very nature ignores: the world of extensional meanings. *The extensional meaning of an utterance is that which it points to in the extensional (physical) world,* referred to in Chapter 2. That is to say, the extensional meaning cannot be expressed in words because it is that which words stand for. An easy way to remember this is *to put your hand over your mouth and point* whenever you are asked to give an extensional meaning.

Of course, we cannot always point to the extensional meanings of the words we use. Therefore, so long as we are *discussing* meanings, we shall refer to that which is being talked about as the *denotation* of an utterance. For example, the denotation of the word "Winnipeg" is the prairie city of that name in southern Manitoba; the denotation of the word "dog" is a class of animals which includes dog_1 (Fido), dog_2 (Rex), dog_3 (Rover) . . . dog_n.

The *intensional meaning* of a word or expression, on the other hand, is that which is *suggested* (connoted) inside one's head. Roughly speaking, whenever we express the meanings of words by uttering more words, we are giving intensional meanings or connotations. To remember this, put your hand over your eyes and let the words spin around in your head.

Utterances may have, of course, both extensional and intensional meaning. If they have no intensional meaning at all—that is, if they start no notions whatever spinning about in our heads—they are meaningless noises, like foreign languages that we do not understand. On the other hand, it is possible for utterances to have no extensional meaning at all, in spite of the fact that they may start many notions spinning about in our heads. The statement, "Angels watch over my bed at night," is one that has intensional but no extensional meaning. This does not mean that there are no angels watching over my bed at night. When we say that the statement has no extensional meaning, we are merely saying that it is not operational, that we cannot see, touch, photograph, or in any scientific manner detect the presence of angels. The result is that, if an argument begins on the subject of whether or not angels watch over my bed, *there is no way of ending the argument to the satisfaction of all disputants,* the Christians and the non-Christians, the pious and the agnostic, the mystical and the scientific. Therefore, whether we believe in angels or not, knowing in advance that any argument on the subject will be both endless and futile, we can avoid getting into fights about it.

When, on the other hand, statements have extensional content, as when we say, "This room is fifteen feet long," arguments can come to a close. No matter how many guesses there are about the length of the room, all discussion ceases when someone produces a tape measure. This, then, is the important difference between extensional and intensional meanings: namely, when utterances have extensional meanings, discussion can be ended and agreement reached; when utterances have intensional meanings only and no extensional meanings, arguments may, and often do, go on indefinitely. Such arguments can result only in conflict. Among individuals, they may break up friendships; in society, they often split organizations into bitterly opposed groups; among nations, they may aggravate existing tensions so seriously as to become real obstacles to the peaceful settling of disputes.

Arguments of this kind may be termed "non-sense arguments," because they are based on utterances about which no sense data can be collected. Needless to say, there are occasions when the hyphen may be omitted—that depends on one's feelings toward the particular argument under consideration. The reader is requested to provide his own examples of "non-sense arguments." Even the foregoing example of the angels may give offense to some people, despite the fact that no attempt is made to deny or affirm the existence of angels. Imagine, then, the uproar that might result from giving a number of examples from theology, politics, law, economics, literary criticism, and other fields in which it is not customary to distinguish clearly sense from non-sense.

The "One Word, One Meaning" Fallacy

Everyone, of course, who has ever given any thought to the meanings of words has noticed that they are always shifting and changing in meaning. Usually, people regard this as a misfortune, because it "leads to sloppy thinking" and "mental confusion." To remedy this condition, they are likely to suggest that we should all agree on "one meaning" for each word and use it only with that meaning. Thereupon it will occur to them that we simply cannot make people agree in this way, even if we could set up an ironclad dictatorship under a committee of lexicographers who would place censors in every newspaper office and microphones in every home. The situation, therefore, appears hopeless.

Such an impasse is avoided when we start with a new premise altogether—one of the premises upon which modern linguistic thought is based: namely, that *no word ever has exactly the same meaning twice.*[2] The extent to which this premise fits the facts can be demonstrated in a number of ways. First, if we accept the proposition that the contexts of an utterance determine its meaning, it becomes apparent that since no two contexts are ever *exactly* the same, no two meanings can ever be exactly the same. How can we "fix the meaning" even for so common an expression as "to believe in" when it can be used in such sentences as the following:

I believe in you (I have confidence in you).
I believe in democracy (I accept the principles implied by the term democracy).
I believe in Santa Claus (It is my opinion that Santa Claus exists).

Second, we can take a word of "simple" meaning, like "kettle," for example. But when John says "kettle," its intensional meanings to him are the common characteristics of all the kettles John remembers. When Peter says "kettle," however, its intensional meanings to him are the common characteristics of all the kettles he remembers. *No matter how small or how negligible the differences may be between John's "kettle" and Peter's "kettle," there is some difference.*

Finally, let us examine utterances in terms of extensional meanings. If John, Peter, Harold, and George each say "my typewriter," we would have to point to four different typewriters to get the extensional meaning in each case: John's new Olivetti, Peter's old Remington, Harold's portable Smith-Corona, and the undenotable intended "typewriter" that George plans to buy someday: "My typewriter, when I buy it, will be an electric." Also, if John says "my typewriter" today, and again "my typewriter" tomorrow, the extensional meaning is different in the two cases, because the typewriter is not exactly the same from one day to the next (nor from one minute to the next): slow processes of wear, change, and decay are going on constantly. Although we can say, then, that the differences in the meanings of a word on one occasion, on another occasion a minute later, and on still another occasion another minute later are negligible, we cannot say that the meanings are *exactly* the same.

To insist dogmatically that we know what a word means *in advance of its utterance* is nonsense. All we can know in advance is *approximately* what it will mean. After the utterance, we interpret what has been said

[2]In the same vein, the Greek philosopher Heraclitus argued that one cannot step into the same river twice.

in the light of both verbal and physical contexts and act according to our interpretation. An examination of the verbal context of an utterance, as well as the examination of the utterance itself, directs us to the intensional meanings; an examination of the physical context directs us to the extensional meanings. When John says to James, "Bring me that book, will you?" James looks in the direction of John's pointed finger (physical context) and sees a desk with several books on it (physical context); he thinks back over their previous conversation (verbal context) and knows which of those books is being referred to.

Interpretation *must* be based, therefore, on the totality of contexts. If it were otherwise, we should not be able to account for the fact that even if we fail to use the right (customary) words in some situations, people can very frequently understand us. For example:

> A: Gosh, look at that second baseman go!
> B (looking): You mean the shortstop?
> A: Yes, that's what I mean.

> A: There must be something wrong with the oil line; the engine has started to balk.
> B: Don't you mean "gas line"?
> A: Yes—didn't I say "gas line"?

Contexts often indicate our meaning so clearly that we do not even have to say what we mean in order to be understood.

Ignoring Contexts

It is clear, then, that the ignoring of contexts in any act of interpretation is at best a stupid practice. At its worst, it can be a vicious practice. A common example is the sensationalistic newspaper story in which a few words by a public personage are torn out of their context and made the basis of a completely misleading account. There is the incident of a Veterans Day speaker, a university teacher, who declared before a high-school assembly that the Gettysburg Address was "a powerful piece of propaganda." The context clearly revealed that "propaganda" was being used, not according to its popular meaning, but rather, as the speaker himself stated, to mean "explaining the moral purposes of a war." The context also revealed that the speaker was a very great admirer of Lincoln. However, the local newspaper, ignoring the context, presented the account in such a way as to suggest that the speaker had called Lincoln a liar. On this basis, the newspaper began a campaign against the instructor. The speaker remonstrated with the editor of the newspaper, who replied, in effect, "I don't care what else you said. You said the Gettysburg Address was propaganda, didn't you?" This appeared to the editor complete proof that Lincoln had been maligned and that the speaker deserved to be discharged from his position at the university. Similar practices may be found in advertisements. A reviewer may be quoted on the jacket of a book as having said, "A brilliant work," while reading of the context may reveal that what he really said was, "It just falls short of being a brilliant work." There are some people who will always be able to find a defense for such a practice in saying, "But he did use the words 'a brilliant work,' didn't he?"

People in the course of argument very frequently complain about words meaning different things to different people. Instead of complaining, they should accept such differences as a matter of course. It would be startling indeed if the word "justice," for example, were to have the same meaning to each of the nine justices of the United States Supreme Court; we should get nothing but unanimous decisions. It would be even more startling if "justice" meant the same thing in the United States as it does in Russia. If we can get deeply into our consciousness the principle that no word ever has the same meaning twice, we will develop the habit of automatically examining contexts, and this will enable us to understand better what others are saying. As it is, however, we are all too likely, when a word sounds familiar, to assume that we understand it, even when we don't. In this way we read into people's remarks meanings that were never intended. Then we waste energy in angrily accusing people of "intellectual dishonesty" or "abuse of words," when their only sin is that they use words in ways unlike our own, as they can hardly help doing, especially if their background has been widely different from ours. There are cases of intellectual dishonesty and abuse of words, of course, but they do not always occur in the places where people think they do.

In the study of history or of cultures other than our own, contexts take on special importance. To say, "There was no running water or electricity in the house," does not condemn an English house in 1570 but says a great deal against a house in Chicago in 1970. Again, if we wish to understand the Constitution of the United States, it is not enough, as our historians now tell us, merely to look up all the words in the dictionary and to read the interpretations written by Supreme Court justices. We must see the Constitution in its historical context: the conditions of life, the state of the arts and industries and transportation, the climate of opinion of the time—all of which helped to determine what words went into the Constitution and what those words meant to those who wrote them. After all, the words "United States of America" stood for quite a different-sized nation and a different culture in 1790 from what they stand for today. When it comes to very big subjects, the range of contexts to be examined—verbal, social, and historical—may become very large indeed.

In personal relations, furthermore, those who ignore psychological contexts often make the mistake of interpreting as insults remarks that are only intended in jest.

The Interaction of Words

All this is not to say, however, that the reader might just as well throw away his dictionary simply because contexts are so important. Any word in a sentence—any sentence in a paragraph, any paragraph in a larger unit—whose meaning is revealed by its context is itself part of the context of the rest of the text. To look up a word in a dictionary, therefore, frequently explains not only the word itself but the rest of the sentence, paragraph, conversation, or essay in which it is found. All words within a given context interact with one another.

Realizing, then, that a dictionary is a historical work, we should understand the dictionary thus: "The word *mother* has most frequently been used in the past among English-speaking people to indicate a female parent." From this we can safely infer, "If that is how it has been used, that is what it *probably* means in the sentence I am trying to understand." This is what we normally do, of course; after we look up a word in the dictionary, we reexamine the context to see if the definition fits. If the context reads, "Mother began to form in the bottle," one may have to look at the dictionary more carefully.

A dictionary definition, therefore, is an invaluable guide to interpretation. Words do not have a single "correct meaning"; they apply to *groups* of similar situations, which might be called *areas of meaning.* It is for defining these areas of meaning that a dictionary is useful. In each use of any word, we examine the particular context and the extensional events denoted (if possible) to discover the *point* intended within the area of meaning.

APPLICATIONS

I. If you were putting together a dictionary and had only the following quotations, what definition would you write for the word "gyxpyx"? Please write a ten- to twenty-word definition of this term; a synonym is not acceptable.

1. His gyxpyx is twenty years old, but it still works.
2. Bill Smith just bought a portable electric gyxpyx.
3. The new girl is fast as blazes with the gyxpyx.
4. One of the keys on the gyxpyx is stuck.
5. I don't care what you say. I think a gyxpyx is better than an abacus.

From the following quotations make up a definition of the word "wanky."

1. He seems to be perpetually wanky.

2. Some people feel most wanky in the early morning, but I get that way just before supper.

3. If you want to get over that wanky feeling, take Johnson's Homogenized Yeast Tablets.

4. . . . the wanky, wanky bluebell
That droops upon its stem. . . .

5. I'm not cross, just wanky.

II. Some readers have assumed from the sound and spelling of the word "extensional" that it is a form of "extension" in the sense of "prolonging or stretching out" and that "intensional" is a form of "intention," meaning "purpose or design." Since these terms will be utilized throughout the remainder of this book, it might be well for the reader to reread pages 52–54.

III. In what contexts are the following questions likely to arise, and in those contexts, which are non-sense questions and which are not? Can you tell why? Can you make any of the non-sense questions verifiable by changing the wording?

1. Is democracy a failure?

SAMPLE ANALYSIS: Unless there is reasonable agreement as to the extensional meaning of "democracy" and "failure," a discussion of this question is not likely to be fruitful. It might be broken up into smaller questions such as these: "Assuming that democracy is a success if 60 or more percent of those able to vote in presidential elections do vote, what was the percentage of voters in the elections of 1960, 1964, 1968 . . . ?" "Assuming that democracy may be said to be reasonably successful if intelligent but underprivileged children are given the opportunity to finish their schooling, what percentage of fourth-grade children with I.Q.'s of over 125 finish high school?" If, however, we talk chiefly in terms of intensional meanings of the terms "democracy" and "failure," disagreement and ill-feelings are likely to result. In many contexts where such a question is brought up for discussion it would seem to be a non-sense question.

2. Is there a life after death?

3. Are women stronger than men?

4. Is the universe expanding or contracting?

5. Is marijuana more harmful than alcohol?

IV. Specify the conditions under which you would say "yes" to the following:

1. Jazz is dying out.

2. Do you love me?

3. Negroes are better athletes than whites.

4. All wars are immoral.

5. DEAR DOROTHY DIX: How can a wife tell when her husband loves her? I have been married ten years and my husband and I quarrel constantly. He beats me and swears at me, and then tells how much he loves me and cries over it all. Now I would like to leave him and go back to my folks, but he won't let me go. Says he can't bear to be separated from me. Please tell me what to do. Do you think he really loves me?

UNHAPPY WIFE, Chicago *Sun-Times*

V. Listen closely to the arguments you hear or overhear in the next few days and ask yourself these questions:

1. What is the question at issue?

2. Is it a non-sense question, or could it be answered by observation of the disputed facts? What would we have to do to tell whether or not it is true?

3. To what extent do the participants reach an agreement? If the argument ends in disagreement, can we think of any procedure that might have helped to bring about agreement?

4. Are there any "key words" around which the dispute seems to resolve?

5. Do the disputants ever take each other's statements out of context, either consciously or unwittingly?

Be prepared to discuss one or more of these arguments in class.

VI. Here is a famous problem related to the "one word, one meaning" fallacy. How would you use the semantic principles discussed in this chapter to resolve the argument? What are the essential points of difficulty?

Some years ago, being with a camping party in the mountains, I returned from a solitary ramble to find everyone engaged in a ferocious metaphysical dispute. The corpus of the dispute was a squirrel—a live squirrel supposed to be clinging to one side of a tree-trunk; while over against the tree's opposite side a human being was imagined to stand. This human witness tries to get sight of the squirrel by moving rapidly around the tree, but no matter how fast he goes, the squirrel moves as fast in the opposite direction and always keeps the tree between himself and the man, so that never a glimpse of him is caught. The resultant metaphysical problem now is this: *Does the man go around the squirrel, or not?* He goes round the tree, sure enough, and the squirrel is on the tree; but does he go round the squirrel? In the unlimited leisure of the wilderness discussion had been worn threadbare. Everyone had taken sides, and was obstinate; and the numbers on both sides were even. Each side, when I appeared, therefore appealed to me to make it a majority. Mindful of the scholastic adage that whenever you meet a contradiction you must make a distinction, I immediately sought and found one, as follows. . . .

WILLIAM JAMES

VII. Many meanings and contexts may affect, sometimes radically, the definitions of words. Take the following words (and any others you may wish to work with) and provide contexts, in sentence form, to clarify their different meanings.

EXAMPLE: *pass*
I hope I pass the exam.
He was about to pass on to his eternal reward.
I was given a pass to the movies.
He caught the pass on the goal line and scored.
It's time to pass the hat.

freedom	love	habit	run
peace	society	groovy	set

VIII. Examine a few advertisements with reference to the distinction between extensional and intensional meaning. What kinds of appeals are being made? Can you describe them as non-sense? Nonsense?

IX. Here are some statements whose meanings can be crucially changed according to context. Below each statement is its context. Before looking at the context, write your immediate response to the statement.

1. STATEMENT: He hasn't had a haircut in four months.
   RESPONSE: He must be rebelling against society or else identifying with the youth subculture.
   ACTUAL CONTEXT: He let his hair grow out for his part in *Hamlet.* "As soon as the play is over, I'm cutting it off," he says.

2. STATEMENT: He looks at me blankly when I speak to him.
   CONTEXT: I therefore suppose that he is still unconscious from the blow.

3. STATEMENT: Of course, son, I'll buy you a new sports car for Christmas.
   CONTEXT: In addition, I'll buy your sister two mink coats, your mother a villa in France, and your grandfather the Brooklyn Bridge.

Tens of thousands of years have elapsed since we shed our tails, but we are still communicating with a medium developed to meet the needs of aboreal man. . . . We may smile at the linguistic illusions of primitive man, but may we forget that the verbal machinery on which we so readily rely, and with which our metaphysicians still profess to probe the Nature of Existence, was set up by him, and may be responsible for other illusions hardly less gross and not more easily eradicable?

C. K. Ogden and I. A. Richards

the double task of language

Connotations

Report language, as we have seen, is *instrumental* in character—that is, instrumental in getting work done; but, as we have seen, language is also used for the direct *expression* of the feelings of the speaker. Considering language from the point of view of the *hearer*, we can say that report language *informs* us but that these expressive uses of language (for example, judgments and also presymbolic functions, which will be discussed in Chapter 6) *affect* us—that is, affect our feelings. When language is affective, it has the character of a kind of force.[1] A spoken insult, for example, provokes a return insult, just as a blow provokes a return blow; a loud and peremptory command compels, just as a push compels; talking and shouting are as much a display of energy as pound-

[1]Such terms as "emotional" and "emotive," which imply misleading distinctions between the "emotional appeals" and "intellectual appeals" of language, should be carefully avoided. In any case, "emotional" applies too specifically to strong feelings. The word "affective," however, in such an expression as the "affective uses of language," describes not only the way in which language can arouse strong feelings, but also the way in which it arouses extremely subtle, sometimes unconscious, responses. "Affective" has the further advantage of introducing no inconvenient distinctions between "physical" and "mental" responses.

ing the chest. And the first of the affective elements in speech, as we have seen, is the tone of voice—its loudness or softness, its pleasantness or unpleasantness, its variations in volume and intonation during the course of the utterance.

Another affective element in language is rhythm. *Rhythm* is the name we give to the effect produced by the repetition of auditory (or kinesthetic) stimuli at fairly regular intervals. From the boom-boom of a childish drum to the subtle nuances of cultivated poetry and music there is a continuous development and refinement of man's responsiveness to rhythm. To produce rhythm is to arouse attention and interest; so affective is rhythm, indeed, that it catches our attention even when we do not want our attention distracted. *Rhyme* and *alliteration* are, of course, ways of emphasizing rhythm in language, through repetition of similar sounds at regular intervals. Political-slogan writers and advertisers therefore have a special fondness for rhyme and alliteration: "Tippecanoe and Tyler Too," "Rum, Romanism, and Rebellion," "Keep Cool with Coolidge," "Order from Horder," "Better Buy Buick," "Take Tea 'n' See," "I Like Ike," "All the Way with L. B. J." These are rather absurd slogans so far as informative value is concerned, but by their sound they set up small rhythmic echoes in one's head that make them annoyingly difficult to forget.

In addition to tone of voice and rhythm, another extremely important affective element in language is the aura of feelings, pleasant or unpleasant, that surrounds practically all words. It will be recalled that in Chapter 4 a distinction was made between denotations (or extensional meaning), pointing to things, and connotations (or intensional meaning), consisting of "ideas," "notions," "concepts," and feelings suggested in the mind. These connotations can be divided into two kinds, the *informative* and the *affective*.

Informative Connotations

The informative connotations of a word are its socially agreed-upon, "impersonal" meanings, *insofar as meanings can be given at all by additional words*. For example, if we talk about a "pig," we cannot give the extensional meaning of the word unless there happens to be an actual pig for us to point to. But we can give its informative connotations: "pig" for English-speaking people means "domesticated mammalian quadruped of the kind generally raised by farmers to be made into pork, bacon, ham, lard. . . ."

Informative connotations may include both the *definition* of a term ("pig" as a "domesticated mammalian . . .") and its *denotation* (pig_1, pig_2, pig_3 . . .). But some terms have a definition, yet lack denotation: for example, a "mermaid" exists by definition only ("a creature half woman and half fish"). The term has no denotation because an extensional mermaid is not to be found. Terms in mathematics which have "logical existence" but no extensional reference can also be said to have informative connotations, but no denotation.

Denotations would seem to offer few problems of interpretation, since we are dealing here with words apart from the personal feelings that they may arouse. But such is not the case, because the same word may denote different things to people in different occupations or in different parts of the English-speaking world. The names of birds, animals, and plants are an interesting example of confusion about denotations. The English "robin" is an entirely different species from the American bird of that name. Many different and unrelated kinds of fish are denoted by the word "bream" (pronounced "brim" in the South). Belgian hares, we are told, are "really rabbits," while the American jackrabbit is "really a hare." The term "crocus," as popularly used, refers in different parts of the country to different flowers. I have also heard from a bird-watcher that the English sparrow is not a sparrow at all, but a weaver finch. House finches are often called linnets. The linnet is a European bird that we don't have in America.

Such differences in popular and regional terminology are among the reasons for establishing scientific names for plants and animals—names which are accepted and used by the entire international scientific community.

Affective Connotations

The affective connotations of a word, on the other hand, are the aura of personal feelings it arouses, as, for example, "pig": "Ugh! Dirty, evil-smelling creatures, wallowing in filthy sties," and so on. While there is no necessary agreement about these feelings—some people like pigs and others don't—it is the existence of these feelings that enables us to use words, under certain circumstances, *for their affective connotations alone,* without regard to their informative connotations. That is to say, when we are strongly moved, we express our feelings by uttering words with the affective connotations appropriate to our feelings, without paying any attention to the informative connotations they may have. We angrily call people "pigs," "rats," "wolves," "old bears," "skunks," or lovingly call them "honey," "sugar," "duck," and "sweetie pie." Indeed, all verbal expressions of feeling make use to some extent of the affective connotations of words.

All words have, according to the uses to which they are put, some affective character. There are many words that exist more for their affective value than for their informative value; for example, we can refer to "that man" as "that gentleman," "that individual," "that person," "that gent," "that guy," "that hombre," "that bird," or "that bozo"—and while the person referred to may be the same in all these cases, each of these terms reveals a difference in our feelings toward him. Dealers in knickknacks frequently write "Gyfte Shoppe" over the door, hoping that such a spelling carries, even if their merchandise does not, the flavor of antiquity. Affective connotations suggestive of England and Scotland are often sought in the choice of brand names for men's suits and overcoats: "Glenmoor," "Regent Park," "Bond Street." Sellers of perfume choose names for their products that suggest France—"Mon Désir," "Indiscret," "Evening in Paris"—and expensive brands always come in "flacons," never in bottles. Consider, too, the differences among the following expressions:

I have the honor to inform Your Excellency . . . .
This is to advise you . . . .
I should like to tell you, sir . . . .
I'm telling you, Mister . . . .
Cheez, boss, git a load of dis . . . .

The parallel columns below also illustrate how affective connotations can be changed while extensional meanings remain the same.

Finest quality filet mignon.	First-class piece of dead cow.
Cubs trounce Giants 15–3.	Score: Cubs 15, Giants 3.
French armies in rapid retreat!	The strategic withdrawal of the French forces to previously prepared positions in the rear was accomplished briskly and efficiently.
Urban Redevelopment Bill steamrollered through Senate.	Senate passes Urban Redevelopment Bill over strong opposition.
She has her husband under her thumb.	She takes a deep interest in her husband's activities.
The governor appeared to be gravely concerned and said that a statement would be issued in a few days, after careful examination of the facts.	The governor was on the spot.

The story is told that, during the Boer War, the Boers were described in the British press as "sneaking and skulking behind rocks and bushes." The British forces, when they finally learned from the Boers how to employ tactics suitable to veldt warfare, were described as "cleverly taking advantage of cover."

A Note on Verbal Taboo

In every language there seem to be certain "unmentionables"—words of such strong affective connotations that they cannot be used in polite discourse. In English, the first of these to come to mind are, of course, words dealing with excretion and sex. We ask movie ushers and filling-station attendants where the "lounge" or "rest room" is, although we usually have no intention of lounging or resting. "Powder room" is another euphemism for the same facility, also known as "toilet," which itself is an earlier euphemism. Indeed, it is impossible in polite society to state, without having to resort to baby talk or a medical vocabulary, what a "rest room" is for. (It is "where you wash your hands.") Another term is "John." There is now a book on the best "Johns" in New York.

Money is another subject about which communication is in some ways inhibited. It is all right to mention *sums* of money, such as $10,000 or $2.50. But it is considered in bad taste to inquire directly into other people's financial affairs, unless such an inquiry is really necessary in the course of business. When creditors send bills, they almost never mention money, although that is what they are writing about. There are many circumlocutions: "We beg to call your attention to what might be an oversight on your part." "We would appreciate your early attention to this matter." "May we look forward to an early remittance?"

The fear of death carries over, quite understandably in view of the widespread confusion of symbols with things symbolized, into fear of the *words* having to do with death. Many people, therefore, instead of saying "died," substitute such expressions as "passed away," "went to his reward," "departed," and "went west." In Japanese, the word for death, *shi*, happens to have the same pronunciation as the word for the number four. This coincidence results in many linguistically awkward situations, since people avoid "*shi*" in the discussion of numbers and prices, and use "*yon*," a word of different origin, instead.

Words having to do with anatomy and sex—and words even vaguely suggesting anatomical or sexual matters—have, especially in American culture, remarkable affective connotations. Ladies of the nineteenth century could not bring themselves to say "breast" or "leg"—not even of chicken—so that the terms "white meat" and "dark meat" were substituted. It was thought inelegant to speak of "going to bed," and "to retire" was used instead. In rural America there are many euphemisms for the word "bull"; among them are "he-cow," "cow-critter," "male cow," "gentleman cow." But Americans are not alone in their delicacy about such matters. When D. H. Lawrence's first novel, *The White Peacock* (1911), was published, the author was widely and vigorously criticized for having used (in innocuous context) the word "stallion." "Our hearts are warm, our bellies are full" was changed to "Our hearts are warm, and we are full" in a 1962 presentation of the Rodgers and Hammerstein musical *Carousel* before the British Royal Family.[2]

These verbal taboos, although sometimes amusing, also produce

[2]See H. W. Fowler's comments on "genteelisms" in his *A Dictionary of Modern English Usage*. 2nd edition.

serious problems, since they prevent frank discussion of sexual matters. Social workers, with whom I have discussed this question, report that young people of junior high school and high school age who contract venereal disease, become pregnant out of wedlock, and get into other serious trouble of this kind are almost always profoundly ignorant of the most elementary facts about sex and procreation. Their ignorance is apparently due to the fact that neither they nor their parents have a vocabulary with which to discuss such matters: the nontechnical vocabulary of sex is to them too coarse and shocking to be used, while the technical, medical vocabulary is unknown to them. The social workers find, therefore, that the first step in helping these young people is usually a linguistic one: the students have to be taught a vocabulary in which they can talk about their problems before they can be helped further.

The stronger verbal taboos have, however, a genuine social value. When we are extremely angry and we feel the need of expressing our anger in violence, uttering these forbidden words provides us with a relatively harmless verbal substitute for going berserk and smashing furniture; that is, the words act as a kind of safety valve in our moments of crisis.

It is difficult to explain why some words should have such powerful affective connotations while others with the same informative connotations do not. Some of our verbal reticences, especially the religious ones, have the authority of the Bible: "Thou shalt not take the name of the Lord thy God in vain; for the Lord will not hold him guiltless that taketh his name in vain" (Exodus 21:7). "Gee," "gosh almighty," and "gosh darn" are ways to avoid saying "Jesus," "God Almighty," and "God damn"; and carrying the biblical injunction one step further, we also avoid taking the name of the Devil in vain by means of such expressions as "the deuce," "the dickens," and "Old Nick." It appears that among all the people of the world, among the civilized as well as the primitive, there is a feeling that the names of the gods are too holy, and the names of evil spirits too terrifying, to be spoken lightly.

The primitive confusion of word with thing, of symbol with thing symbolized, manifests itself in some parts of the world in a belief that the name of a person is *part of* that person. To know someone's name, therefore, is to have power over him. Because of this belief, it is customary among some peoples for children to be given at birth a "real name" known only to the parents and never used, as well as a nickname or public name to be called by in society. In this way the child is protected from being put in anyone's power. The story of Rumpelstiltskin is a European illustration of this belief in the power of names.

Thomas Mann, in *Joseph and His Brethren*, gives the following dramatic account of the power of names, according to ancient Jewish belief:

> [Joseph, speaking of a lion.] "But if he had come, with lashing tail, and roared after his prey, like the voice of the chanting seraphim, yet thy child would have been little affrighted or not at all before his rage. . . . For knoweth not my father that the beasts fear and avoid man, for that God gave him the spirit of understanding and taught him the orders into which single things fall; doth he not know how Shemmael shrieked when the man of earth knew how to name the creation as though he were its master and framer . . . ? And the beasts too they are ashamed and put the tail between their legs because we know them and have power over their names and can thus render powerless the roaring might of the single one, by naming him. If now he had come, with long slinking tread, with his hateful nose, mewing and spitting, terror would not have robbed me of my senses, nor made me pale before his riddle. 'Is thy name Blood-Thirst?' I would have asked of him making merry at his expense. 'Or Springing Murder?' But there I would have sat upright and cried out: 'Lion! Lo, Lion art thou, by nature and species, and thy riddle lieth bare before me, so that I speak it out and with a laugh it is plain.' And he would have blinked before the name and gone meekly away before the word, powerless to answer unto me. For he is quite unlearned and knows nought of writing tools."

Words with Built-in Judgments

The fact that some words arouse both informative and affective connotations simultaneously gives a special complexity to discussions involving religious, racial, national, and political groups. To many people, the word "communist" means simultaneously "one who believes in communism" (informative connotations) *and* "one whose ideals and purposes are altogether repellent" (affective connotations). Words applying to occupations of which one disapproves ("pickpocket," "racketeer," "prostitute"), like those applying to believers in philosophies of which one may disapprove ("atheist," "heretic," "materialist," "Holy Roller," "radical," "liberal"), likewise often communicate *simultaneously* a fact and a judgment on the fact.

In some parts of the southwestern United States there is strong prejudice against Mexicans, both immigrant and American-born. The strength of this prejudice is indirectly revealed by the fact that newspapers and polite people have stopped using the word "Mexican" altogether, using the expression "Spanish-speaking person" instead. "Mexican" has been used with contemptuous connotations for so long that it has become, in the opinion of many people in the region, unsuitable for polite conversation. In some circles, the word is reserved for lower-class Mexicans, while the "politer" term is used for the upper class. There are also terms, such as "chicano" and "Latino," that Mexican-American and Spanish-speaking groups have chosen to describe themselves.

In dealing with subjects about which strong feelings exist, we are compelled to talk in roundabout terms if we wish to avoid arousing tradi-

A spade calling a spade a spade

tional prejudices, which hinder clear thinking. Hence we have not only such terms as "Spanish-speaking persons" but also, in other contexts, "problem drinkers" instead of "drunkards," and "Hansen's disease" instead of "leprosy."

These verbal stratagems are necessitated by the strong affective connotations as well as by the often misleading implications of their blunter alternatives; they are not merely a matter of giving things fancy names in order to fool people, as the simple-minded often believe. Because the old names are "loaded," they dictate traditional patterns of behavior toward those to whom they are applied. When everybody "knew" what to do about "little hoodlums," they threw them in jail and "treated 'em rough." Once in jail, little hoodlums showed a marked tendency to grow up into big hoodlums. When thoughtful people began to observe such facts, they started rethinking the problem, using different terminologies. What is the best way of describing these troubled and troublesome youths? Shall they be described as "defectives" or "psychopathic personalities"? Or as "maladjusted" or "neurotic"? Shall we say they are "deprived," "disadvantaged," "frustrated," or "socially displaced"? Shall we say they are "troubled by problems of identity"? Are they in need of "confinement," "punishment," "treatment," "education," or "rehabilitation"? It is through trying out many, many possible terms such as these that new ways of dealing with the problem are discovered and devised.

The meaning of words, as we have observed, changes from speaker to speaker and from context to context. The words "Japs" and "niggers," for instance, although often used both as a designation and an insult, are sometimes used with no intent to offend. In some classes of society and in some geographical areas, there are people who know no other words for Japanese, and in other areas there are people who know no other words for Negroes. Ignorance of regional and class differences of dialect often results in feelings being needlessly hurt. Those who believe that the meaning of a word is *in the word* often fail to understand this simple point of differences in usage. For example, an elderly Japanese woman of my acquaintance used to squirm at the mention of the word

"Jap," even when used in an innocuous or complimentary context. "Whenever I hear that word," she used to say, "I feel dirty all over."

The word "nigger" has a similar effect on most Negroes. A distinguished Negro sociologist tells of an incident in his adolescence when he was hitchhiking far from home in regions where Negroes are hardly ever seen. He was befriended by an extremely kindly white couple who fed him and gave him a place to sleep in their home. However, they kept calling him "little nigger"—a fact which upset him profoundly, even while he was grateful for their kindness. He finally got up courage to ask the man not to call him by that "insulting term."

> "Who's insultin' you, son?" said the man.
> "You are, sir—that name you're always calling me."
> "What name?"
> "Uh . . . you know."
> "I ain't callin' you no names, son."
> "I mean your calling me 'nigger.'"
> "Well, what's insultin' about that? You are a nigger, ain't you?"

As the sociologist says now in telling the story, "I couldn't think of an answer then, and I'm not sure I can now."

In case the sociologist reads this book, we are happy to provide him with an answer, although it may be twenty-five years late. He might have said to his benefactor, "Sir, in the part of the country I come from, white people who treat colored people with respect call them Negroes, while those who wish to show their contempt for colored people call them niggers. I hope the latter is not your intention." And the man might have replied, had he been kindly in thought as he was in deed, "Well, you don't say! Sorry I hurt your feelings, son, but I didn't know." And that would have been that. Many black people have rejected the term "Negro" as itself an insulting term and prefer to be called blacks or Afro-Americans. Some "hip" terms that Negroes use for themselves are "moulenjam," "splib," "member," "blood," and "boots."

Negroes, having for a long time been victims of unfair persecution because of race, are often even more sensitive about racial appellations than the Japanese woman previously mentioned. It need hardly be said that Negroes suffer from the confusion of informative and affective connotations just as often as white people—or Japanese. Such Negroes, and those white sympathizers with the Negro cause who are equally naive in linguistic matters, tend to feel that the entire colored "race" is vilified whenever and wherever the word "nigger" occurs. They bristle even when it occurs in such expressions as "niggertoe" (the name of an herb; also a dialect term for Brazil nut), "niggerhead" (a type of chewing tobacco), "niggerfish" (a kind of fish found in West Indian and Floridan waters)—and even the word "niggardly" (of Scandinavian origin, unrelated, of course, to "Negro") has to be avoided before some audiences.

Such easily offended people sometimes send delegations to visit dictionary offices to demand that the word "nigger" be excluded from future editions, being unaware that dictionaries, as has already been said (Chapter 4), perform a historical, rather than legislative, function. To try to reduce racial discrimination by getting dictionaries to stop including the word "nigger" is like trying to cut down the birth rate by shutting down the office of the county register of births. When racial discrimination against Negroes is done away with, the word will either disappear or else lose its present connotations. By losing its present connotations, we mean, first, that people who need to insult their fellow men will have found more interesting grounds on which to base their insults and, second, that people who are called "niggers" will no longer fly off the handle any more than a person from New England does at being called a "Yankee."

One other curious fact needs to be recorded about words applied to such hotly debated issues as race, religion, political heresy, and economic dissent. Every reader is acquainted with certain people who, according to their own flattering descriptions of themselves, "believe in being frank" and like to "tell it like [sic] it is." By "telling it like it is," they usually mean calling anything or anyone by the term which has the strongest and most disagreeable affective connotations. Why people should pin medals on themselves for "candor" for performing this nasty feat has often puzzled me. Sometimes it is necessary to violate verbal taboos as an aid to clearer thinking, but more often "calling a spade a spade" is to provide our minds with a greased runway down which we may slide back into old *and discredited* patterns of evaluation and behavior.

Everyday Uses of Language

The language of everyday life, then, differs from "reports" such as those discussed in Chapter 3. As in reports, we have to be accurate in choosing words that have the informative connotations we want; otherwise the reader or hearer will not know what we are talking about. But in addition, we have to give those words the affective connotations we want in order that he will be interested or moved by what we are saying and feel toward things the way we do. This double task confronts us in almost all ordinary conversation, oratory, persuasive writing, and literature. Much of this task, however, is performed intuitively; without being aware of it, we choose the tone of voice, the rhythms, and the affective connotations appropriate to our utterance. Over the informative connotations of our utterances we exercise somewhat more conscious control. Improvement in our ability to understand language, as well as in our ability to use it, depends therefore not only upon sharpening our sense for the informative connotations of words but *also upon the sharpening of our insight into the affective elements in language through social experience, through contact with many kinds of people in many kinds of situations, and through literary study.*

The following, finally, are some of the things that can happen in any speech event:

1. The informative connotations may be inadequate or misleading, but the affective connotations may be sufficiently well directed so that we are able to interpret correctly. For example, when someone says, "Imagine who I saw today! Old What's-his-name—oh, you know who I mean—Whoosis, that old buzzard that lives on, oh—what's the name of that street!" there are means, certainly not clearly informative, by which we manage to understand who is being referred to.
2. The informative connotations may be correct enough and the extensional meanings clear, but the affective connotations may be inappropriate, misleading, or ludicrous. This happens frequently when people try to write elegantly: "Jim ate so many bags of *Arachis hypogaea*, commonly known as peanuts, at the ball game today that he was unable to do justice to his evening repast."
3. Both informative and affective connotations may "sound all right," but there may be no "territory" corresponding to the "map." For example: "He lived for many years in the beautiful hill country just south of Chicago." There is no hill country just south of Chicago.
4. Both informative and affective connotations may be *consciously* used to create "maps" of "territories" that do not exist. There are many reasons, only two of which need be mentioned now, why we should wish on occasion to do this. First, we may wish to give pleasure:

> Yet mark'd I where the bolt of Cupid fell:
> It fell upon a little western flower,
> Before milk-white, now purple with love's wound,
> And maidens call it, Love-in-idleness.
> Fetch me that flower; the herb I show'd thee once:
> The juice of it on sleeping eyelids laid
> Will make or man or woman madly dote
> Upon the next live creature that it sees.
>
> *A Midsummer Night's Dream*

A second reason is to enable us to plan for the future. For example, we can say, "Let us suppose there is a bridge at the foot of this street; then the heavy traffic on High Street would be partly diverted over the new bridge; shopping would be less concentrated on High Street. . . ." Having visualized the condition that would result, we can recommend or oppose the bridge according to whether or not we like the probable results. The relationship of present words to future events is a subject we must leave for Chapter 7.

APPLICATIONS

I. Be prepared to discuss the following passage in the light of what you have read about affective connotations. Have you encountered similar situations in the social gatherings you have attended?

> . . . I remember once hearing a Negro friend have an intellectual discussion at a party for half an hour with a white girl who was a few years out of college. The Negro literally could not read or write, but he had an extraordinary ear and a fine sense of mimicry. So as the girl spoke, he would respond to one or another facet of her doubts. When she would finish what she felt was a particularly well-articulated idea, he would smile privately and say, "Other-direction . . . do you really believe in that?"
>
> "Well . . . No," the girl would stammer, "now that you get down to it, there is something disgusting about it to me," and she would be off again for five more minutes.
>
> Of course the Negro was not learning anything about the merits and demerits of the argument, but he was learning a great deal about a type of girl he had never met before, and that was what he wanted. Being unable to read or write, he could hardly be interested in ideas nearly as much as in lifemanship, and so he eschewed any attempt to obey the precision or lack of precision in the girl's language, and instead sensed her character (and the values of her social type) by swinging with the nuances of her voice.
>
> NORMAN MAILER, *The White Negro*

II. Bertrand Russell, on a British Broadcasting Company radio program called the Brains Trust, gave the following "conjugation" of an "irregular verb":

I am firm.

You are obstinate.

He is a pig-headed fool.

The *New Statesman and Nation,* quoting the above as a model, offered prizes to readers who sent in the best "irregular verbs" of this kind. Here are some of the published entries.

I am sparkling. You are unusually talkative. He is drunk.

I am righteously indignant. You are annoyed. He is making a fuss about nothing.

I am fastidious. You are fussy. He is an old woman.

I am a creative writer. You have a journalistic flair. He is a prosperous hack.

I am beautiful. You have quite good features. She isn't bad-looking, if you like that type.

I day dream. You are an escapist. He ought to see a psychiatrist.

I have about me something of the subtle, haunting, mysterious fragrance of the Orient. You rather overdo it, dear. She stinks.

"Conjugate," in a similar way, the following statements:

1. I am slender.
2. I am a trifle overweight.
3. I don't dance very well.
4. Naturally I use a little make-up.
5. I collect rare, old objects of art.
6. I don't like to play bridge with people who are too serious about it.
7. I have a sense of humor.
8. I have a cocktail or two before dinner.
9. I love my country.
10. I am cautious.
11. I speak my mind frankly.

III. Think about the following questions in terms of the discussion on verbal taboos and connotations. (See pages 65–68.)

What's in a name? To what degree "are" we our names? We associate certain qualities with names such as "Otis," "Lance," "Percy," or "Rock." Why? Certain classes and ethnic groups can be associated with certain names. Can you think of any examples? Would a different name have made any difference in your life?

IV. Many people have names that are strangely fitting for their jobs. Can you think of some amusing examples from real life? There are many such characters in literature. In *Miss Lonelyhearts,* Nathanael West's celebrated novel, there is a character named Shrike who acts like one, and the hero of the story is a man known as "Miss Lonelyhearts" who writes a lonelyhearts column for a newspaper. In *Volpone* (fox) we find characters named Voltore (vulture), Corbaccio (raven), and Corvino (crow). Can you recall others?

V. After reading the following passage, reread the section on "Words with Built-in Judgments." Do you think the Mexican-Americans described below are being "too thin-skinned" or oversensitive about their image?

Sunday newspaper supplements in nearly 70 cities carried a full-page color advertisement last month in which Emiliano Zapata, the Mexican national hero, glared forbiddingly out at readers, a belt of bullets strapped across his chest.

Two modern Elgin watches glittered on the photograph, and the caption declared: "Your new Elgin is better than the Elgins Zapata was willing to kill for in 1914."

The ad outraged a good many Americans of Mexican descent. The Mexican-American Anti-Defamation Committee, Inc. has denounced the Elgin company for "fostering prejudice against Mexican Americans." Mexican Americans have picketed the Chicago Tribune, which ran the ad, and complained to many other papers across the country.

In the process, the Zapata ad has become the focal point of the anti-defamation group's efforts to combat the U.S. media portrayal of Mexicans in an unfavorable light.

"Every American is convinced that every Mexican is either a bandit or is sleeping under a tree wearing a sombrero," said Jose Carlos Gomez, publisher of a Spanish language newspaper in Chicago and leader of the protests there. Mexican Americans, Gomez said, "are saying, 'we don't want to be the white man's newest nigger.'"

San Francisco Sunday Examiner and Chronicle, July 12, 1970

VI. Consider the following passage:

Today's Uncle Tom doesn't wear a handkerchief on his head. This modern twentieth-century Uncle Thomas now often wears a top hat. He's usually well-dressed and well-educated. He's often the personification of culture and refinement. The twentieth-century Uncle Thomas sometimes speaks with a Yale or Harvard accent. Sometimes he is known as Professor, Doctor, Judge, and Reverend, even Right Reverend Doctor. This twentieth-century Uncle Thomas is a *professional* Negro . . . by that I mean his profession is being a Negro for the white man.

The Autobiography of Malcolm X

What does Malcolm X mean when he says that some people are professional Negroes? What difference is there between "Negro" and "black" and "Afro-American"? Which term do you think should be used? Why? Explain your answer in a 500-word essay.

VII. Think about this passage from *Newsweek*.

I play it cool
and dig all jive.
That's the reason
I stay alive . . .

This verse by Negro poet Langston Hughes points up a problem faced by Negroes and Puerto Ricans in U.S. ghetto schools. While the teen-ager learns to dig all the jive of the streets, the task of learning standard English —which he must also dig to stay alive outside his ghetto—can be a harrowing experience. He often must overcome barriers caused by differences in pronunciation, intonation, syntax and vocabulary.

To break down some of these barriers, Frank Riessman, professor of educational sociology at New York University, and John Dawkins of Science Research Associates, Inc., have written an English exercise book called "Play It Cool," based on the unorthodox assumption that ghetto or hip English is a valid form of the language and can be used as well as the standard words and syntax of newspapers, TV and English teachers. "Language," explains Dawkins, "is a very deep part of each of us. We are profoundly offended if someone attacks our language or laughs at it. This is why the ghetto kid doesn't talk in class. He thinks his own way of speaking has been outlawed by the teacher."

As a class project, compile a glossary of "hip" terms. Whenever possible, "explain" these terms using your knowledge of semantics to deal with their affective connotations, intensional meanings, and such matters. Do you think "hip" language should be "allowed" in the classroom?

> *Two little dogs sat by the fire*
> *Over a fender of coal dust;*
> *Said one little dog to the other little dog,*
> *"If you don't talk, why, I must."*
>
> Mother Goose

> *Are words in Phatic Communion ["a type of speech in which ties of union are created by a mere exchange of words"] used primarily to convey meaning, the meaning which is symbolically theirs? Certainly not! They fulfil a social function and that is their principal aim, but they are neither the result of intellectual reflection, nor do they necessarily arouse reflection in the listener.*
>
> Bronislaw Malinowski

the language of social cohesion

Noises as Expression

What complicates the problems of interpretation is the fact that informative uses of language are intimately fused with older and deeper functions of language, so that only a small proportion of utterances in everyday life can be described as purely informative. We have every reason to believe that the ability to use language for strictly informative purposes was developed relatively late in the course of linguistic evolution. Long before we developed language as we now know it, we probably made, like the lower animals, all sorts of cries, expressive of such internal conditions as hunger, fear, loneliness, sexual desire, and triumph. We can recognize a variety of such noises and the conditions of which they are symptoms in our domestic animals. Gradually such noises seem to have become more and more differentiated; consciousness expanded. Grunts and gibberings became language. Therefore, although we have developed language in which accurate reports may be given, we almost universally tend to *express* our internal conditions *first,* then to follow up with a report if necessary: "Ow! (expression) My tooth hurts (report)." Many utterances are, as we have seen with regard to "snarl-words" and "purr-words," vocal equivalents of expressive gestures, such as crying in pain, baring the teeth in anger, nuzzling to express friendliness, dancing with delight, and so on. When words are used as vocal equivalents of expressive gestures, we shall say that language is being used in *presymbolic* ways. These presymbolic uses of language coexist with our symbolic systems, and the talking we do in everyday life is a thorough blending of symbolic and presymbolic.

Indeed, the presymbolic factors in everyday language are always most apparent in expressions of strong feeling of any kind. If we carelessly step off a curb when a car is coming, it doesn't much matter whether someone yells, "Look out!" or "Kiwotsuke!" or "Hey!" or "Prends garde!" or simply utters a scream, so long as whatever noise is made is uttered loudly enough to alarm us. It is the fear expressed in the *loudness* and *tone* of the cry that conveys the necessary sensations, and not the words. Similarly, commands given sharply and angrily usually produce quicker results than the same commands uttered tonelessly. The quality of the voice itself, that is to say, has a power of expressing feelings that is almost independent of the symbols used. We can say, "I hope you'll come to see us again," in a way that clearly indicates that we hope the visitor never comes back. Or again, if a young lady with whom we are strolling says, "The moon is bright tonight," we are able to tell by the tone whether she is making a meteorological observation or indicating that she wants to be kissed.

Very small infants understand the love, the warmth, or the irritation in a mother's voice long before they are able to understand her words. Most children retain this sensitivity to presymbolic elements in language. It even survives in some adults; they are the people credited with "intuition" or "unusual tact." Their talent lies in their ability to interpret tones of voice, facial expressions, "body language," and other symptoms of the internal condition of the speaker: they listen not only to *what* is said, but to *how* it is said. On the other hand, people who have spent much of their lives in the study of *written* symbols (scientists, intellectuals, bookkeepers) are often relatively deaf to everything but the surface sense of the words. If a lady wants a person of this kind to kiss her, she usually has to tell him to in so many words.

Noise for Noise's Sake

Sometimes we talk simply for the sake of hearing ourselves talk; that is, for the same reason that we play golf or dance. The activity gives us a pleasant sense of being alive. Children prattling, adults singing in the bathtub, are alike enjoying the sound of their voices. Sometimes large groups make noises together, as in group singing, group recitation, or group chanting, for similar presymbolic reasons. In all this, the significance of the words used is almost completely irrelevant. We may, for example, chant the most lugubrious words about a desire to be carried back to a childhood home in old Virginny, when in actuality we have never been there and haven't the slightest intention of going.

What we call social conversation is again largely presymbolic in character. When we are at a tea or dinner party, for example, we all have to talk—about anything: the weather, the performance of the Green Bay Packers, Norman Mailer's latest book, or Raquel Welch's most recent picture. Rarely, except among very good friends, are the remarks made during these conversations important enough to be worth making for their informative value. Nevertheless, it is regarded as rude to remain silent. Indeed, in such matters as greetings and farewells—"Good morning"—"Lovely day"—"And how's your family these days?"—"It was a pleasure meeting you"—"Do look us up the next time you're in town"—it is regarded as a social error not to say these things even if we do not mean them. There are numberless daily situations in which we talk simply because it would be impolite not to. Every social group has its own form of this kind of talking—"the art of conversation," "small talk," or the mutual kidding that Americans love so much.[1] From these social practices it is possible to state, as a general principle, that *the prevention of silence is itself an important function of speech,* and that it is completely impossible for us in society to talk only when we "have something to say."

This presymbolic talk for talk's sake is, like the cries of animals, a form of activity. We talk together about nothing at all and thereby establish friendships. The purpose of the talk is not the communication of information, as the symbols used would seem to imply ("I see the Dodgers are out in the lead again"), but the establishment of communion. Human beings have many ways of establishing communion among themselves: breaking bread together, playing games together, working together. But talking together is the most easily arranged of all these forms of collective

[1] Among American men, this mutual kidding has something of the quality of an initiation rite. During World War II a Jewish scientist, recently fled from Germany, served as a professor of physics on the faculty of a Midwestern college. Also on the faculty was a professor of chemistry, a bluff, outgoing, cheerful man who was always kidding others in the faculty dining room. The chemist would joke with the physicist in what many of us felt to be a crude way: "Hey, Max, what did you Jews do that they kicked you out of Germany?" Professor Max, still sensitive and bitter after his persecution by the Nazis, would simply look miserable and not reply.

One day, however, Professor Max caught the idea. He said to the chemist, "Professor Schlemmer, isn't yours a *German* name?" "Why, yes," said Professor Schlemmer, "my grandparents came here from Germany in the 1880's." "Aha," said Professor Max, "they kicked your family out *two generations* before they kicked out mine!" Professor Schlemmer roared with laughter and put his arm around Professor Max's shoulder. See Martin Grotjahn's *Beyond Laughter* (1957) for an analysis of the significance of "kidding."

Frantic escape from the burden of silence

activity. The *togetherness* of the talking, then, is the most important element in social conversation; the subject matter is only secondary.

There is a principle at work, therefore, in the selection of subject matter. Since the purpose of this kind of talk is the establishment of communion, *we are careful to select subjects about which agreement is immediately possible.* Consider, for example, what happens when two strangers feel the necessity or the desire to talk to each other:

> "Nice day, isn't it?"
> "It certainly is." (Agreement on one point has been established. It is safe to proceed.)
> "Altogether, it's been a fine summer."
> "Indeed it has. We had a nice spring, too." (Agreement on two points having been established, the second party invites agreement on a third point.)
> "Yes, it was a lovely spring." (Third agreement reached.)

The togetherness, therefore, is not merely in the talking itself, but in the opinions expressed. Having agreed on the weather, we go on to further agreements—that it is nice farming country around here, that it certainly is scandalous how prices are going up, that New York is certainly an interesting place to visit but it would be awful to have to live there, and so on. *With each new agreement, no matter how commonplace or how obvious, the fear and suspicion of the stranger wears away, and the possibility of friendship enlarges.* When further conversation reveals that we have friends or political views or artistic tastes or hobbies in common, a friend is made, and genuine communication and cooperation can begin.

Here is how these conversational exchanges are likely to go among young people:

> BOY: Like to dance?
> GIRL: Yes, I would.
> BOY: My name's Charlie.
> GIRL: I'm Joan. Groovy party, isn't it?
> BOY: Yes, it sure is. One of the best since I've been in school.
> GIRL: Oh, do you go to school here?
> BOY: Yeah. You?

GIRL: No . . . well, I came with a friend who does, though. How many years have you been going here?
BOY: Two.
GIRL: What's your major?
BOY: I don't know yet.
GIRL: That's a pretty popular major around here, isn't it.
BOY: Guess so. How about something to drink?
GIRL: Okay.
BOY: I'll be right back then.

The Value of Unoriginal Remarks

An incident in my own experience illustrates how necessary it sometimes is to give people the opportunity to agree. Early in 1942, a few weeks after the beginning of the war and at a time when rumors of Japanese spies were still widely current, I had to wait two or three hours in a railroad station in Oshkosh, Wisconsin, a city in which I was a stranger. I became aware as time went on that the other people waiting in the station were staring at me suspiciously and feeling uneasy about my presence. One couple with a small child were staring with special uneasiness and whispering to each other. I therefore took occasion to remark to the husband that it was too bad that the train should be late on so cold a night. The man agreed. I went on to remark that it must be especially difficult to travel with a small child in winter when train schedules were so uncertain. Again the husband agreed. I then asked the child's age and remarked that the child looked very big and strong for his age. Again agreement—this time with a slight smile. The tension was relaxing.

After two or three more exchanges, the man asked, "I hope you don't mind my bringing it up, but you're Japanese, aren't you? Do you think the Japs have any chance of winning this war?"

"Well," I replied, "your guess is as good as mine. I don't know any more than I read in the papers. (This was true.) But the way I figure it, I don't see how the Japanese, with their lack of coal and steel and oil and their limited industrial capacity, can ever beat a powerfully industrialized nation like the United States."

My remark was admittedly neither original nor well informed. Hundreds of radio commentators and editorial writers were saying exactly the same thing during those weeks. But just because they were, the remark *sounded familiar* and was *on the right side*, so that it was easy to agree with. The man agreed at once, with what seemed like genuine relief. How much the wall of suspicion had broken down was indicated in his next question, "Say, I hope your folks aren't over there while the war is going on."

"Yes, they are. My father and mother and two young sisters are over there."

"Do you ever hear from them?"

"How can I?"

"Do you mean you won't be able to see them or hear from them till after the war is over?" Both he and his wife looked troubled and sympathetic.

There was more to the conversation, but the result was that within ten minutes after it had begun they had invited me to visit them in their city and have dinner with them in their home. And the other people in the station, seeing me in conversation with people who *didn't* look suspicious, ceased to pay any attention to me and went back to reading their papers and staring at the ceiling.[2]

Maintenance of Communication Lines

Such presymbolic uses of language not only establish new lines of communication, but keep old lines open. Old friends like to talk even when they have nothing especially to say to each other. In the same way that long-distance telephone operators, ship radio officers, and army signal corps outposts chatter with each other even when there are no official messages to communicate, so do people who live in the same household or work in the same office continue to talk to each other even when there is nothing much to say. The purpose in both cases seems to be partly to relieve tedium, but partly, and more importantly, to keep the lines of communication open.

Hence the situation between many a married couple:

WIFE: Wilbur, why don't you talk to me?
HUSBAND (interrupted in his reading of Schopenhauer or *The Racing Form*): What's that?
WIFE: Why don't you talk to me?
HUSBAND: But there isn't anything to say.
WIFE: You don't love me.
HUSBAND (thoroughly interrupted, and somewhat annoyed): Oh, don't be silly. You know I do. (Suddenly consumed by a passion for logic.) Do I run around with other women? Don't I turn my paycheck over to you? Don't I work my head off for you and the kids?
WIFE (way out on a logical limb, but still not satisfied): But still I wish you'd say something.
HUSBAND: Why?
WIFE: Well, because.

Of course, in a way the husband is right. His actions are an extensional demonstration of his love. They speak louder than words. But, in a different way, the wife is right. How does one know that the lines of

[2]Perhaps it should be added that I was by no means *consciously* applying the principles of this chapter during the incident. This account is the result of later reflection. I was simply groping, as anyone else might do, for a way to relieve my own loneliness and discomfort in the situation.

communication are still open unless one keeps them at work? When a sound engineer says into a microphone, "One . . . two . . . three . . . four . . . testing . . ." he isn't saying anything much. But it is nevertheless important at times that he say it.

Presymbolic Language in Ritual

Sermons, political caucuses, conventions, pep rallies, and other ceremonial gatherings illustrate the fact that all groups—religious, political, patriotic, scientific, and occupational—like to gather together at intervals for the purpose of sharing certain accustomed activities, wearing special costumes (vestments in religious organizations, regalia in lodges, uniforms in patriotic societies, and so on), eating together (banquets), displaying the flags, ribbons, or emblems of their group, and marching in processions. Among these ritual activities is always included a number of speeches, either traditionally worded or specially composed for the occasion, whose principal function is *not* to give the audience information it did not have before, *not* to create new ways of feeling, but something else altogether.

What this something else is, we shall analyze more fully in Chapter 7, the chapter on "The Language of Social Control." However, we can now analyze one aspect of language as it appears in ritual speeches. Let us look at what happens at a pep rally such as precedes college football games. The members of "our team" are "introduced" to a crowd that already knows them. Called upon to make speeches, the players mutter a few incoherent and often ungrammatical remarks, which are received with wild applause. The leaders of the rally make fantastic promises about the mayhem to be performed on the opposing team the next day. The crowd utters "cheers," which normally consist of animalistic noises arranged in extremely primitive rhythms. *No one comes out any wiser or better informed than he was before he went in.*

To some extent religious ceremonies are equally puzzling at first glance. The priest or clergyman in charge utters set speeches, *often in a language incomprehensible to the congregation* (Hebrew in orthodox Jewish synagogues. Coptic in Egyptian Christian churches, Sanskrit in Chinese and Japanese temples), with the result that, as often as not, no information whatsoever is communicated to those present.[3]

If we approach these linguistic events from a detached point of view, and if we also examine our own reactions when we enter into the spirit of such occasions, we cannot help observing that, whatever the words

[3]The Roman Catholic Church has only recently eliminated Latin in the liturgy in favor of the vernacular. Will the "common speech" now employed in the services harden once more into incomprehensibility with the passage of centuries?

used in ritual utterance may signify, we often do not think very much about their signification during the course of the ritual. Most of us, for example, have often repeated the Lord's Prayer or sung "The Star-Spangled Banner" without thinking about the words at all. As children we are taught to repeat such sets of words before we can understand them, and many of us continue to say them for the rest of our lives without bothering about their signification. Only the superficial, however, will dismiss these facts as "simply showing what fools human beings are." We cannot regard such utterances as "meaningless," because they have a genuine effect upon us. We may come out of church, for example, with no clear memory of what the sermon was about, but with a sense nevertheless that the service has somehow "done us good."

What is the "good" that is done us in ritual utterances? It is the *reaffirmation of social cohesion:* the Christian feels closer to his fellow-Christians, the Elk feels more united with his brother Elks, the American feels more American and the Frenchman more French, as the result of these rituals. Societies are held together by such bonds of common reactions to sets of linguistic stimuli.

Ritualistic utterances, therefore, whether made up of words that have symbolic significance at other times, of words in foreign or obsolete tongues, or of meaningless syllables, may be regarded as consisting in large part of presymbolic uses of language: that is, *accustomed sets of noises* which convey no information, but to which feelings (often group feelings) are attached. Such utterances rarely make sense to anyone not a member of the group. The abracadabra of a lodge meeting is absurd to anyone not a member of the lodge. When language becomes ritual, then its effect becomes to a considerable extent independent of whatever significations the words once possessed.

Advice to the Literal-Minded

Presymbolic functions of language have this characteristic in common: their effectiveness does not depend on the use of words. They can even be performed without recognizable speech at all. Group feeling may be established, for example, among animals by collective barking or howling, and among human beings by college cheers, community singing, and other collective noise-making activities. Indications of friendliness such as we give when we say "Good morning" or "Nice day, isn't it?" can be given by smiles, gestures, or, as among animals, by nuzzling or sniffing. Frowning, laughing, smiling, jumping up and down, can satisfy a large number of needs for expression, without the use of verbal symbols. But the use of verbal symbols is more customary among human beings, so that instead of expressing our feelings by knocking a man down, we often verbally blast him to perdition; instead of forming social groups by huddling together like puppies, we write constitutions and bylaws and invent rituals for the vocal expression of our cohesion.

To understand the presymbolic elements that enter into our everyday language is extremely important. We cannot restrict our speech to the giving and asking of factual information; we cannot confine ourselves strictly to statements that are literally true, or we should often be unable to say even "Pleased to meet you" when the occasion demanded. The intellectually persnickety often tell us that we should always say what we mean and mean what we say, and talk only when we have something to talk about. These are, of course, impossible prescriptions.

Ignorance of the existence of these presymbolic uses of language is not so common among uneducated people (who often perceive such things intuitively) as it is among the educated. The educated often listen to the chatter at teas and receptions, and conclude from the triviality of the conversation that all the guests (except themselves) are fools. They may discover that people often come away from church services without any clear memory of the sermon and conclude that churchgoers are either fools or hypocrites. Listening to political oratory, they may wonder "how anybody can believe such rot," and then conclude that people in general are so unintelligent that democracy is unworkable. Almost all such gloomy conclusions about the stupidity or hypocrisy of our friends and neighbors are unjustifiable on such evidence, because they usually come from applying the standards of symbolic language to linguistic events that are either partly or wholly presymbolic in character.

One further illustration may make this clearer. Let us suppose that we are on the roadside struggling with a flat tire. A not-very-bright-looking but friendly youth comes up and asks, "Got a flat tire?" If we insist upon interpreting his words literally, we will regard this as an extremely silly question and our answer may be, "Can't you see I have, you dumb ox?" If we pay no attention to what the words say, however, and understand his meaning, we will return his gesture of friendly interest by showing equal friendliness, and in a short while he may be helping us to change the tire.[4] In a similar way, many situations in life demand that we pay no attention to what the words say, since the meaning may often be a great deal more intelligent and intelligible than the surface *sense* of the words

[4]Dr. Karl Menninger, in *Love Against Hate* (1942), comments on this passage and offers the following translation of "Got a flat tire?" in terms of its psychological meaning: "Hello—I see you are in trouble. I'm a stranger to you but I might be your friend now that I have a chance to be if I had any assurance that my friendship would be welcomed. Are you approachable? Are you a decent fellow? Would you appreciate it if I helped you? I would like to do so but I don't want to be rebuffed. This is what my voice sounds like. What does your voice sound like?" Why does not the youth simply say directly, "I would be glad to help you"? Dr. Menninger explains: "But people are too timid and mutually distrustful to be so direct. *They want to hear one another's voices. People need assurance that others are just like themselves.*" (Italics added.)

themselves. A great deal of our pessimism about the world, about humanity, and about democracy probably derives from the fact that unconsciously we apply the standards of symbolic language to presymbolic utterances.

APPLICATIONS

I. Try the following "experiment" at your next lunch or coffee break. No one is to say anything except "Urglu" (though you may say "Urglu" with whatever variation of pitch or tone you think necessary to express different meanings). See what you *can* and *cannot* communicate when limited to this single word. You may use whatever gestures and facial expressions you can think up to aid in communicating.

II. The next time you attend a club meeting or watch a television panel show in which group discussion is important, pay particular attention to the way presymbolic language is used. Notice presymbolic language in the comic pages, where there is a whole "vocabulary" of grunts, groans and other such utterances. Analyze the presymbolic utterances in a comic book and explain how they are significant. Where else can you find a great reliance on presymbolic language?

III. Consider the following matters which deal with sound and silence.

1. Why is it so important for people to prevent silence? Notice that this is an important principle in radio and television broadcasting, where any gaps in programming are usually the results of errors or of the breakdown of equipment. What significance does the transistor radio have in this respect? It is now possible for people to be bombarded with news and music wherever they are, without having to make an effort to talk or make noise. ("We are becoming a nation of mutes," argues a friend of mine. "Ever since I got my son a transistor radio he never talks to anyone; he seems to spend all his time listening to it.")

2. To what degree do we depend upon words that do not actually mean what they say, but rather serve as crutches and are really little more than noise? Eliminate the following and note how difficult a conversation becomes.

   tremendous groovy great damned
   interesting like, I mean . . . you know

   What other crutch-words (and phrases) can you think of? Try this experiment in class: two members of the class are to have a conversation but one of them can only use the words listed above, or any similar expressions you may wish to add or substitute.

3. Do you think it would be a good idea if, after any remark, etiquette required a ten-second period of thoughtful silence before any reply

could be given? One of the Roman Caesars made it a practice to recite the letters of the alphabet to himself whenever someone had angered him. This habit, he asserted, kept him from issuing many rash retorts (or commands for punishment).

IV. Record the different ways your friends greet you during the day. What patterns do you observe? Are there differences between the way men greet other men, and women greet other women? If so, what are they? Small children often have not developed presymbolic means of securing rapport with others. Observe with special care how a child and an adult who are strangers start a conversation.

V. Over-literalness is a standard technique in humor. It is, for example, the basic mechanism upon which Moron jokes work.

QUESTION: Why did the Moron put on a wet shirt?
ANSWER: Because the label said "Wash and Wear."

What other jokes (and kinds of jokes) are based on over-literalness? Why is over-literalness funny?

VI. The rich variety of social conventions within the ethnic groups of America produce a wide variety of presymbolic expressions. If you are acquainted with more than one nationality group, you might compare the presymbolic expressions utilized in these groups. Which group's expressions seem to be the most graceful or frank, joking or serious, expressive or matter-of-fact? Do members of the groups use different presymbolic forms for "outsiders"? Do first-generation and second-generation immigrants use different expressions? Do presymbolic usages vary from state to state or region to region, regardless of the ethnic origin of the populace?

VII. The dramatic representation of presymbolic language is one of the playwright's most effective devices for establishing the mood and manner of the society he is portraying. By recognizing and analyzing these presymbolic forms, we may perceive something of how life in other times and other societies was and is carried on. What do the following selections tell you about the society in which such presymbolic forms were operating?

MILLWOOD: Sir! the surprise and joy—
BARNWELL: Madam—
MILLWOOD: This is such a favor. (Advancing)
BARNWELL: Pardon me, madam.
MILLWOOD: So unhoped for. (Barnwell salutes her and retires in confusion) To see you here. Excuse the confusion—
BARNWELL: I fear I am too bold.

MILLWOOD: Alas, sir! All my apprehensions proceed from my fears of your thinking me so. Please, sir, to sit. I am as much at a loss how to receive this honor as I ought, as I am surprised at your goodness in conferring it . . .

BARNWELL: Madam, you may command my poor thoughts on any subject. I have none that I would conceal.

GEORGE LILLO, *The London Merchant* (1731)

SCENE: *The fireman's forecastle of an ocean liner—an hour after sailing from New York.*

VOICES: Gif me a trink dere, you!
Ave a wet!
Salute!
Gesundheit!
Skoal!
Drunk as a lord, God stiffen you!
Here's how!
Luck!
Pass back that bottle, damn you!
Pourin' it down his neck!
Ho, Groggy! Where the devil have you been?
La Touraine.
Jenkins—the first—he's a rotten swine.
And the coppers nabbed—and I run—
I like peer better. It don't pig head gif you.
A slut, I'm sayin'! She robbed me aslape—
To hell with 'em all!
You're a bloody liar!
Say dot again!

EUGENE O'NEILL, *The Hairy Ape* (1922)

The effect of a parade of sonorous phrases upon human conduct has never been adequately studied.

Thurman W. Arnold

Yet the layman errs in his belief that this lack of precision and finality is to be ascribed to the lawyers. The truth of the matter is that the popular notion of the possibilities of legal exactness is based upon a misconception. The law always has been, is now, and will ever continue to be, largely vague and variable. And how could this well be otherwise? The law deals with human relations in their most complicated aspects. The whole confused, shifting helter-skelter of life parades before it—more confused than ever, in our kaleidoscopic age.

Jerome Frank

the language of social control

Making Things Happen

The most interesting and perhaps least understood relationship between words and the world is that between words and future events. When we say, for example, "Come here!" we are not describing the extensional world about us, nor are we merely expressing our feelings; we are trying to *make something happen.* What we call "commands," "pleas," "requests," and "orders" are the simplest ways we have of making things happen by means of words.

There are, however, more roundabout ways. When we say, for example, "Our candidate is a great American," we are of course making an enthusiastic purr about him, but we may also be influencing other people to vote for him. Again, when we say, "Our war against the enemy is God's war. God wills that we must triumph," we are saying something which, though unverifiable, may influence others to help in the prosecution of the war. Or if we merely state as a fact, "Milk contains vitamins," we may be influencing others to buy milk.

Consider, too, such a statement as "I'll meet you tomorrow at two o'clock in front of the Palace Theater." Such a statement about *future* events can only be made, it will be observed, in a system in which symbols are independent of things symbolized. The future, like the recorded past, is a specifically human dimension. To a dog, the expression "hamburger *tomorrow*" is meaningless—he will look at you expectantly, hoping for the extensional meaning of the word "hamburger" to be produced *now*. Squirrels, to be sure, store food for "next winter," but the fact that they store food regardless of whether or not their needs are adequately provided for demonstrates that such behavior (usually called "instinctive") is governed neither by symbols nor by other interpreted stimuli. Human beings are unique in their ability to react meaningfully to such expressions as "next Saturday," "on our next wedding anniversary," "twenty years from now I promise to pay," "some day, perhaps five hundred years from now." That is to say, maps can be made, even though the territories they stand for are not yet actualities. Guiding ourselves by means of such maps of territories-to-be, we can impose a certain predictability upon future events.

With words, therefore, we influence and to an enormous extent *control future events.* It is for this reason that writers write; preachers preach; employers, parents, and teachers scold; propagandists send out news releases; statesmen give speeches. All of them, for various reasons, are trying to influence our conduct—sometimes for our good, sometimes for their own. These attempts to control, direct, or influence the future actions of fellow human beings with words may be termed *directive uses of language.*

Now it is obvious that if directive language is going to direct, it cannot be dull or uninteresting. If it is to influence our conduct, it *must* make use of every affective element in language: dramatic variations in tone of voice, rhyme and rhythm, purring and snarling, words with strong affective connotations, endless repetition. If meaningless noises will move the audience, meaningless noises must be made; if facts move them, facts must be given; if noble ideals move them, we must make our proposals appear noble; if they will respond only to fear, we must scare them stiff.

The nature of the affective means used in directive language is limited, of course, by the nature of our aims. If we are trying to direct people to be more kindly toward each other, we obviously do not want to arouse feelings of cruelty or hate. If we are trying to direct people to think and act more intelligently, we obviously should not use subrational appeals. If we are trying to direct people to lead better lives, we use affective appeals that arouse their finest feelings. Included among directive utterances, therefore, are many of the greatest and most treasured works of literature: the Christian and Buddhist scriptures, the writings of Confucius, Milton's *Areopagitica,* and Lincoln's Gettysburg Address.

There are, however, occasions when it is felt that language is not sufficiently affective by itself to produce the results wanted. We supplement directive language, therefore, by *nonverbal affective appeals* of many kinds. We supplement the words "Come here" by gesturing with our hands. Advertisers are not content with saying in words how beautiful their products will make us; they supplement their words by the use of colored inks and by pictures. Newspapers are not content with saying that communism is a menace; they supply political cartoons depicting communists as criminally insane people placing sticks of dynamite under magnificent buildings labeled "American way of life." The affective appeal of sermons and religious exhortations may be supplemented by costumes, incense, processions, choir music, and church bells. A political candidate seeking office reinforces his speechmaking with a considerable array of nonverbal affective appeals: brass bands, flags, parades, picnics, barbecues, and free cigars.[1] Often a candidate's smile or, as in the case of President Kennedy, his wife's appearance and charm were a powerful influence upon the voter.

Now, if we want people to do certain things and if we are indifferent as to *why they do them,* then no affective appeals need be excluded. Some political candidates want us to vote for them regardless of our reasons for doing so. Therefore, if we hate the rich, they will snarl at the rich for us; if we dislike strikers, they will snarl at the strikers; if we like clambakes, they will throw clambakes; if the majority of us like hillbilly music, they may say nothing about the problems of government, but travel among their constituencies with hillbilly bands. Again, many business firms want us to buy their products regardless of our reasons for doing so; therefore, if delusions and fantasies will lead us to buy

[1]The following are excerpts from reports of the Republican National Convention of 1948: "There on the stage a gigantic photograph of the candidate, tinted somewhat too vividly, gazed steadily out over the throngs. Around the balcony hung other photographs: the Dewey family playing with their Great Dane; the Deweys at the circus; Dewey on the farm. Dewey infantrymen passed out soft drinks and small favors to gawking visitors and gave every 200th visitor a door prize. William Horne, a Philadelphia bank employee, was clocked in as the 45,000th visitor and got a sterling silver carving aid." *Time* (July 5, 1948). "Over loudspeakers of the Bellevue-Stratford came a constant stream of official exhortations against undue crowding at the entrance to the Dewey headquarters. The warnings were part of the game, but they were also justified. Why wouldn't the Dewey headquarters be jammed when prizes—from chewing gum and pocket combs to silk lingerie and dresses—were being doled out with the largess of a radio quiz show? At one point the Dewey people even staged a fashion show, complete with eight bathing beauties. A bewildered foreign newspaperman asked a fellow-reporter, 'How can I explain to France what this has to do with electing a President?' . . . The Stassen managers appeared to be saving up their circus talent for Convention Hall, where it turned out to be considerable, ranging from an Indian chief in full regalia to a shapely girl in sailor pants who did a nautical rumba on the rostrum." *The Nation* (July 3, 1948).

their products, they will seek to produce delusions and fantasies; if we want to be popular with the other sex, they will promise us popularity; if we like pretty girls in bathing suits, they will show pretty girls in bathing suits with their products whether they are selling shaving cream, automobiles, summer resorts, ice-cream cones, house paint, or hardware. Only the law keeps them from presenting pretty girls without bathing suits. The records of the Federal Trade Commission, as well as the advertising pages of many magazines, show that some advertisers will stop at practically nothing.

The Promises of Directive Language

Almost all directive utterances say something about the future. They are "maps," either explicitly or by implication, of *"territories" that are to be.* They direct us to do certain things with the stated or implied promise that if we do these things, certain consequences will follow: "If you adhere to the Bill of Rights, your civil rights too will be protected." "If you vote for me, I will have your taxes reduced." "Live according to these religious principles, and you will have peace in your soul." "Read this magazine, and you will keep up with important current events." "Take Lewis's Licorice Liver Pills and enjoy that glorious feeling that goes with regularity." Needless to say, some of these promises are kept, and some are not. Indeed, we encounter promises daily that are obviously incapable of being kept.

There is no sense in objecting as some people do to advertising and political propaganda—the only kind of directives they worry about—

Television suckling its young

on the ground that they are based on "emotional appeals." Unless directive language has affective power of some kind, it is useless. We do not object to campaigns that tell us, "Give to the Community Chest and enable poor children to enjoy better care," although that is an "emotional appeal." Nor do we resent being reminded of our love of home, friends, and nation when people issue moral or patriotic directives at us. The important question to be asked of any directive utterance is, "Will things happen as promised if I do as I am directed to do? If I accept your philosophy, will I achieve peace of mind? If I vote for you, will my taxes be reduced? If I use Lifeguard Soap, will my boy friend really come back to me?"

We rightly object to advertisers who make false or misleading claims and to politicians who ignore their promises, although it must be admitted that, in the case of politicians, they are sometimes compelled to make promises that later circumstances prevent them from keeping. Life being as uncertain and as unpredictable as it is, we are constantly trying to find out what is going to happen next, so that we may prepare ourselves. Directive utterances undertake to tell us how we can bring about certain desirable events and how we can avoid undesirable events. If we can rely upon what they tell us about the future, the uncertainties of life are reduced. When, however, directive utterances are of such a character that things do *not* happen as predicted—when, after we have done as we were told, the peace in the soul has not been found, the taxes have not been reduced, the boy friend has not returned, there is disappointment. Such disappointments may be trivial or grave; in any event, they are so common that we do not even bother to complain about some of them. They are, nevertheless, all serious in their implications. *Each of them serves, in greater or lesser degree, to break down that mutual trust that makes cooperation possible and knits people together into a society.*[2]

Every one of us, therefore, who utters directive language, with its concomitant promises, stated or implied, is morally obliged to be as certain as he can, since there is no absolute certainty, that he is arousing no false expectations. Politicians promising the immediate abolition of poverty, national advertisers suggesting that tottering marriages can be restored to bliss by a change in the brand of laundry detergent used in the family, newspapers threatening the collapse of the nation if the party they favor is not elected—all such utterers of nonsense are, for the reasons stated, menaces to the social order. It does not matter much whether such misleading directives are uttered in ignorance and error or with conscious intent to deceive, because the disappointments they cause are all similarly destructive of mutual trust among human beings.

[2]For an examination of television commercials in this respect, see Arthur A. Berger, "Commercials Ad Nauseam," *ETC.*, XXVI No. 4 (1969), 481–487.

The Foundations of Society

What we call society is a vast network of mutual agreements. We agree to refrain from murdering our fellow citizens, and they in turn agree to refrain from murdering us; we agree to drive on the right-hand side of the road, and others agree to do the same; we agree to deliver specified goods, and others agree to pay us for them; we agree to observe the rules of an organization, and the organization agrees to let us enjoy its privileges. This complicated network of agreements, into which almost every detail of our lives is woven and upon which most of our expectations in life are based, consists essentially of *statements about future events which we are supposed, with our own efforts, to bring about.* Without such agreements, there would be no such thing as society. We would all be huddling in caves, not daring to trust anyone, and life would be, as Hobbes put it, "nasty, brutish, and short." With such agreements, and a will on the part of the vast majority of people to live by them, behavior begins to fall into relatively predictable patterns; cooperation becomes possible; peace and freedom are established.

Therefore, in order that we shall continue to exist as human beings, we *must* impose patterns of behavior on each other. We must make citizens conform to social and civic customs; we must make husbands dutiful to their wives; we must make soldiers courageous, judges just, priests pious, and teachers solicitous for the welfare of their pupils. In early stages of culture the principal means of imposing patterns of behavior was, of course, physical coercion. But such control can also be exercised, as human beings must have discovered extremely early in history, by *words*—that is, by directive language. Therefore, directives about matters which society as a whole regards as essential to its own safety are made especially powerful, so that no individual in that society will fail to be impressed with a sense of his obligations. To make doubly sure, society further reinforces the directives by the assurance that punishment, possibly including imprisonment and death, may be visited upon those who fail to heed the words.

Directives with Collective Sanction

These directive utterances with collective sanction, which try to impose patterns of behavior upon the individual in the interests of the whole group, are among the most interesting of linguistic events. Not only are they usually accompanied by ritual; they are usually the central purpose of ritual. There is probably no kind of utterance that we take more seriously, that affects our lives more deeply, that we quarrel about more bitterly. Constitutions of nations and of organizations, legal contracts, and oaths of office are utterances of this kind; in marriage vows, confirmation exercises, induction ceremonies, and initiations, they are the essential constituent. Those terrifying verbal jungles called *laws* are simply such directives, accumulated, codified, and systematized through the centuries. In its laws, society makes its mightiest collective effort to impose predictability upon human behavior.

Directive utterances made under collective sanction may exhibit any or all of the following features:

1. Such language is almost always phrased in *words that have affective connotations,* so that people will be appropriately impressed and awed. Archaic and obsolete vocabulary or stilted phraseology quite unlike the language of everyday life is employed. For example: "Wilt thou, John, take this woman for thy lawful wedded wife?" "This lease, made this tenth day of July, A.D. One Thousand Nine Hundred and Sixty-three, between Samuel Smith, hereinafter called the Lessor, and Jeremiah Johnson, hereinafter called Lessee, WITNESSETH, that Lessor, in consideration of covenants and agreements hereinafter contained and made on the part of the Lessee, hereby leases to Lessee for a private dwelling, the premises known and described as follows, to wit . . ."
2. Such directive utterances are often accompanied by *appeals to supernatural powers,* who are called upon to help us carry out the vows, or to punish us if we fail to carry them out. An oath, for example, ends with the words, "So help me God." Prayers, incantations, and invocations accompany the utterance of important vows in practically all cultures, from the most primitive to the most civilized. These further serve, of course, to impress our vows on our minds.
3. The *fear of direct punishment* is also invoked. If God does not punish us for failing to carry out our agreements, it is made clear either by statement or implication that our fellow men will. For example, we all realize that we can be imprisoned for desertion, nonsupport, or bigamy; sued for "breach of contract"; "unfrocked" for activities contrary to priestly vows; "cashiered" for "conduct unbecoming an officer"; "impeached" for "betrayal of public trust"; hanged for "treason."
4. The formal and public utterance of the vows may be preceded by *preliminary disciplines* of various kinds: courses of training in the meaning of the vows one is undertaking; fasting and self-mortification, as before entering the priesthood; initiation ceremonies involving physical torture, as before induction into the warrior status among primitive peoples or membership in college fraternities.
5. The utterance of the directive language may be accompanied by other *activities or gestures calculated to impress the occasion on*

the mind. For example, everybody in a courtroom stands up when a judge is about to open a court; huge processions and extraordinary costumes accompany coronation ceremonies; academic gowns are worn for commencement exercises; for many weddings, an organist and a soprano are procured and special clothes are worn.

6. The uttering of the vows may be immediately followed by *feasts, dancing, and other joyous manifestations*. Again the purpose seems to be to reinforce still further the effect of the vows. For example, there are wedding parties and receptions, graduation dances, banquets for the induction of officers, and even in the most modest social circles, some form of "celebration" when a member of the family enters into a compact with society. In primitive cultures, initiation ceremonies for chieftains may be followed by feasting and dancing that last for several days or weeks.

7. In cases where the first utterance of the vows is not made a special ceremonial occasion, the effect on the memory is usually achieved by *frequent repetition*. The flag ritual ("I pledge allegiance to the flag of the United States of America . . .") is repeated daily in most schools. Mottoes, which are briefly stated general directives, are repeated frequently; sometimes they are stamped on dishes, sometimes engraved on a warrior's sword, sometimes inscribed in prominent places such as on gates, walls, and doorways, where people can see them and be reminded of their duties.

The common feature of all these activities that accompany directive utterances, as well as of the affective elements in the language of directive utterances, is the deep effect they have on the memory. Every kind of sensory impression from the severe pain of initiation rites to the pleasures of banqueting, music, splendid clothing, and ornamental surroundings may be employed; every emotion from the fear of divine punishment to pride in being made the object of special public attention may be aroused. This is done in order that the individual who enters into his compact with society—that is, the individual who commits himself to the "map" of the not-yet-existent "territory"—shall never forget to try to bring that "territory" into existence.

For these reasons, such occasions as when a cadet receives his commission, when a Jewish boy has his *bar mitzvah*, when a priest takes his vows, when a policeman receives his badge, when a foreign-born citizen is sworn in as a citizen of the United States, or when a president takes his oath of office—these are events one never forgets. Even if, later on, a person realizes that he has not fulfilled his vows, he cannot shake off the feeling that he should have done so. All of us, of course, use and respond to these ritual directives. The phrases and speeches to which we respond reveal our deepest religious, patriotic, social, professional, and political allegiances more accurately than do the citizenship papers or membership cards that we may carry in our pockets or the badges that we may wear on our coats. A man who has changed his religion after reaching adulthood will, on hearing the ritual he was accustomed to hearing in childhood, often feel an urge to return to his earlier form of worship. In such ways, then, do human beings use words to reach out into the future and control each other's conduct.

It should be remarked that many of our social directives and many of the rituals with which they are accompanied are antiquated and somewhat insulting to adult minds. Rituals that originated in times when people had to be scared into good behavior are unnecessary to people who already have a sense of social responsibility. For example, a five-minute marriage ceremony performed at the city hall for a mature, responsible couple may "take" much better than a full-dress church ceremony performed for an infantile couple. In spite of the fact that the strength of social directives obviously lies in the willingness, the maturity, and the intelligence of the people to whom the directives are addressed, there is still a widespread tendency to rely upon the efficacy of ceremonies as such. This tendency is due, of course, to a lingering belief in word-magic, the notion that, by *saying* things repeatedly or in specified ceremonial ways, we can cast a spell over the future and force events to turn out the way we said they would. ("There'll always be an England!") An interesting manifestation of this superstitious attitude toward words and rituals is to be found among those members of patriotic societies who seem to believe that the way to educate school children in democracy is to stage bigger and better flag-saluting ceremonies and to treble the occasions for singing "God Bless America."

What Are "Rights"?

What, extensionally, is the meaning of the word "my" in such expressions as "my real estate," "my book," "my automobile"? Certainly the word "my" describes no characteristics of the objects named. A check changes hands and "your" automobile becomes "mine" but no change results in the automobile. What has changed?

The change is, of course, in *our social agreements covering our behavior* toward the automobile. Formerly, when it was "yours," you felt free to use it as you liked, while I did not. Now that it is "mine," I use it freely and you may not. The meaning of "yours" and "mine" lies not in the external world, but in *how we intend to act.* And when society as a whole recognizes my "right of ownership" (by issuing me, for example, a certificate of title), it agrees to protect me in my intentions to use the automobile and to frustrate, by police action if necessary, the intentions of those who may wish to use it without my permission. Society makes this agreement with me in return for my obeying its laws and paying my share of the expenses of government.

Are not, then, all assertions of ownership and statements about "rights" directives? Cannot "This is *mine*" be translated "I am going to use this object; you keep your hands off"? Cannot "Every child has a *right* to an education" be translated "*Give* every child an education"? And is not the difference between "moral rights" and "legal rights" the difference between agreements which people believe *ought* to be made, and those which, through collective, legislative sanction, *have been* made?

Directives and Disillusionment

A few cautions may be added before we leave the subject of directive language. First, it should be remembered that, since words cannot "say all" about anything, the promises implied in directive language are never more than "outline maps" of "territories-to-be." The future will fill in those outlines, often in unexpected ways. Sometimes the future will bear no relation to our "maps" at all, in spite of all our endeavors to bring about the promised events. We swear always to be good citizens, always to do our duty, and so on, but we never quite succeed in being good citizens *every* day of our lives or in performing *all* our duties. A realization that directives cannot *fully* impose any pattern on the future saves us from having impossible expectations and therefore from suffering needless disappointments.

Secondly, one should distinguish between directive and informative utterances, which often look alike. Such statements as "A boy scout is clean and chivalrous and brave" or "Policemen are defenders of the weak" *set up goals* and do not necessarily describe the present situation. This is extremely important, because all too often people understand such definitions as descriptive and are then shocked and disillusioned when they encounter a boy scout who is not chivalrous or a policeman who is a bully. They decide that they are "through with the boy scouts" or "disgusted with all policemen," which, of course, is nonsense. They have, in effect, inferred an informative statement from what is to be taken only as a very general directive.

A third source of disappointment and disillusionment arising from the improper understanding of directives results from reading into directives promises that they do not make. A common instance is provided by advertisements of the antiseptics and patent medicines which people buy under the impression that the cure or prevention of colds was promised. Because of the rulings of the Federal Trade Commission, the writers of these advertisements carefully avoid saying that their preparations will prevent or cure anything. Instead, they say that they "help reduce the severity of the infection," "help relieve the symptoms of a cold," or "help guard against sniffling and other discomforts." If after reading these advertisements you feel that prevention or cure of colds has been promised, you are exactly the kind of sucker they are looking for. (Of course, if you buy the product knowing clearly what was promised and what was not, that is a different matter.)

Another way of reading into directives things that were not said is by believing promises to be more specific and concrete than they really are. When, for example, a candidate for political office promises to "help the farmer," and you vote for him, and then you discover that he helps the *cotton* farmer without helping the *potato* farmer (and you grow potatoes)—you cannot exactly accuse him of having broken his promise. Or, if another candidate promises to "protect union labor," and you vote for him, and he helps to pass legislation that infuriates the officials of your union (he calls it "legislation to protect union members from their own racketeering leadership")—again you cannot exactly accuse him of having broken his promise, since his action may well have been sincerely in accord with his notion of "helping union labor." The ambiguities of campaign oratory are notorious.

Politicians are often accused of breaking their promises. No doubt many of them do. But it must be remarked that they often do not promise as much as their constituents think they do. The platforms of the major parties are almost always at high levels of abstraction ("they mean all things to all men," as the cynical say), but they are often understood by voters to be more specific and concrete (i.e., at lower levels of abstraction) than they are. If one is "disillusioned" by the acts of a politician, sometimes the politician is to blame, but sometimes the voter is to blame for having had the illusion to start with—or, as we shall say, for having *confused different levels of abstraction.* What is meant by this expression will be more fully explained in ensuing chapters.

APPLICATIONS

I. The following statements, in the contexts in which they are usually found, are directives. Which of these directives have collective sanction and which have not? What rewards (if any) are promised to those who follow the directives, and what punishments (if any) are threatened to those who do not? What is the likelihood, in each case, of the consequences following as promised?

1. And remember, ladies and gentlemen of the radio audience, whenever you say "Blotto Coffee" to your grocer, you are saying "thank you" to us.

SAMPLE ANALYSIS: This is directive language since it attempts to influence the future behavior of the listener. Happily, we are free to disregard this directive since it is in the interests of a business concern and, therefore, does not have collective sanction. There is an implied promise that if the listener will show his gratitude by purchasing Blotto Coffee, the manufacturer will continue to provide him with programs such as precede this announcement. If enough people obey this directive, the likelihood of this promise being kept is quite great.

2. Jaguar: the car that makes Great Britain a Great sports car power, can make you one, too.

3. Somehow you feel more important on TWA.

4. You're in Good Hands with Allstate.

5. You can be sure, if it's Westinghouse.

6. It's the real thing. Coke.

7. We hold these truths to be self-evident, that all men are created equal, that they are endowed by their Creator with certain inalienable Rights, that among these are life, liberty and the pursuit of happiness.
The Declaration of Independence

8. When you're out of Schlitz, you're out of beer.

9. *To the Virgins to Make Much of Time*

Gather ye rose-buds while ye may,
  Old Time is still a-flying:
And this same flower that smiles today,
  Tomorrow will be dying.
The glorious lamp of heaven, the Sun,
  The higher he's a-getting
The sooner will his race be run,
  And nearer he's to setting.
That age is best which is the first,
  When youth and blood are warmer;
But being spent, the worse, and worst
  Times, still succeed the former.
Then be not coy, but use your time;
  And while ye may, go marry:
For having lost but once your prime,
  You may for ever tarry.

ROBERT HERRICK

10. *The New Colossus: Inscription for the Statue of Liberty*

Not like the brazen giant of Greek fame,
With conquering limbs astride from land to land
Here at our sea-washed sunset gates shall stand
A mighty woman with a torch, whose fame
Is the imprisoned lightning, and her name
Mother of Exiles. From her beaconhand
Glows world-wide welcome; her mild eyes command
The air-bridged harbour that twin cities frame.
"Keep, ancient lands, your storied pomp," cries she
With silent lips. "Give me your tired, your poor,
Your huddled masses yearning to breathe free.
The wretched refuse of your teeming shore,
Send these, the homeless, the tempest-tost to me,
I lift my lamp beside the golden door!"

EMMA LAZARUS

11. Let us eat and drink; for to-morrow we shall die.

Isaiah 22:13

II. The disappointments we suffer when the promises of directive language do not come true help break down mutual trust and alienate people. Is it possible that our advertisements are turning us (and especially the generation brought up on television) into cynics? If so, what should be done about this? Do advertisers have the "right" to sell products any way they see fit? Do people have the "right" to be protected against misleading advertisements? Two valuable studies which deal with the social significance of television are S. I. Hayakawa, "Who's Bringing Up Your Children?", *ETC., XXV*, No. 3 (1968) and Nicholas Johnson, *How to Talk Back to Your Television Set* (1970).

III. Organize a campaign (real or imaginary) on behalf of the Red Cross, Friends of the Earth, or a similar organization. What forms of appeal would you use in trying to persuade people to support your cause? Could you, if you so desired, devise means to persuade people to contribute money where they otherwise might not? Is it possible to go too far in resorting to affective appeals, even for a worthy cause? If so, where do you draw the line between ethical and unethical appeals?

IV. In this chapter, the concept of ownership was discussed in terms of how we intend to act. Ownership, in this light, is a set of directive agreements, sanctioned by society, as to who may use what things. However, the word "my" may not denote ownership in this strict sense at all times. Explain the different extensional meanings of the word "my" in these phrases:

my girl friend	*my* country
my mortgage	*my* hotel room
my belief in God	*my* size shoe

V. During the next national or local election, gather as many examples of political promises as you can find. Especially stunning promises may be found in the campaign literature of third-party candidates. Recalling what you read in Chapter 4 about contexts, ask yourself how many of the candidates' promises could be "kept" by supplying the appropriate context, as in the hypothetical case of the farmers quoted above.

During election years, many candidates or their official representatives are available for public questioning, either directly, by phone, or by mail. Can you devise a set of questions precise enough to find out *exactly* where he stands on any given issue? Could you have saved the potato farmer from disappointment—or, at least, saved him from believing he had been lied to—by formulating the right set of questions for him to ask of the candidate who promised to "help the farmer"?

VI. What major events in your life have been accompanied by directive or ritual language? Can you recall the words used in religious ceremonies, or in the marriage ceremony? Many fraternal organizations—even academic honor societies—have certain phrases and symbols that members are sworn never to repeat outside the fraternity. Even less secretive institutions, such as labor unions, universities, and medical groups issue certificates worded in lofty or ornate language. Do you think that such uses of language are merely ostentatious, or do they perform a function for the organizations that issue such certificates?

VII. Many books deal with the subject matter discussed in this chapter. Here are some of particular interest.

Jules Henry, *Culture Against Man* (1963), an anthropological study of American culture, with particular attention to advertising (seen as a "philosophical system") and youth culture.

Edward T. Hall, *The Silent Language* (1959), an analysis of various ways we have of communicating, and of the complications that arise when people from different cultures try to communicate with one another.

Edward C. Banfield, *The Unheavenly City* (1970), which argues that cities are not beyond redemption and our society is not so corrupt that it must be destroyed. Banfield believes that much of the current talk about society is based on misinformation—maps that are little related to their territories.

Orrin E. Klapp, *The Collective Search for Identity* (1969), a wide-ranging treatment of social movements seeking "identity" in modern society. Klapp suggests that many of our ills are caused by social systems which do not give us adequate psychic support.

Thurman Arnold, *The Folklore of Capitalism* (1938), a famous book which shows how certain political and economic beliefs become conventional wisdom, and prevent societies from seeing their problems clearly and solving them.

B. F. Skinner, *Walden Two* (1948), a novel dealing with a utopian society fashioned, or made possible, by advancements in behavioral psychology, especially the principle of "positive reinforcement." Some see this community as a totalitarian one, while others see it as a somewhat unconventional democracy.

Other books of interest are: Marshall McLuhan, *The Mechanical Bride* (1951); J. A. C. Brown, *Techniques of Persuasion: From Propaganda to Brainwashing* (1963); Walter Lippmann, *Public Opinion* (1922); Carl G. Jung, *Man and His Symbols* (1968).

What I call the "auditory imagination" is the feeling for syllable and rhythm, penetrating far below the conscious levels of thought and feeling, invigorating every word; sinking to the most primitive and forgotten, returning to the origin and bringing something back, seeking the beginning and the end. It works through meanings, certainly, or not without meanings in the ordinary sense, and fuses the old and obliterated and the trite, the current, and the new and surprising, the most ancient and the most civilized mentality.

T. S. Eliot

"What's all this about 'one man, one vote'?" asked the Nottingham miner.

"Why, one bloody man, one bloody vote," Bill replied.

"Well, why the 'ell can't they say so?"

Hugh R. Walpole

One must know and recognize not merely the direct but the secret power of the word.

Knut Hamsun

the language of affective communication

The language of reports is instrumental in getting done the work necessary for life, but it does not tell us anything about what life feels like in the living. We can communicate scientific facts to each other without knowing or caring about each other's feelings; but before love, friendship, and community can be established among men so that we *want* to cooperate and become a society, there must be, as we have seen, a flow of sympathy between one man and another. This flow of sympathy is established, of course, by means of the affective uses of language. Most of the time, after all, we are not interested in keeping our feelings out of our discourse, but rather we are eager to express them as fully as we can. Let us examine, then, some more of the ways in which language can be made to work affectively.

Verbal Hypnotism

First, it should be pointed out again that fine-sounding speeches, long words, and the general *air* of saying something important are affective in result, regardless of what is being said. Often when we are hearing or reading impressively worded sermons, speeches, political addresses, essays, or "fine writing," we stop being critical altogether, and simply allow ourselves to feel as excited, sad, joyous, or angry as the author wishes us to feel. Like snakes under the influence of a snake charmer's flute, we are swayed by the musical phrases of the verbal hypnotist. If the author is a man to be trusted, there is no reason why we should not enjoy ourselves in this way now and then. But to listen or read like this all the time is a debilitating habit.

There is a kind of churchgoer who habitually listens in this way, however. He enjoys any sermon, no matter what the moral principles recommended, no matter how poorly organized or developed, no matter how shabby its rhetoric, so long as it is delivered in an impressive tone of voice with proper musical and physical settings. Such listeners are by no means to be found only in churches. I have frequently been upset when, after having spoken before women's clubs on problems about which I wished to arouse thoughtful discussion, certain ladies have remarked, "That was such a lovely address, professor. You have such a nice voice."

Some people, that is, never listen to *what* is being said, since they are interested only in what might be called the gentle inward massage that the *sound* of words gives them. Just as cats and dogs like to be stroked, so do some human beings like to be verbally stroked at fairly regular intervals; it is a form of rudimentary sensual gratification. Because listeners of this kind are numerous, intellectual shortcomings are rarely a barrier to a successful career in public life, on the stage or the networks, on the lecture platform, or in the ministry.

More Affective Elements

The affective power of repetition of similar sounds, as in catchy titles and slogans, has already been mentioned. Somewhat higher on the scale are repetitions not only of sounds but of grammatical structures, as in:

> First in war,
> first in peace,
> first in the hearts of his countrymen . . .
>
> Government of the people,
> by the people,
> for the people . . .

Elements of discourse such as these are, from the point of view of scientific reporting, extraneous; but without them, these phrases would not have impressed people. Lincoln could have signified just as much for informative purposes had he said "government of, by, and for the people," or even more simply, "a people's government." But he was not writing a scientific monograph. He hammers the word "people" at us three times, and with each apparently unnecessary repetition he arouses deeper and more affecting connotations of the word. While this is not the place to discuss in detail the complexities of the affective qualities of language that reside in sound alone, it is important to remember that many of the attractions of literature and oratory have a simple phonetic basis—rhyme, alliteration, assonance, crossed alliteration, and all the subtleties of rhythm. All these sound effects are used to reinforce, wherever possible, the other affective devices.

Another affective device is the *direct address* to the listener or reader, as: "Keep off the grass. This means YOU!" The most painful example of this device is, of course, the spurious friendliness and intimacy with which the announcer of television commercials "personally" addresses each of several million listeners. But direct appeal to an audience is by no means limited to the advertising poster and television announcer. It softens the impersonality of formal speeches, so that when a speaker or writer feels a special urgency about his message, he can hardly help using it. It occurs, therefore, in the finest rhetoric as well as in the simplest. An interesting variant of the "you" device occurs in the college classroom, when the learned professor says, "You will recall what Kropotkin says in his *Mutual Aid: A Factor in Evolution* . . ." although he knows very well that Mr. Merkle, sprawling in his chair at the back of the class, has never even heard of Kropotkin before.[1]

Almost as common as the "you" device is the "we" device. The writer in this case allies the reader with himself, in order to carry the reader along with him in seeing things as he does: "*We* shall now consider . . ." "Let *us* take, for example . . ." "*Our* duty is to go forward . . ." This device is particularly common in the politer forms of exhortation used by preachers and teachers though recently the use of the first person "I"

[1]Thanks to the computer, many people now receive "personal" letters during elections with their own names in the body of the letter. Computers can run typewriters now; this is the latest development in spurious friendliness.

has become standard; it is used in this book. The "we" device is also often heard in kindergarten and the lower elementary grades, where teachers use it to sugar-coat their disciplinary directives: "Now, Ricky, now, Penny, we don't fight and call each other names here. We'll all say we're sorry and sit down and be friends again, *won't we*?" (Children usually believe that the word "cooperate" means "obey.")

In such rhetorical devices as the *periodic sentence* there is distortion of grammatical order for affective purposes. A periodic sentence is one in which the completion of the thought is, for the sake of the slight dramatic effect that can be produced by keeping the reader in suspense for a while, delayed. Then there are such devices as *antithesis*, in which strongly opposed notions are placed together or even laid side by side in parallel phonetic or grammatical constructions, so that the reader feels the contrast and is stirred by it: "Born a serf, he died a king." "The sweetest songs are those that tell of saddest thought." "The hungry judges soon the sentence sign,/And wretches hang that jurymen may dine."

Metaphor and Simile

As we have seen, words have affective connotations in addition to their informative value, and this accounts for the fact that statements of the kind: "I've been waiting *ages* for you—you're an hour overdue!" "He's got *tons* of money!" "I'm so tired I'm simply *dead!*"—which are nonsensical if interpreted literally—nevertheless "make sense." The inaccuracy or inappropriateness of the informative connotations of our words are often irrelevant from the point of view of affective communication. Therefore we may refer to the moon as "a piece of cheese," "a lady," "a silver ship," "a fragment of angry candy," or anything else, so long as the words arouse the desired feelings toward the moon or toward the whole situation in which the moon appears. This, incidentally, is the reason literature is so difficult to translate from one language to another: a translation that follows informative connotations will often falsify the affective connotations, and vice versa, so that readers who know both the language of the original and the language of the translation are almost sure to be dissatisfied, feeling either that the "spirit of the original has been sacrificed" or else that the translation is "full of inaccuracies."

In translations, a further problem is presented by the fact that a well-understood metaphor in one culture may have entirely different meanings in another part of the world. The United Nations once made a short movie in which an owl was shown, to indicate wisdom. It completely misfired in certain Asiatic countries where the movie was shown, and the footage had to be reshot. Why? Because in those countries it was found that the owl was a traditional image of stupidity and an object of amusement.

During the long time in which *metaphor* and *simile* were regarded as "ornaments" of speech—that is, as if they were like embroidery, which improves the appearance of our linen but adds nothing to its utility—the psychology of such communicative devices was neglected. We tend to assume, in ways that will be discussed more fully in later chapters, that things that create in us the same responses are identical with each other. If, for example, we are revolted by the conduct of an acquaintance at dinner and we have had such a sense of revulsion before only when watching pigs at a trough, our first, unreflecting reaction is naturally to say, "He is a pig." So far as our feelings are concerned, the man and the pig are identical with each other. Again, the soft winds of spring may produce in us agreeable sensations; the soft hands of lovely young girls also produce agreeable sensations; therefore, "Spring has soft hands." This is the basic process by which we arrive at metaphor. Metaphors are not "ornaments of discourse"; they are direct expressions of evaluations and are bound to occur whenever we have strong feelings to express. They are to be found in special abundance, therefore, in all primitive speech, in folk speech, in the speech of the unlearned, in the speech of children, and in the professional argot of theater people, of gangsters, and of those in other lively occupations.

So far as our feelings are concerned, there is no distinction between animate and inanimate objects. Our fright *feels* the same whether it is a creature or object that we fear. Therefore, in the expression of our feelings, a car may "lie down and die," the wind "kisses" our cheeks, the waves are "angry" and "roar" against the cliffs, the roads are icy and "treacherous," the mountains "look down" on the sea, machine guns "spit," revolvers "bark," volcanoes "vomit" fire, and the engine "gobbles" coal. This special kind of metaphor is called *personification* and is ordinarily described in textbooks of rhetoric as "making animate things out of inanimate." It is better understood, however, if we describe it as *a reaction that does not distinguish between the animate and the inanimate.*

Simile

However, even at rudimentary stages of evaluation it becomes apparent that calling a person a pig does not take sufficiently into consideration the differences between the person and the pig. Further reflection compels one to say, in modification of the original statement, "He is *like* a pig." Such an expression is called a *simile*—the pointing out of the similarities in our feelings toward the person and the pig. The simile, then, is something of a compromise stage between the direct, unreflective expression of feeling and the report, but of course closer to the former than the latter.

Adequate recognition has never been given to the fact that what we call slang and vulgarism works on exactly the same principles as poetry does. Slang makes constant use of metaphor and simile: "sticking his neck out," "out like a light," "way out on a limb," "baloney (no matter how thin you slice it)," "punch-drunk," "slick chick," "keep your shirt on," "as phony as a three-dollar bill." Clarence "Pinetop" Smith, one of the founders of the boogie-woogie style of piano-playing, used to admonish his friends: "Take it easy, greasy; there's a long way to slide!"

The imaginative process by which phrases such as these are coined is the same as that by which poets arrive at poetry. In poetry, there is the same love of seeing things in scientifically outrageous but emotionally expressive language:

> The hunched camels of the night
> Trouble the bright
> And silver waters of the moon.
>
> FRANCIS THOMPSON

> The snow doesn't give a soft white
> damn Whom it touches.
>
> E. E. CUMMINGS

> . . . the leaves dead
> Are driven, like ghosts from an enchanter fleeing,
> Yellow, and black, and pale, and hectic red,
> Pestilence-stricken multitudes.
>
> PERCY BYSSHE SHELLEY

> Sweet are the uses of adversity,
> Which like the toad, ugly and venomous,
> Wears yet a precious jewel in his head;
> And this our life, exempt from public haunt,
> Finds tongues in trees, books in the running brooks,
> Sermons in stones, and good in everything.
>
> WILLIAM SHAKESPEARE

> I saw Eternity the other night
> Like a great ring of pure and endless light.
>
> HENRY VAUGHAN

What is called slang, therefore, might well be regarded as the poetry of everyday life, since it performs much the same function as poetry; that is, it vividly expresses people's feelings about life and about the things they encounter in life.

Dead Metaphor

Metaphor, simile, and personification are among the most useful communicative devices we have, because by their quick affective power they often make unnecessary the inventing of new words for new things or new feelings. They are so commonly used for this purpose, indeed, that we resort to them constantly without realizing that we are doing so. For example, when we talk about the "head" of a cane, the "face" of a cliff, the "bowels" of a volcano, the "arm" of the sea, the "hands" of a watch, the "branches" of a river or an insurance company, we are using metaphor. A salesman "covers" an area; an engine "knocks"; people pass "rubber" checks which "bounce"; a theory is "built up" and then "knocked down"; a government "drains" the taxpayers, and corporations "milk" the consumers. Even in so unpoetical a source as the financial page of a newspaper, metaphors are to be found: stock is "watered," shares are "liquidated," prices are "slashed" or "stepped up," markets are "flooded," the exchange is "bullish"; in spite of government efforts to "hamstring" business and "strangle" enterprise, there are sometimes "melons" to be "sliced"; although this is—but here we leave the financial page—"pure gravy" for some, others are left "holding the bag." The "rings" both of "political rings" and "hydrocarbon rings" are metaphorical, as are the "chains" in "chain stores" and "chain reactions."

Metaphors are so useful that they often pass into the language as part of its regular vocabulary. Metaphor is probably the most important of all the means by which language develops, changes, grows, and adapts itself to our changing needs. Sometimes, however, metaphors get overworked—"ball-and-chain" (wife), "head-shrinker," "a horse of a different color," "a pretty kettle of fish"—so that they turn into linguistic deadwood (another metaphor!), or *clichés.*[2] When metaphors are successful, they "die"—that is, they become so much a part of our regular language that we cease thinking of them as metaphors at all.

To object to arguments, as is often done, on the ground that they are based on metaphors or on "metaphorical thinking" is rarely just. The question is not whether metaphors are used, but whether the metaphors represent useful similarities.

Allusion

Still another affective device is *allusion.* If we say, for example, standing on a bridge in St. Paul, Minnesota, in the early morning:

> Earth has not anything to show more fair;
> Dull would he be of soul who could pass by
> A sight so touching in its majesty . . .

we are evoking, in the mind of anyone familiar with the poem, such feelings as Wordsworth expressed at the sight of London in the early morning light in September 1802, and we are applying them to St. Paul. Thus, by a kind of implied simile, we can give expression to our feelings. Allusion, then, is an extremely quick way of expressing and also of creating in our hearers shades of feeling. With a Biblical allusion ("Hasten ye, O generation of vipers, and pay me heed") we can often arouse

[2]The word "cliché" conceals still another metaphor; see its etymology as given in *Webster's Third New International Dictionary.*

reverent or penitential attitudes; with a historical allusion, such as saying that New York is "the modern Babylon," we can say quickly and effectively that we feel New York to be a luxurious and extremely wicked city, doomed to destruction because of its sinfulness; by a literary allusion, we can evoke the exact feelings found in a given story or poem as a way of feeling toward the event before us.

But allusions work as an affective device only when the hearer is familiar with the history, literature, people, or events alluded to. Family jokes (which are allusions to events or memories in the family's experience) have to be explained to outsiders; classical allusions in literature have to be explained to people not familiar with the classics. Nevertheless, whenever a group of people—the members of a single family or the members of a whole civilization—have memories and traditions in common, extremely subtle and efficient affective communications become possible through the use of allusion.

The foreigner, however well he may have studied English before coming to America, will fail to detect the sources of the allusions in such expressions as, "He is a regular Lower Slobbovian" or, "He communicates good, like a semanticist should." The number of times we find it necessary to stop and explain things when we converse with foreigners indicates the degree to which we rely upon allusions in everyday discourse.

One of the reasons, therefore, that the young in every culture are made to study the literature and history of their own linguistic or national groups is that they may be able to understand and share in the communications of the group. Those who fail to understand passing allusions to well-known figures in European or American history, to well-known lines in Chaucer, Shakespeare, Milton, Wordsworth, or the King James version of the Bible, or to well-known characters in Dickens, Thackeray, or Mark Twain, may be said to be outsiders to an important part of the traditions of English-speaking people. The study of history and of literature, therefore, is not merely the idle acquisition of social polish, as practical men are fond of believing, but a necessary means both of increasing the efficiency of our communications with others and of increasing our understanding of what others are trying to communicate to us.

Irony, Pathos, and Humor

A somewhat more complex device, upon which much of humor, pathos, and irony depends, is the use of a metaphor, simile, or allusion that is very obviously inappropriate to the subject at hand. The result of the incongruous comparison is a feeling of conflict, a conflict between our more obvious feelings toward that which we are talking about and the feelings aroused by the expression. In such a case, the conflicting feelings resolve themselves into a *third, new feeling.* Let us suppose, returning to our example above, that we are looking at an extremely ugly part of St. Paul, so that our obvious feelings are those of distaste. Then we arouse, with the Wordsworth quotation, the feeling of beauty and majesty. The result is a feeling suggested neither by the sight of the city alone nor by the allusion alone, but one that is a product of the *conflict* of the two—a sharp sense of incongruity that compels us either to laugh or to weep, depending on the rest of the context. There are many complex shades of feeling that can hardly be aroused in any other way. If a village poet is referred to as the "Mudville Milton," for example, the conflict between the inglorious connotations of "Mudville" and the glorious connotations of "Milton" produces an effect of the ludicrous, so that the poet is exposed to contempt (although, if Craigenputtock can produce a Carlyle, there is no reason that Mudville should not produce a Milton). The rather complex device that we have been discussing may be represented graphically by a diagram borrowed from mathematics:

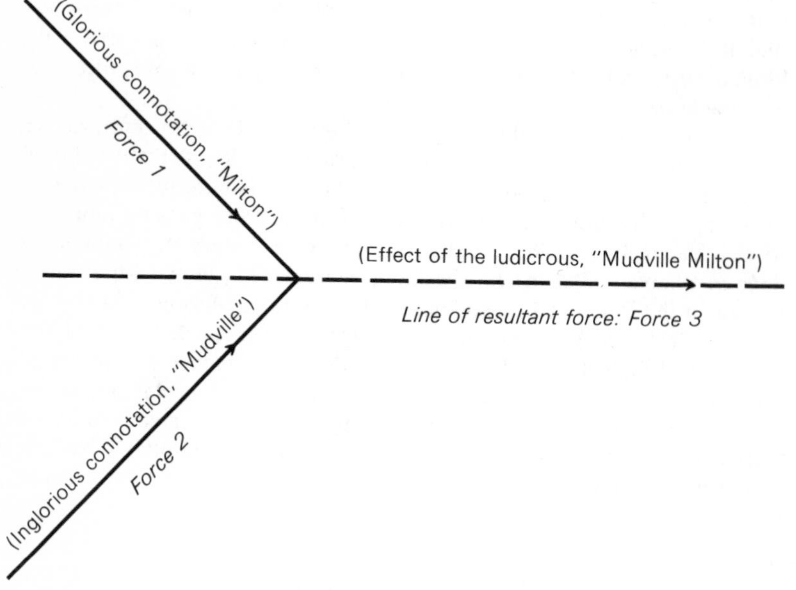

The Affectiveness of Facts

The following account of an automobile accident is quoted from the Chicago *Sun-Times:*

> One [victim], Alex Kuzma, 63, of 808 North Maplewood Avenue, was hit with such impact that his right forearm was carried off on the car of the hit-run motorist who struck him. Kuzma was struck Sunday as he crossed Chicago Avenue at Campbell Avenue. Witnesses saw the car slow down, douse its headlights and speed away. After searching futilely for the dead man's missing arm, police expressed belief it must have lodged in some section of the speeding auto.

There are few readers who will not have some kind of affective reaction to this story—at least a mild horror at the gruesomeness of the accident and some indignation at the driver who failed to stop after striking someone. Facts themselves, *especially at lower levels of abstraction,* can be affective without the use of special literary devices to make them more so.

There is, however, one important difference between the affectiveness of facts and the other affective elements in language. In the latter, the writer or speaker is expressing his own feelings; in the former, he is "suppressing his feelings"—that is to say, stating things in a way that would be verifiable by all observers, regardless of one's feelings.

Often, as in the example given, a report with accurately stated facts is more affective in result than outright and explicit judgments. By bringing the report down to even lower levels of abstraction—describing the blood on the victim's face and torn clothing, the torn ligaments hanging out of the remaining stump of his arm, and so on—one can make it even more affective. Instead of telling the reader, "It was a ghastly accident!" *we can make the reader say it for himself.* The reader is, so to speak, *made to participate in the communicative act by being left to draw his own conclusions.* A skillful writer is often, therefore, one who is especially expert at selecting the facts that are sure to move his readers in the desired ways. We are more likely to be convinced by such descriptive and factual writing than by a series of explicit judgments, because the writer does not ask us to take his word for it that the accident was ghastly. Such a conclusion becomes, in a sense, our own discovery rather than his.

Levels of Writing

Reliance upon the affectiveness of facts—that is, reliance upon the reader's ability to arrive at the judgment we want him to arrive at—varies considerably, of course, with the audience and with the subject being treated.

In this light, it is interesting to compare magazines and stories at different levels: the "pulp" and "confession" magazines, the "slicks" (*Ladies' Home Journal, Cosmopolitan, McCall's, Commentary,* and so on), and the "quality" magazines (*Harper's,* the *Atlantic,* the *New Yorker Commentary,* for example). In the magazines of mass appeal, the writers rarely rely on the reader's ability to arrive at his own conclusions. In order to save any possible strain on the reader's intelligence, the writers *make the judgments for us.* The "slicks" do this less than the "pulps," while in the "quality" group, the tendency is to rely a great deal on the reader: to give no judgments at all when the facts "speak for themselves," or to give enough facts with every judgment so that the reader is free to make a different judgment if he so wishes.

The following passages from *True Confessions* give an example of judgments made for the reader so that he doesn't have to figure them out for himself:

> Telling Mrs. Peters and Mrs. Jenks, watching grief engulf them, was nightmare enough, but telling Edie was worst of all. She just stood there in frozen silence, her eyes wide with horror and disbelief, her face getting whiter and whiter.
>
> "I did everything possible to save them!" I cried. "It was an accident—an unpreventable accident!"
>
> But Edie's eyes were bitterly accusing as she choked, "*Accident!* If you hadn't insisted on taking them, there would have been no accident!" Tears streamed down her ravaged face and her voice rose hysterically. "I never want to see you again as long as I live! You—*you murderer!*" she screamed.
>
> I stared at her for what seemed a lifetime of horror before I turned and fled, a million shrieking demons screaming in my ear, *She's right! You're a murderer! Murderer!*
>
> The coroner's verdict called the boat's overloading "a tragic error of judgment." . . . But nothing could lighten that feeling of guilt in my heart or remove the sound of Edie's voice screaming, "Murderer!" It rang in my ears day and night, making work impossible—sleep even more impossible. Until I sought forgetfulness in the only way I could find it—by getting blind drunk and staying that way.
>
> I was lurching through the door of a cheap bar weeks later when . . .

> Jim was big and strong with huge shoulders and a great shock of yellow hair. Just looking at him made me excited and breathless. His great laugh could stir me to laughter. The touch of his hand filled me with a sweet, frightening delight. The day he invited me to the senior prom I thought I'd die of happiness.
>
> Then I told Mother. I can still see her thin, fine-featured face pinched as if with frost. There was cold retreat in her eyes, and the wry smile on her lips made my heart turn over. . . .

The prose style of Ernest Hemingway is perhaps the classic example of the opposite technique—a highly sophisticated one, needless to say—of stating externally observable facts in the form of bare reports and of letting the reported facts have their impact on the reader. The following passage is the famous ending of *A Farewell to Arms:*

> I went into the room and stayed with Catherine until she died. She was unconscious all the time, and it did not take her very long to die.
>
> Outside the room, in the hall, I spoke to the doctor, "Is there anything I can do tonight?"

"No. There is nothing to do. Can I take you to your hotel?"

"No, thank you. I am going to stay here a while."

"I know there is nothing to say. I cannot tell you—"

"No," I said. "There's nothing to say."

"Good-night," he said. "I cannot take you to your hotel?"

"No, thank you."

"It was the only thing to do," he said "The operation proved—"

"I do not want to talk about it," I said.

"I would like to take you to your hotel."

"No, thank you."

He went down the hall. I went to the door of the room.

"You can't come in now," one of the nurses said.

"Yes I can," I said.

"You can't come in yet."

"You get out," I said. "The other one too."

But after I had got them out and shut the door and turned off the light it wasn't any good. It was like saying good-by to a statue. After a while I went out and left the hospital and walked back to the hotel in the rain.

What Literature Is For

From what has been said, our first and most obvious conclusion is that since the expression of individual feelings is central to literature, affective elements are of the utmost importance in all literary writing. In the evaluation of a novel, poem, play, or short story, as well as in the evaluation of sermons, moral exhortations, political speeches, and directive utterances generally, the usefulness of the given piece of writing as a "map" of actual "territories" is often secondary—sometimes quite irrelevant. If this were not the case, *Gulliver's Travels, Alice in Wonderland, The Scarlet Letter,* or Emerson's Essays would have no excuse for existence.

Secondly, when we say that a given piece of affective writing is true, we do not mean "scientifically true." We may merely mean that we agree with the sentiment; we may also mean that we believe that an attitude has been accurately expressed; again, we may mean that the attitudes evoked seem such as will lead us to better social or personal conduct.

The word "true" has many meanings. People who feel that science and literature or science and religion are in necessary conflict do so because they habitually think in opposites of black and white, true and false, good and evil. To such people, if science is "true," then literature or religion is nonsense; if literature or religion is "true," science is merely "pretentious ignorance." What should be understood when people tell us that certain statements are "scientifically true" is that they are useful and verifiable formulations, suitable for the purposes of organized cooperative workmanship. What should be understood when people tell us that the plays of Shakespeare or the poems of Milton or Dante are "eternally true" is that they produce in us attitudes toward our fellow men, an understanding of ourselves, or feelings of deep moral obligation that are valuable to humanity under any conceivable circumstances.

Thirdly, let us consider an important shortcoming of the language of reports and of scientific writing. John Smith in love with Mary is not William Brown in love with Jane; William Brown in love with Jane is not Henry Jones in love with Anne; Henry Jones in love with Anne is not Robert Browning in love with Elizabeth Barrett. Each of these situations is unique; no two loves are exactly alike—in fact, no love even between the same people is *exactly* the same from day to day. Science, seeking as always laws of the widest possible applicability and the greatest possible generality, would abstract from these situations *only what they have in common*. But each of these lovers is conscious only of the *uniqueness* of his own feelings: each feels, as we all know, that he is the first one in the world ever to have so loved. Literature creates the sense of what life feels like in the living.

How is that sense of difference conveyed? It is here that affective uses of language play their most important part. The infinity of differences in our feelings toward all the many experiences that we undergo are too subtle to be reported; they must be expressed. And we express them by the complicated manipulation of tones of voice, of rhythms, of connotations, of affective facts, of metaphors, of allusions, of every affective device of language at our command.

Frequently the feelings to be expressed are so subtle or complex that a few lines of prose or verse are not enough to convey them. It is sometimes necessary, therefore, for authors to write entire books, carrying their readers through numbers of scenes, situations, and adventures, pushing their sympathies now this way and now that, arousing in turn their fighting spirit, their tenderness, their sense of tragedy, their laughter, their superstitiousness, their cupidity, their sensuousness, their piety. Sometimes it is only in such ways that the *exact* feelings an author wants to express can be recreated in his readers. This, then, is the reason that novels, poems, dramas, stories, allegories, and parables exist: to convey such propositions as "Life is tragic" or "Susanna is beautiful," not by telling us so, but by putting us through a whole series of experiences that make us feel toward life or toward Susanna as the author did. *Literature is the most exact expression of feelings, while science is the most exact kind of reporting.* Poetry, which condenses all the affective resources of language into patterns of infinite rhythmical subtlety, may be said to be *the language of expression at its highest degree of efficiency.*

Symbolic Experience

In a very real sense, then, people who have read good literature have lived more than people who cannot or will not read. To have read *Gulliver's Travels* is to have had the experience, with Jonathan Swift, of turning sick at one's stomach at the conduct of the human race; to read *Huckleberry Finn*[3] is to feel what it is like to drift down the Mississippi River on a raft; to have read Byron is to have suffered with him his rebellions and neuroses and to have enjoyed with him his nose-thumbing at society; to have read *Native Son* is to know how it feels to be frustrated in the particular way in which many Negroes in Chicago are frustrated. This is the great task that affective communication performs: it enables us to feel how others felt about life, even if they lived thousands of miles away and centuries ago. It is not true that we have only one life to live; if we can read, we can live as many more lives and as many kinds of lives as we wish.

Here, the reader may object by asking, are we not twisting language somewhat to talk about "living" other lives than one's own? In one sense, the objection is correct; two different meanings of the word "live" are involved in the expressions "living one's own life" and "living other people's lives in books." Human life, however, is "lived" at more than one level; we inhabit both the extensional world and the world of words (and other symbols). "Living other people's lives in books" means, as we shall use the expression here, *symbolic experience*—sometimes called "vicarious experience."

In the enjoyment and contemplation of a work of literary or dramatic art—a novel, a play, a moving picture—*we find our deepest enjoyment when the leading characters in the story to some degree symbolize ourselves.* Jessie Jenkins at the movie, watching Elizabeth Taylor being kissed by a handsome man, sighs as contentedly as if she herself were being kissed—and *symbolically,* she is. In other words, she identifies herself with Elizabeth Taylor and her role in the story. Kirk Douglas fighting a villain is watched by thousands of men who clench their hands as if *they* were doing the fighting—which they are, *symbolically.* As we identify ourselves with the people in the story, the dramatist or the novelist puts us through *organized sequences of symbolic experiences.*

The differences between actual and symbolic experiences are great —one is not scarred by watching a moving-picture battle, nor is one nourished by watching people in a play having dinner. Furthermore, actual experiences come to us in highly disorganized fashion: meals,

[3]Huckleberry Finn was important as a "model" for American youth. For a discussion of this idea see Robert Lee White's "Little Lord Fauntleroy as Hero" in *Challenges in American Culture* (Bowling Green, Ohio, 1970).

arguments with the landlady, visits to the doctor about one's fallen arches, and so on, interrupt the splendid course of romance. The novelist, however, *abstracts* only the events relevant to his story and then *organizes* them into a meaningful sequence. This business of abstracting (selecting) events and organizing them so that they bear some meaningful relationship to each other and to the central theme of a novel or play constitutes the storyteller's art. Plot construction, development of character, narrative structure, climax, denouement, and all the other things one talks about in technical literary criticism have reference to this organizing of symbolic experiences so that the whole complex of symbolic experiences (i.e., the finished story or play) will have the desired impact on the reader.

All literary and dramatic enjoyment, whether of nursery tales in childhood or of moving pictures later on or of "great literature," appears to involve to some degree the reader's imaginative identification of himself with the roles portrayed and his projection of himself into the situations described in the story.[4] Whether a reader is able to identify himself with the characters of a story depends both on the maturity of the story and the maturity of the reader. If a mature reader finds difficulty identifying himself with the hero of a cowboy story, it is because he finds the hero too simple-minded a character to serve as an acceptable symbol for himself, and the villains and the events too improbable to serve as symbols for his own enemies and his own problems.

However, the simple-mindedness of the people and the improbability of the events of cowboy and western movies contribute much to their popularity on television. We live in a complex civilization, in which the vast majority of us lead peaceful, unaggressive lives. When we are troubled by problems—when sales fall off or profits decline or our jobs are threatened or shipments do not arrive on time or customers complain—many, many things may be to blame: manufacturers, middlemen, the stock market, the labor unions, high taxes, high rentals, the railroads, the government, local zoning regulations, or the problems of communication inevitable in large and complex societies. There is as a rule no single villain or group of villains, no one agency, that can be the object of our wrath when things go wrong. Hence, the world of the television western is comforting to come home to when the day's work is done: the "good guys" (in white hats) and the "bad guys" (in black hats) are clearly distinguishable, and all troubles are dissolved in a happy ending when the "bad guys" are defeated or dead after a heroic gun-fight. (Pictures in which the "good guys" wear black hats are known as "adult westerns.")

[4]At what age does the capacity for imaginative identification of oneself with the roles portrayed in a story begin? I would suggest, on the basis of very limited observation, that it begins around the age of two or earlier. An interesting test case is to read the story of the Three Bears to a very small child to see when he begins to identify himself with Baby Bear.

One of the reasons for calling some people immature is that they are incapable of confronting defeat, tragedy, or unpleasantness of any kind. Such persons usually cannot endure an "unhappy ending" *even in a set of symbolic experiences.* Hence the widespread passion for happy endings in popular literature, so that even stories about unhappy events have to be made, in the end, to "come out all right." The immature constantly need to be reassured that everything will always come out all right.

Readers who mature as they grow older, however, steadily increase the depth and range and subtlety of their symbolic experiences. Under the guidance of skilled writers who have accurately observed the world and have been able to organize their observations in significant ways, the mature reader may symbolically experience murder, guilt, religious exaltation, bankruptcy, the loss of friends, the discovery of gold mines or new philosophical principles, or the sense of desolation following a locust invasion in North Dakota. Each new symbolic experience means the enrichment of his insight into people and events.

As we progress in our reading, our consciousness widens. Gradually, the "maps" which we have inside our heads become fuller, more accurate pictures of the actual "territories" of human character and behavior under many different conditions and in many different times. Gradually, too, our increased insight gives us sympathy with our fellow human beings everywhere. The kings of Egypt, the Tibetan priest behind his ceremonial mask, the Roman political exile, and the embittered Harlem youth are presented to us by the novelist, the poet, and the playwright, at levels of vivid and intimate description, so that we learn how they lived, what they worried about, and how they felt. When the lives of other people, of whatever time and place, are examined in this way, we discover to our amazement that they are all people. This discovery is the basis of all civilized human relationships. If we remain uncivilized—whether in community, industrial, national, or international relationships—it is largely because most of us have not yet made this discovery. Literature is one of the important instruments to that end.

Science and Literature

By means of scientific communication, with its international systems of weights and measures, international systems of botanical and zoological nomenclature, international mathematical symbols, we are enabled to exchange information with each other, pool our observations, and acquire collective control over our environment. By means of affective communication—by conversation and gesture when we can see each other, but by literature and other arts when we cannot—we come to understand each other, to cease being brutishly suspicious of each other, and gradually to realize the profound community that exists between us and our fellow men. Science, in short, makes us able to cooperate; the arts enlarge our sympathies so that we become willing to cooperate.

APPLICATIONS

I. All literary criticism that tries to discover exactly what an author is saying presupposes, of course, knowledge of principles such as those discussed in this chapter. Their real application can only be in abundant and careful reading and in the development of taste through *consciousness of what is going on* in every piece of literature one reads, whether it be a magazine serial, a Eudora Welty short story, or an Elizabethan play.

A useful practice, even for an experienced reader, is to take short passages of prose and verse—especially passages he has long been familiar with—and to find out by careful analysis (a) what the author is trying to communicate; (b) what affective elements help him to convey his meaning; (c) what elements, if any, obscure his communication; and (d) how successful, on the whole, the author is in conveying his ideas and feelings to the reader. The following passages may serve as material for this kind of analysis:

1. It was a crisp and spicy morning in early October. The lilacs and laburnums, lit with the glory fires of autumn, hung burning and flashing in the upper air, a fairy bridge provided by kind Nature for the wingless wild things that have their home in the tree tops and would visit together; the larch and the pomegranate flung their purple and yellow flames in brilliant broad splashes along the slanting sweep of the woodland; the sensuous fragrance of innumerable deciduous flowers rose upon the swooning atmosphere; far in the empty sky a solitary oesophagus slept upon motionless wing; everywhere brooded stillness, serenity, and the peace of God.

SAMUEL L. CLEMENS, "A Double-Barreled Detective Story"

2. O say, can you see, by the dawn's early light,
What so proudly we hailed at the twilight's last gleaming?
Whose broad stripes and bright stars, through the perilous fight,
O'er the ramparts we watched, were so gallantly streaming!
And the rockets' red glare, the bombs bursting in air,
Gave proof through the night that our flag was still there:
O say, does that star-spangled banner yet wave
O'er the land of the free and the home of the brave?

FRANCIS SCOTT KEY

3. PARIS—Dive as deep as you like into that closet full of last winter's moth-proofed clothes and you will find little to resemble the over-stretched and well-swaddled silhouette now centered on the Paris fashion stage. The emerging blueprint sketched by top couturiers creates an elongated woman, drawn out like a winter's night. Her clothes are fitted to the body, but they skip the curves in a general mood of austerity, backed by a preference for the more melancholic colors and an absence of distracting detail.

Outdoors, she is covered in more layers than an onion. So little of the face is visible that a new heavy-handed way with make-up makes eyes larger than ever. Sketched in black pencil and haloed in green mascara, they require half an hour of skilled attention and seven successive applications of color. They emerge, framed between a small hat clamped down to the hairline (and sometimes covered by a hood) and a tall collar rising into the chin.

Necks vanish inside a soft ring of fur, or a stole as narrow as a stocking. Shoulders are shrugged under cocoon capes or coachman capelets. At the other end of the line, charming little bootees with Edwardian overtones climb up to the calf, to afford similar protection.

Fashion page of the San Francisco *Sunday Chronicle*

4. The value of philosophy is, in fact, to be sought largely in its very uncertainty. The man who has no tincture of philosophy goes through life imprisoned in the prejudices derived from common sense, from the habitual beliefs of his age or his nation, and from convictions which have grown up in his mind without the co-operation or consent of his deliberate reason. To such a man the world tends to become definite, finite, obvious; common objects rouse no questions, and unfamiliar possibilities are contemptuously rejected. As soon as we begin to philosophize, on the contrary, we find, as we saw in our opening chapters, that even the most everyday things lead to problems to which only very incomplete answers can be given. Philosophy, though unable to tell us with certainty what is the true answer to the doubts which it raises, is able to suggest many possibilities which enlarge our thoughts and free them from the tyranny of custom. Thus, while diminishing our feeling of certainty as to what things are, it greatly increases our knowledge as to what they may be; it removes the somewhat arrogant dogmatism of those who have never travelled into the region of liberating doubt, and it keeps alive our sense of wonder by showing familiar things in an unfamiliar aspect.

BERTRAND RUSSELL, *Essays*

5. There is no history of mankind, there is only an indefinite number of histories of all kinds of aspects of human life. And one of these is the history of political power. This is elevated into the history of the world. But this, I hold, is an offense against every decent conception of mankind. It is hardly better than to treat the history of embezzlement or of robbery or of poisoning as the history of mankind. *For the history of power politics is nothing but the history of international crime and mass murder* (including, it is true, some of the attempts to suppress them). This history is taught in schools, and some of the greatest criminals are extolled as its heroes.

KARL POPPER, *The Open Society and Its Enemies*

6. *The Guitarist Tunes Up*

With what attentive courtesy he bent
Over his instrument;
Not as a lordly conquerer who could
Command both wire and wood,
But as a man with a loved woman might,
Inquiring with delight

What slight essential things she had to say
Before they started, he and she, to play.

FRANCES CORNFORD

7. In dread there is no annihilation of the whole of what-is in itself; but equally we cannot negate what-is-in-totality in order to reach Nothing. Apart from the fact that the explicitness of a negative statement is foreign to the nature of dread as such, we would always come too late with any such negation intended to demonstrate Nothing. For Nothing is anterior to it. As we said, Nothing is "at one with" what-is as this slips away in totality.

MARTIN HEIDEGGER, *Time and Being*

II. The opening of a story, poem, essay, or book has special significance in setting the point of view, establishing the mood, gaining the reader's attention and interest. What can be inferred about the author's purpose from these beginnings?

1. Chicago is the great American city. New York is one of the capitals of the world and Los Angeles is a constellation of plastic, San Francisco is a lady, Boston has become Urban Renewal, Phildelphia and Baltimore and Washington wink like dull diamonds in the smog of Eastern Megalopolis, and New Orleans is unremarkable past the French Quarter. Detroit is a one-trade town, Pittsburgh has lost its golden triangle, St. Louis has become the golden arch of the corporation, and nights in Kansas City close early. The oil depletion allowance makes Houston and Dallas naught but checkerboards for this sort of game. But Chicago is a great American city. Perhaps it is the last of the great American cities.

NORMAN MAILER, *Miami and the Siege of Chicago*

2. St. Agnes' Eve—Ah, bitter chill it was!
The owl, for all his feathers, was a-cold;
The hare limped trembling through the frozen grass,
And silent was the flock in woolly fold:
Numb were the Beadsman's fingers while he told
His rosary, and while his frosted breath,
Like pious incense from a censer old,
Seemed taking flight for heaven, without a death,
Past the sweet Virgin's picture, while his prayer he saith.

JOHN KEATS, "The Eve of St Agnes"

3. In the village of Lapschitz lived a tailor named Shmul-Leibele with his wife, Shoshe. Shmul-Leibele was half tailor, half furrier, and a complete pauper. He never mastered his trade. When filling an order for a jacket or a gabardine, he inevitably made the garment either too high or too low, the lapels never matched, the vent was off center. It was said that he had once sewn a pair of trousers with the fly off to one side. Shmul-Leibele could not count the wealthy citizens among his customers. Common people brought him their shabby garments to have patched and turned, and the peasants gave him their old pelts to reverse. As is usual with bunglers, he was also slow. He would dawdle over a garment for weeks at a time. Yet despite his shortcomings, it must be said that Shmul-Leibele was an honorable man. He used only strong thread and none of his seams ever gave. If one ordered a lining from Shmul-Leibele, even one of common sackcloth or cotton, he bought only the very best

material, and thus lost most of his profit. Unlike other tailors who hoarded every bit of remaining cloth, he returned all scraps to his customers.

ISAAC BASHEVIS SINGER, "Short Friday"

4. As Gregor Samsa awoke one morning from uneasy dreams he found himself transformed in his bed into a gigantic insect. He was lying on his hard, as it were armor-plated, back and when he lifted his head a little he could see his dome-like brown belly divided into stiff arched segments on top of which the bed quilt could hardly keep in position and was about to slide off completely. His numerous legs, which were pitifully thin compared to the rest of his bulk, waved helplessly before his eyes.

FRANZ KAFKA, "Metamorphosis"

5. Now the shadow of the column—the column which supports the southwest corner of the roof—divides the corresponding corner of the veranda into two equal parts. This veranda is a wide, covered gallery surrounding the house on three sides. Since its width is the same for the central portion as for the sides, the line of shadow cast by the column extends precisely to the corner of the house; but it stops there, for only the veranda flagstones are reached by the sun, which is still too high in the sky. The wooden walls of the house—that is, its front and west gable-end—are still protected from the sun by the roof (common to the house proper and the terrace). So at this moment the shadow of the outer edge of the roof coincides exactly with the right angle formed by the terrace and the two vertical surfaces of the corner of the house.

ALAIN ROBBE-GRILLET, *Jealousy*

6. The Chevalier Tannhauser, having lighted off his horse, stood doubtfully for a moment beneath the ombre gateway of the mysterious hill, troubled with an exquisite fear lest a day's travel should have too cruelly undone the labored niceness of his dress. His hand, slim and gracious as La Marquise du Deffand's in the drawing by Carmontelle, played nervously about the gold hair that fell upon his shoulders like a finely-curled peruke, and from point to point of a precise toilet the fingers wandered, quelling the little mutinies of cravat and ruffle.

AUBREY BEARDSLEY, "Under the Hill"

III. A reader may make two kinds of identification with characters in a story. First, he may recognize in the story-character a more or less realistic representation of himself. (For example, the story-character is shown misunderstood by his parents, while the reader, because of the vividness of the narrative, recognizes his own experiences in those of the story-character.) Secondly, the reader may find, by identifying himself with the story-character, the fulfillment of his own desires. (For example, the reader may be poor, not very handsome, and not popular with girls, but he may find symbolic satisfaction in identifying himself with a story-character who is represented as rich, handsome, and madly sought after by hundreds of beautiful women.) It is not easy to draw hard-and-fast lines between these two kinds of identification, but basically the former kind (which we may call "identification by self-recognition") rests upon the *similarity* of the reader's experiences with those of the story-character, while the latter kind ("identification for wish-fulfillment") rests upon the *dissimilarity* between the reader's dull life and the story-character's interesting life. Many (perhaps most) stories engage (or seek to engage) the reader's identification by *both* means.

Study carefully a story in a love-story, confession, or male adventure magazine or a television western, analyzing plot and characterization to see in what ways and to what degree "identification by self-recognition" and "identification for wish-fulfillment" are produced in the reader by the author. Do *not* begin this analysis with literature of greater sophistication or higher quality, since the mechanisms are most clearly and simply revealed in fiction addressed to an unsophisticated audience.

IV. The above exercise rests on the assumption that the reader, not being a pulp magazine fan, will have performed his analysis "from the outside," as one whose own emotions were not involved in the story analyzed. Next, the same task of analysis may be performed with a story, novel, or play which the reader has found interesting and absorbing. The reader might ask himself such questions as these: "What *in me* responded to what elements in the story? What does my enthusiasm for this story reveal about the story and about myself? Ten years from now, is it likely that I shall be sufficiently like my present self to continue to be moved and delighted by this story?

V. There is a great deal of controversy about popular culture, its relation to our psychological development (or lack of development) and to the social order. The following books deal with popular culture in its various manifestations—comic strips and comic books, cartoons, movies, detective stories, science fiction, radio, television, and advertising.

Bernard Rosenberg and David Manning White, editors, *Mass Culture* (1957), a collection of articles, critical for the most part and strongly influenced by European social thought.

Stuart Hall and Paddy Whannel, *The Popular Arts* (1964), an attempt to discriminate between good and bad popular art and to promote understanding of the social function of the popular arts.

Jonathan Eisen, *The Age of Rock* (1969), Volumes 1 and 2, which describes itself as an analysis of "the sights and sounds of the American cultural revolution" as reflected in rock music.

Gilbert Seldes, *The Seven Lively Arts* (1924), a classic but somewhat dated treatment of the arts, by one of the earliest and most influential critics of popular culture. Another of his books, *The Public Arts* (1956), is a discussion of popular culture of the fifties, and of theoretical and political concerns.

Arthur Asa Berger, *Li'l Abner: A Study in American Satire* (1970), an analysis of the social and political implications of Al Capp's famous strip, and a methodology for interpreting the comic strip as an art form. Berger also has written *The Evangelical Hamburger* (1971), a book dealing with hamburger joints, sports, comics, and other commonplaces.

Marshall McLuhan, *Understanding Media* (1964), the book that made McLuhan a media guru. (There is now a flourishing business in explaining McLuhan.) *The Mechanical Bride* (1951), his first book, is very perceptive and is probably his most readable book.

Other important books on popular culture are: Denys Thompson, editor, *Discrimination and Popular Culture* (1964); Robert Warshaw, *The Immediate Experience* (1962); Russel Nye, *The Unembarrassed Muse: The Popular Arts in America* (1970). A scholarly magazine, *The Journal of Popular Culture*, deals with the subject in a lively and imaginative way. Take a topic such as "the western" or "adventure comics" and see what some of the sources mentioned above have to offer. Write a 500-word report about your findings.

VI. In the conclusion to his article, "The Concept of Formula in the Study of Popular Literature," John Cawelti, a professor at the University of Chicago, writes:

> My argument, then, is that formula stories like the detective story, the Western, the seduction novel, the biblical epic, and many others are structures of narrative conventions which carry out a variety of cultural functions in a unified way. We can best define these formulas as principles for the selection of certain plots, characters, and settings, which possess in addition to their basic narrative structure the dimensions of collective ritual, game and dream . . . Once we have understood the way in which particular formulas are structured, we will be able to compare them, and also to relate them to the cultures which use them.
>
> *Journal of Popular Culture*, III:3, p. 390.

What are the basic formulas in the various kinds of popular literature we are familiar with? What "taboos" exist? Are we still a "happy ending" country or do you think some changes have taken place in that respect?

But my position is this: that if we try to discover what the poem is doing for the poet, we may discover a set of generalizations as to what poems do for everybody.

Kenneth Burke

A well-chosen anthology [of verse] is a complete dispensary of medicine for the more common mental disorders, and may be used as much for prevention as cure.

Robert Graves

art and tension

Bearing the Unbearable

Animals know their environment by direct experience only; man crystallizes his knowledge and his feelings in phonetic symbolic representations; by written symbols he accumulates knowledge and passes it on to further generations of men. Animals feed themselves where they find food, but man, coordinating his efforts with the efforts of others by linguistic means, feeds himself abundantly and with food prepared by a hundred hands and brought great distances. Animals exercise but limited control over each other, but man, again by employing symbols, establishes laws and ethical systems, which are linguistic means of imposing order and predictability upon human conduct. Acquiring knowledge, securing food, establishing social order—these activities make sense to the biologist because they contribute to survival. For human beings, each of these activities involves a symbolic dimension—a dimension of which lower animals have no inkling.

Let us attempt to state the functions of literature in scientifically verifiable terms—in other words, in terms of biological "survival value." Granted that this is a difficult task in the present state of psychological knowledge, it is necessary that we try to do so, since most explanations of the necessity or value of literature (or the other arts) take the form of purr-words—which are really no explanations at all. For example, Wordsworth speaks of poetry as "the breath and finer spirit of all knowledge"; Coleridge speaks of it as "the best words in the best order." The explanations of literature given by many teachers and critics follow a similar purr-word pattern, usually reducible to "You should read great literature because it is very, very great." If we are to give a scientific account of the functions of literature, we shall have to do better than that.

Having included under the term "literature" all the affective uses of language, we are helped in our inquiry by recent psychological and psychiatric investigations, as well as by the insights of critics and students of literature. These sources indicate that, from the point of view of the utterer, one of the most important functions of the utterance is the relieving of *tensions.* We have all known the relief that comes from uttering a long and resounding series of impolite vocables under the stress of great irritation. The same releasing of psychological tensions—Aristotle called it *catharsis*—appears to be effected at all levels of affective utterance, if we are to believe what writers themselves have said about the creative process. The novel, the drama, the poem, like the oath or the expletive, arise at least in part out of internal necessity when the organism experiences a serious tension, whether resulting from joy, grief, disturbance, or frustration. And as a result of the utterances made, the tension is, to a greater or lesser degree—perhaps only momentarily—mitigated.

A frustrated or unhappy animal can do relatively little about its tensions.[1] A human being, however, with an extra dimension (the world of symbols) to move around in, not only undergoes experience, but also *symbolizes his experience to himself.* Our states of tension—especially the unhappy tensions—*become tolerable* as we manage to *state what is wrong—to get it said*—whether to a sympathetic friend, or on paper to a hypothetical sympathetic reader, or even to oneself.[2] If our symbolizations are adequate and sufficiently skillful, our tensions are brought

[1] See the account of "substitutive, or symbolic" behavior among cats under conditions of experimentally induced neurosis in Jules Masserman's *Behavior and Neurosis* (1943). It can hardly be denied, in the face of Dr. Masserman's evidence, that an extremely rudimentary form of what might be called "pre-poetic" behavior, analogous to the treasuring of a lock of a loved one's hair, is to be found even among cats. The cats, when hungry, fondle the push-button that *used to* trip a mechanism that brought them food, although they appear to know (since they no longer move to the food box after touching the button) that it no longer works.

[2] An indication of the importance of "getting it said" is given in the research of Charles W. Slack of the Harvard Psychological Clinic. Dr. Slack "hired," at modest hourly wages, unemployed young men hanging around street corners in Cambridge. He asked them to be "research consultants" to help inquire into the question of "how guys foul up." Their task was to talk into tape-recorders about themselves and their problems. A dramatic improvement in behavior was shown by almost all the boys who took part in the project: they got jobs and held them; the number of arrests among them dropped by half.

symbolically under control. To achieve this control, we may employ what Kenneth Burke has called "symbolic strategies"—that is, ways of reclassifying our experiences so that they are "encompassed" and easier to bear.[3] Whether by processes of "pouring out our hearts" or by "symbolic strategies" or by other means, we may employ symbolizations as mechanisms of relief when the pressures of a situation become intolerable.

As we all know, language is social, and for every speaker there may be hearers. An utterance that relieves a tension for the speaker can relieve a similar tension, should one happen to exist, in the hearer. And because human experience remains fairly constant, this process is possible even when speaker and hearer are separated by centuries or by different cultures. The symbolic manipulation by which John Donne "encompassed" his feelings of guilt in one of his Holy Sonnets enables us too, at another time and under another set of circumstances, to encompass our feelings of guilt about, in all probability, a different set of sins.

William Ernest Henley confronted the fact of his chronic invalidism—he had been ill since childhood and had spent long periods of his life in hospitals—by stating, in his well-known poem "Invictus," his refusal to be defeated:

Out of the night that covers me,
Black as the pit from pole to pole,
I thank whatever gods may be
For my unconquerable soul.

In the fell clutch of circumstance
I have not winced nor cried aloud,
Under the bludgeonings of chance
My head is bloody, but unbowed.

Beyond this place of wrath and tears
Looms but the horror of the shade,
And yet the menace of the years
Finds, and shall find me, unafraid.

It matters not how strait the gate,
How charged with punishments the scroll,
I am the master of my fate:
I am the captain of my soul.

How, at a different time and under different circumstances, other people can use Henley's utterance to take arms against a different sea of troubles is shown by the fact that this poem has been one of the favorite poems of American Negroes and is sometimes recited or sung chorally by Negro organizations. The extra meaning of the word "black" in the second line when the poem is said by Negroes makes it perhaps an even more pointed utterance for the Negro reader than it was for the original

[3]See Kenneth Burke, *Philosophy of Literary Form* (1941). An infielder for the Chicago White Sox some years ago made four errors in four consecutive chances. Naturally, he found his performance difficult to face. His "symbolic strategy" was reported by a Chicago *Times* writer who quoted the infielder as saying, "Anyway, I bet it's a *record!*"

author. Indeed, the entire poem takes on different meanings depending on what a reader, putting himself into the role of the speaker of the poem, projects into the words "the night that covers me."[4]

Poetry has often been spoken of as an aid to sanity. Kenneth Burke calls it "equipment for living." It would appear that we can take these statements seriously and work out their implications in many directions. What are, for example, some of the kinds of symbolic manipulation by which we attempt to equip ourselves in the face of the constant succession of difficulties and tensions, great and small, that confront us day by day? Of course, the stimulus of social tension is not necessary for all literature, but unquestionably it is often a significant spur to creation.

Some "Symbolic Strategies"

First of all, of course, there is what is called literary "escape"—a tremendous source of literature, poetry, drama, comic strips, and other forms of affective communication. Edgar Rice Burroughs, confined to a sickbed, symbolically traipsed through the jungle, in the person of Tarzan, in a series of breath-taking and triumphant adventures—and by means of this symbolic compensation made his sickbed endurable. At the same time he made life endurable for millions of undersized, frustrated, and feeble people. One may not think much of the author and the readers of the Tarzan stories; still, one must admit that in order to derive what relief they offer from pain or boredom, it takes, both in the telling and in the reading of such stories, the symbolic process, and hence a *human* nervous system.

Let us take another example of symbolic strategy. When a disgruntled employee calls his employer a "half-pint Hitler," is he not using a "strategy" that, by means of introducing his employer (a petty tyrant) into a perspective which includes Hitler (a great tyrant), symbolically reduces his employer to what Kenneth Burke calls manageable proportions? And did not Dante likewise, unable to punish his enemies as they deserved to be punished, symbolically put them in their places in the most uncomfortable quarters in Hell? There is a world of difference between the completeness and adequacy of such a simple epithet as "half-pint Hitler" and Dante's way of disposing of his enemies—and Dante accomplished many more things in his poem besides symbolically punishing his enemies

[4]Anyone saying, as I do, that a poem may mean different things to different people, lays himself open to the charge that his relativistic position makes it impossible "to distinguish between right and wrong readings of a poem." It is perhaps necessary, therefore, to clarify what is asserted here: saying that a poem may have different meanings for different people is *not* the same as saying that a poem can mean anything at all.

Incidentally, another example of a poem acquiring a changed meaning in a changed context is provided by the Freedom Riders who "sat in" and refused to budge from segregated premises. They responded to threats with the old hymn, "We shall not be, we shall not be moved," endowing the words with a meaning not found when sung in church.

—but are they not both symbolic manipulations by means of which the utterers derive a measure of relief or relaxation of psychological tensions?

Let us take another example. Upton Sinclair was deeply disturbed by the stockyards as they were in 1906. He could have tried to forget them; he could have buried himself in reading or writing about other things, such as idyllic lands long ago and far away or entirely nonexistent —as do the readers and writers of escape literature. He could have tried, by a different symbolic manipulation, to show that present evil was part of greater good "in God's omniscient plan." This has been the strategy of many religions as well as of many authors. Still another possibility would have been actually to reform conditions at the stockyards so that he could contemplate them with equanimity—but he would have had to be an important official in a packing company or in the government to initiate a change in conditions. What he did, therefore, was to *socialize his discontent*—pass it on to others—on the very good theory that if enough people felt angry or disgusted with the situation, they could collectively change the stockyards in such a way that one could adjust oneself to them. Sinclair's novel, *The Jungle,* upset so many people that it led to a federal investigation of the meat industry and to the enactment of legislation controlling some of its practices.

As is now well known, when tensions are experienced constantly, and permitted to accumulate, they may lead to more or less serious psychological maladjustment. Adjustment, as modern psychology sees the process, is no static condition of unreflective bliss that comes from neither knowing nor caring what is wrong with the world. It is a dynamic, day-to-day, moment-to-moment process, and it involves changing the environment to suit one's personality as much as it involves adapting one's feelings to existing conditions. The greater resources one has for achieving and maintaining adjustment, the more successful will the process be. Literature appears to be one of the available resources.

Both the production and enjoyment of literature, then, being human symbolic devices employed in the day-to-day process of equipping ourselves for living, appear to be extensions of our adjustment mechanism beyond those provided for us by that part of our biological equipment which we have in common with lower animals. If a man were to spend years of his life trying to discover the chemical constituency of salt water without bothering to find out what has already been said on the subject in any elementary chemistry book, we should say that he was making very imperfect use of the resources which our symbolic systems have made available to us. Similarly, can it not be said that people, worrying themselves sick over their individual frustrations, constantly suffering from petty irritations and hypertensions, are making extremely imperfect use of the available human resources of adjustment when they fail to strengthen and quiet themselves through contact with literature and the other arts?

What all this boils down to, then, is that poetry (along with the other arts), whether it be good or bad and at whatever level of crudity or refinement, exists to fulfill a necessary biological function for a symbol-using class of life, that of *helping us to maintain psychological health and equilibrium.*

"Equipment for Living"

Psychiatrists recognize no distinct classes of the "sane" and the "unsane." Sanity is a matter of degree, and "sane" people are all capable of becoming more sane, or less, according to the experiences they encounter and the strength and flexibility of the internal equipment with which they meet them. Even as one's physical health has to be maintained by food and exercise, it would appear that one's psychological health too has to be maintained in the very course of living by "nourishment" at the level of affective symbols: literature that introduces us to new sources of delight; literature that makes us feel that we are not alone in our misery; literature that shows us our own problems in a new light; literature that suggests new possibilities to us and opens new areas of possible experience; literature that offers us a variety of "symbolic strategies" by means of which we can "encompass" our situations.

But there are certain kinds of literature, like certain kinds of processed food, that look very much like nourishment but contain none of the essential vitamin ingredients, so that great quantities can be consumed without affecting one's spiritual undernourishment.[5] (One could mean by "essential vitamin ingredients" in this context, "maps" of actual "territories" of human experience, directives that are both realistic and helpful, and so on.) Certain kinds of popular fiction claim to throw light on given problems in life—stories with such titles as "The Office Wife—Was She Playing Fair?"—but, like patent medicines, these offer apparent soothing to surface symptoms and ignore underlying causes. Other kinds of fiction, like drugs and liquor, offer escape from pain and again leave causes untouched, so that the more of them you take the more you need. Fantasy-living—which is one of the important characteristics of schizophrenia—can be aggravated by the consumption of too much of this narcotic literature. Still other kinds of fiction, movies, television programs, and the like give a false, prettified picture of the world—a world that can be adjusted to *without effort.* But readers who adjust themselves to this unreal world naturally become progressively less adjusted to the world as it is. Such "adjustment to unreality" must lead to an enormous amount of disappointment and heartbreak among the

[5] Wendell Johnson of the University of Iowa refers to television-viewing, reading the Sunday papers, and similar diversions as "semantic thumb-sucking": you go through the motions of getting nourishment without getting any.

young and unsophisticated when they discover that the world is not as it was depicted in romantic tales.

On the other hand, it will not do to apply too crudely the principle of literature as an aid to sanity. Some might be tempted to say that, if literature is an instrument for maintaining sanity, the writings of many not-too-sane geniuses will have to be thrown out as unhealthy. It would seem, on the contrary, that the symbolic strategies devised by extremely tortured people like Dostoyevsky or Donne or Shelly for the encompassing of their situations are valuable in the extreme. They mixed themselves powerful medicines against their ills, and their medicines not only help us to encompass whatever similar tortures we may be suffering from, but may serve also as antitoxins for future sufferings.

Furthermore, when a work of literature is said to be "permanent," "lasting," or "great," does it not mean that the symbolic strategy by which the author encompassed his disturbance (achieved his equilibrium) works for other people troubled by other disturbances at other times and places? Is it possible, for example, to read Sinclair's strategic handling of the Chicago stockyards without awareness that it applies more or less adequately to other people's disturbances about factory conditions in Turin, or Manchester, or Kobe, or Montreal? And if it applies especially well to, say, Detroit, does not the Detroiter regard Sinclair's book as having lasting value? And if, under changing conditions, there are no longer social situations which arouse similar tensions, or if the strategies seem no longer adequate, do we not consider the author to be "dated," if not "dead"?[6] But if an author has adequately dealt with tensions that people in all times and under all conditions appear to experience, do we not call his writings "universal" and "undying"?

The relationship between literature and life is a subject about which little is known scientifically at the present time. Nevertheless, in an unorganized way, we all feel that we know something about that relationship, since we have all felt the effects of some kind of literature at some time in our lives. Most of us have felt, even if we have not been able to prove, that harmful consequences can arise from the consumption of such literary fare as is offered in many movies, in popular magazines,

[6] *The Jungle* is, in my opinion, very much dated in most respects, although still powerful in some. Working people in the United States (and in many other parts of the world as well) are simply not treated as badly as they are in this novel, partly because of unionization, of course, and also partly because of advances in technology and a more highly developed public conscience. But ever since its publication in 1906, it has been widely read by working classes all over the world: few American books have been translated into so many languages.

The symbolic strategies of works of great literary art, unlike those of *The Jungle*, are usually too complex and subtle for such a rough analysis as has been attempted here. *The Jungle* has been chosen for discussion because books like this, which are far from being great masterpieces and yet give a great deal of profoundly felt insight into segments of human experience, are especially helpful in the understanding of the theories of literature proposed in this chapter. The strategies, being not too subtle, can be clearly seen and described.

and in the so-called comic books. But the imperfection of our scientific knowledge is revealed by the fact that, when there is widespread argument as to whether or not comic books should be banned, equally imposing authorities on both sides are able to "prove" their cases; some say that comic books stimulate children's imaginations in unhealthy ways and lead them into crime, while others say that the crimes are committed by psychopathic children who would have committed them anyway, and that comic books, by offering to normal children a symbolic release of their aggressive tendencies, actually help to calm them down. It appears to be anybody's guess.

Because no one yet has answers to such questions, it would seem to be extremely desirable for students of literature and of psychology to work together. If they do, perhaps they will some day be able to state, in the interests of everyday sanity, what kinds of literature contribute to maturity and what kinds help to keep us permanently infantile and immature in our evaluations.

Art as Order

At least one other important element enters into our pleasure both in the writing and reading of literature—but about this there is still less available scientific knowledge. It pertains to what are called the artistic or esthetic values of a work of the imagination.

In Chapter 8, we spoke of the relationships, for example in a novel, of the incidents and characters to each other—that is, the meaningful arrangement of experiences that makes a novel different from a jumbled narrative. Before we speak of a narrative as a "novel" and therefore as a "work of art," we must be satisfied that, regardless of whether or not we could "live the story" through imaginative identification with the characters, the incidents are arranged in some kind of *order*. Even when we don't happen to like the story, if we find a complex, but discernible and interesting, order to the incidents in a novel, we are able to say, "It certainly is beautifully put together." Indeed, sometimes the internal order and neat relationships of the parts to each other in a novel may be so impressive that we enjoy it in spite of a lack of sympathy with the kinds of incidents or people portrayed. Why is order interesting almost of itself?

I would suggest that if an answer is to be found to this question, it will have to be found in terms of human symbolic processes and the fact that symbols of symbols, symbols of symbols of symbols, and so on, can be manufactured indefinitely by the human nervous system. This fact, already explained in Chapter 2 (and to be explained further in Chapter 10), can be given a special application that may enable us to understand the functions of literature.

Animals, as we have remarked, live in the extensional world—they have no symbolic world to speak of. There would seem to be no more "order" in an animal's existence than the order of physical events as they impinge on its life. Man, however, both *lives* (at the extensional level) and *talks about his life to himself* (at the symbolic level, either with words or, in the case of painters and musicians and dancers, with nonverbal symbols). A human being is not satisfied simply to know his way around extensionally; he can hardly help talking to himself about what he has seen and felt and done.

The data of experience, when talked about, are full of contradictions. Mrs. Robinson loves her children, but ruins them through misdirected love; the illiterate peasants of a Chinese village show greater social and personal wisdom than the educated people of great cities; people say crime doesn't pay, but in some cases it pays extremely well; a young man who is by temperament a scholar and a poet feels compelled to commit a political murder; a faithful wife of twenty years deserts her husband for no apparent reason; a ne'er-do-well acts courageously in a dangerous situation—these and a thousand other contradictions confront us in the course of our lives. Unordered, and bearing no relationship to each other, our statements about experience are not only disconnected, but they are difficult to use.

Insofar as we are aware of these contradictions, this disorder among our statements is itself a source of tension. Such contradictions provide us with no guide to action; hence they leave us with the tensions of indecision and bewilderment. These tensions are not resolved until we have, *by talking to ourselves about our talking* (symbolizing our symbols), "fitted things together," so that, as we say, things don't seem to be "meaningless" any more. Religions, philosophies, science, and art are equally, and through different methods, ways of resolving the tensions produced by the contradictory data of experience by talking about our talking, then talking about our talking about our talking, and so on, until some kind of *order* has been established among the data.

Talking about things, talking about talking, talking about talking about talking, etc., represent what we shall call talking at different *levels of abstraction.* The imposition of order upon our pictures of the world is, it appears, what we mean by "understanding." When we say that a scientist "understands" something, does it not mean that he has ordered his observations at the objective, descriptive, and higher inferential levels of abstraction into a workable system in which all levels are related to other levels in terms of a few powerful generalizations? When a great religious leader or philosopher is said to "understand" life, does it not mean that he has also ordered his observations into a set of attitudes, often crystallized into exceedingly general and powerful directives? And when a novelist is said to "understand" the life of any segment of humanity (or humanity as a whole), has he not also ordered his observations at many different levels of abstraction —the particular and concrete, the general, and the more general? (Fuller explanation of "levels of abstraction" will be found in Chapter 10.) However, the novelist presents that order not in a scientific, ethical, or philosophical system of highly abstract generalizations, but in a set of symbolic experiences at the descriptive level of affective reports, involving the reader's feelings through the mechanism of identification. And these symbolic experiences, in the work of any competent novelist, are woven together to frame a consistent set of attitudes, whether of scorn, or compassion, or admiration of courage, or sympathy with the downtrodden, or a sense of futility, depending on his outlook.

Some of the ways of organizing a set of experiences for literary purposes are purely mechanical and external: these are the "rules" governing the proper construction of the novel, the play, the short story, the sonnet, and so on. But more important are the ways of organization suggested by the materials of the literary work—the experiences which the writer wishes to organize. When the materials of a story do not fit into the conventional pattern of a novel, the novelist may create a new organization altogether, more suited to the presentation of his experiences than the conventional patterns. In such a case, critics speak of the materials as "creating their own form." In such a case, too, the order may seem like disorder at first—one thinks of Laurence Sterne's *Tristram Shandy* and James Joyce's *Ulysses*—because the principles of organization, being new, have to be discovered in the course of reading. The reason a poem, novel, or play assumes the shape it ultimately does is the concern of the technical literary critic. He studies the interplay of external and internal demands which has finally shaped the materials into a "work of art."

To symbolize one's experiences adequately and then to order them into a coherent whole constitute an integrative act. The great novelist, or dramatist, or poet is one who has successfully integrated and given coherence to vast areas of human experience. Literary greatness requires, therefore, great extensional awareness of the range of human experience as well as great powers of ordering that experience meaningfully. This is why the discipline of the creative artist is endless: there is always more to learn, both about human experience (which is the material to be ordered) and about the techniques of his craft (which are the means of ordering).

From the point of view of the reader, the fact that language is social is again of central importance. The ordering of experiences and attitudes accomplished linguistically by the writer produces, in the reader, some ordering of his own experiences and attitudes. The reader becomes, as a result of this ordering, somewhat better organized himself. That's what art is for.

APPLICATIONS

I. Discuss the following selections on art, in terms of the ideas presented in this chapter. In what ways do the selections support or conflict with the tension-reduction theory of art? What other ways of explaining art do you find in these passages? How satisfactory are they? Write a 1,000 word essay on "Art, Tension, and Society" or a similar topic making use of some of the ideas you have just encountered.

1. Art in those times was still wrapped up in life. Its function was to fill with beauty the forms assumed by life. . . . The task of art was to adorn all these concepts [religion, chivalry, love] with charm and colour; it is not desired for its own sake, but to decorate life with the splendor which it could bestow. Art was not yet a means, as it is now, to step out of the routine of everyday life to pass some moments in contemplation; it had to be enjoyed as an element of life itself, as the expression of life's significance . . . Consequently, we might venture the paradox that the Middle Ages knew only applied art. They wanted works of art only to make them subservient to some practical use. Their purpose and their meaning always preponderated over their purely aesthetic value.

J. HUIZINGA, *The Waning of the Middle Ages*

2. Art is not and never has been subordinate to moral values. Moral values are social values; aesthetic values are human values. Moral values promote and protect a particular way of life; aesthetic values promote and protect life itself, as a vital principle. . . . Morality seeks to restrain the feelings, art seeks to define them by externalizing them, by giving them significant form. Morality has only one aim—the ideal good; art has quite another aim—the objective truth. Morality finds expression in precept and commandment; art in symbol and myth.

HERBERT READ, *The Grass Roots of Art*

3. Art is anything you can get away with.

MARSHALL McLUHAN, *The Medium Is the Massage*

4. All Nature is but art, unknown to thee
All chance, direction, which thou canst not see
All discord, harmony not understood;
All partial evil, universal good
And, spite of pride, in erring reason's spite,
One truth is clear: Whatever IS, is right.

ALEXANDER POPE, *Essay on Man*

5. Art, including fiction, is neither a means of avoiding pain nor of dulling oneself to it: neither a renunciation nor a narcotic. Like play, fantasy, and wit, which are its close relations, it represents an attempt to augment the meager satisfactions offered by experience through the creation of a more harmonious world to which one can repair, however briefly, for refuge, solace, and pleasure.

SIMON LESSER, *Fiction and the Unconscious*

6. A classic is a work which gives pleasure to the minority which is intensely and permanently interested in literature. It lives on because the minority, eager to renew the sensation of pleasure, is eternally curious and is therefore engaged in an eternal process of rediscovery. A classic does not survive for any ethical reason. It does not survive because it conforms to certain canons, or because neglect would kill it. It survives because it is a source of pleasure and because the passionate few can no more neglect it than a bee can neglect a flower. The passionate few do not read "the right things" because they are right. That is to put the cart before the horse. "The right things" are the right things solely because the passionate few *like* reading them. . . .

   Nobody at all is quite in a position to choose with certainty among modern works. To sift the wheat from the chaff is a process that takes an exceedingly long time. Modern works have to pass before the bar of the taste of successive generations; whereas, with classics, which have been through the ordeal, almost the reverse is the case. *Your taste has to pass before the bar of the classics.* That is the point. If you differ with a classic, it is you who are wrong, and not the book. If you differ with a modern work, you may be wrong or you may be right, but no judge is authoritative to decide. Your taste is unformed. It needs guidance and it needs authoritative guidance.

   ARNOLD BENNET, *Literary Taste: How to Form It*

7. The business of art is to reveal the relation between man and his circumambient universe, at the living moment. As mankind is always struggling in the toils of old relationships, art is always ahead of the "times," which themselves are always far in the rear of the living moment.

   When van Gogh paints sunflowers, he reveals, or achieves, the vivid relation between himself, as man, and the sunflower, as sunflower, at that quick moment of time. His painting does not represent the sunflower itself. We shall never know what the sunflower is. And the camera will *visualize* the sunflower far more perfectly than van Gogh can.

   The vision on the canvas is a third thing, utterly intangible and inexplicable, the offspring of the sunflower itself and van Gogh himself. The vision on the canvas is for ever incommensurable with the canvas, or the paint, or van Gogh as a human organism, or the sunflower as a botanical organism. You cannot weigh nor measure nor even describe the vision on the canvas. . . .

   It is a revelation of the perfected relation, at a certain moment, between a man and a sunflower. . . . And this perfected relation between man and his circumambient universe is life itself, for mankind. . . . Man and the sunflower both pass away from the moment, in the process of forming a new relationship. The relation between all things changes from day to day, in a subtle stealth of change. Hence art, which reveals or attains to another perfect relationship, will be for ever new.

   If we think about it, we find that our life *consists in* this achieving of a pure relationship between ourselves and the living universe about us. This is how I "save my soul" by accomplishing a pure relationship between me and another person, me and other people, me and a nation, me and a race of men, me and animals, me and the trees or flowers, me and the earth, me and the skies and sun and stars, me and the moon:

an infinity of pure relations, big and little. . . . This, if we knew it, is our life and our eternity: the subtle, perfected relation between me and my whole circumambient universe. . . .

Now here we see the beauty and the great value of the novel. Philosophy, religion, science, they are all of them busy nailing things down, to get a stable equilibrium. Religion, with its nailed down One God . . . ; philosophy, with its fixed ideas; science with its "laws": they, all of them, all the time, want to nail us on some tree or other.

But the novel, no. The novel is the highest example of subtle interrelatedness that man has discovered. . . .

D. H. LAWRENCE, "Morality and the Novel," *Phoenix*

II. Be prepared to discuss the impact of violence in comics or television upon the individual "psyche" and upon society at large. If the mass media are part of our "equipment for living," what kind of a job do they do in this respect? The following passages offer some different opinions on this topic.

1. The first comic books appeared in 1935. Not having anything connected or literary about them, and being as difficult to decipher as the *Book of Kells,* they caught on with the young. The elders of the tribe, who had never noticed that the ordinary newspaper was as frantic as a surrealist art exhibition, could hardly be expected to notice that the comic books were as exotic as eighth century illuminations. So, having noticed nothing about the *form,* they could discern nothing of the *contents,* either. The mayhem and violence were all they noted. Therefore, with naive literary logic, they waited for violence to flood the world. Or, alternatively, they attributed existing crime to the comics. The dimmest-witted convict learned to moan, "It wuz comic books done this to me."

   Meanwhile, the violence of an industrial and mechanical environment had to be lived and given meaning and motive in the nerves and viscera of the young. To live and experience anything is to translate its direct impact into many indirect forms of awareness. We provided the young with a shrill and raucous asphalt jungle, beside which any tropical animal jungle was as quiet and tame as a rabbit hutch. We called this normal. We paid people to keep it at the highest pitch of intensity because it paid well. When the entertainment industries tried to provide a reasonable facsimile of the ordinary city vehemence, eyebrows were raised.

   MARSHALL McLUHAN, *Understanding Media*

2. Whether crime and violence programs arouse a lust for violence, reinforce it when it is present, show a way to carry it out, teach the best method to get away with it, or merely blunt a child's (and adult's) awareness of its wrongness, television has become a school for violence.

   In this school young people are never, literally never, taught that violence is, in itself, reprehensible. The lesson they do get is that violence is the great adventure and the sure solution, and he who is best at it wins. We are training not only a peace corps but also a violence corps. I do not advocate that violence should be entirely eliminated from TV. But it should be presented as a fact of life, not as life itself.

   FREDERIC WERTHAM, "School for Violence," *The New York Times,* July 5, 1964.

III. In the light of what has been said in this chapter, study the following poems to see:

a. What tensions of his own the author seems to be trying to remove;

b. What symbolic strategies he employs;

c. Whether these strategies might be applicable to other people and other situations;

d. To what extent the author has succeeded in ordering his experiences into a coherent, meaningful whole;

e. In what particular ways, if any, each of these poems is likely to serve as "equipment for living."

1. *Curiosity*

may have killed the cat; more likely
the cat was just unlucky, or else curious
to see what death was like, having no cause
to go on licking paws, or fathering
litter on litter of kittens, predictably.

Nevertheless, to be curious
is dangerous enough. To distrust
what is always said, what seems,
to ask odd questions, interfere in dreams,
leave home, smell rats, have hunches
does not endear him to those doggy circles
where well-smelt baskets, suitable wives, good lunches
are the order of things, and where prevails
much wagging of incurious heads and tails.

Face it. Curiosity
will not cause him to die—
only lack of it will.
Never to want to see
the other side of the hill,
or that improbable country
where living is an idyll
(although a probable hell)
would kill us all.
Only the curious
have, if they live, a tale
worth telling at all.

Dogs say he loves too much, is irresponsible,
is changeable, marries too many wives,
deserts his children, chills all dinner tables
with tales of his nine lives.
Well, he is lucky. Let him be
nine-lived and contradictory,
curious enough to change, prepared to pay
the cat price, which is to die
and die again and again,
each time with no less pain.
A cat minority of one
is all that can be counted on

to tell the truth. And what he has to tell
on each return from hell
is this: that dying is what the living do,
that dying is what the loving do,
and that dead dogs are those who do not know
that hell is where, to live, they have to go.

ALASTAIR REID

2. *Dream Deferred*

What happens to a dream deferred?

Does it dry up
like a raisin in the sun?
Or fester like a sore—
And then run?
Does it stink like rotten meat?
Or crust and sugar over—
like a syrupy sweet?

Maybe it just sags
like a heavy load.

Or does it explode?

LANGSTON HUGHES

3. My poems are always unfinished:
for,
written at the peak of a fancy,

all the loves die—
and I have no energy to chronicle
the endings,
Sad little half-polished stones,
they lie in my closet;
just as well incomplete,
for the imagined beauty beneath
the roughness
is better than the truth of
the faults.

HUNTER HEATH III

4. Myself when young did eagerly frequent
Doctor and Saint, and heard great Argument
About it and about: but evermore
Came out by the same door where in I went.

OMAR KHAYYAM

5. *Brahma*

If the red slayer think he slays,
Or if the slain think he is slain,
They know not well the subtle ways
I keep, and pass, and turn again.

Far or forgot to me is near;
Shadow and sunlight are the same;
The vanquished gods to me appear;
And one to me are shame and fame.

They reckon ill who leave me out;
    When me they fly, I am the wings;
I am the doubter and the doubt,
    And I the hymn the Brahmin sings.

The strong gods pine for my abode,
    And pine in vain the sacred Seven;
But thou, meek lover of the good!
    Find me, and turn thy back on heaven.

RALPH WALDO EMERSON

6. *Fire and Ice*

Some say the world will end in fire,
Some say in ice.
From what I've tasted of desire
I hold with those who favor fire.
But if it had to perish twice,
I think I know enough of hate
To say that for destruction ice
Is also great
And would suffice.

ROBERT FROST

IV. Read, ponder, and digest:

1. The worst *does* sometimes happen. As men we have to count on that possibility, have to arm ourselves against it, and above all we have to realize that since absurdities necessarily occur, and nowadays manifest themselves with more and more forcefulness, we can prevent ourselves from being destroyed by them and can make ourselves relatively comfortable upon this earth only if we humbly include these absurdities in our thinking, reckon with the inevitable fractures and distortions of human reason when it attempts honestly to deal with reality.

FRIEDRICH DUERRENMATT, *The Pledge*

2. *A Study of Reading Habits*

When getting my nose in a book
Cured most things short of school
It was worth ruining my eyes
To know I could still keep cool,
And deal out the old right hook
To dirty dogs twice my size.

Later, with inch-thick specs,
Evil was just my lark:
Me and my cloak and fangs
Had ripping times in the dark.
The women I clubbed with sex!
I broke them up like meringues.

Don't read much now: the dude
Who lets the girl down before
The hero arrives, the chap
Who's yellow and keeps the store,
Seems far too familiar. Get stewed:
Books are a load of crap.

PHILIP LARKIN

BOOK TWO

language and thought

He [the student of politics] must also be on his guard against the old words, for the words persist when the reality that lay behind them has changed. It is inherent in our intellectual activity that we seek to imprison reality in our description of it. Soon, long before we realize it, it is we who become the prisoners of the description. From that point on, our ideas degenerate into a kind of folklore which we pass to each other, fondly thinking we are still talking of the reality around us.

Thus we talk of free enterprise, of capitalist society, of the rights of free association, of parliamentary government, as though all of these words stand for the same things they formerly did. Social institutions are what they do, not necessarily what we say they do. It is the verb that matters, not the noun.

If this is not understood, we become symbol worshipers. The categories we once evolved and which were the tools we used in our intercourse with reality become hopelessly blunted. In these circumstances the social and political realities we are supposed to be grappling with change and reshape themselves independently of the collective impact of our ideas. We become the creature and no longer the partner of social realities. As we fumble with outworn categories our political vitality is sucked away and we stumble from one situation to another, without chart, without compass, and with the steering-wheel lashed to a course we are no longer following.

This is the real point of danger for a political party and for the leaders and thinkers who inspire it. For if they are out of touch with reality, the masses are not.

Aneurin Bevan
In Place of Fear

foreword

The Story of A-town and B-ville: Second Semantic Parable

Once upon a time, said the Professor, there were two small communities, spiritually as well as geographically situated at a considerable distance from each other. They had, however, these problems in common: both were hard hit by a recession, so that in each of the towns there were about one hundred heads of families unemployed.

The city fathers of A-town, the first community, were substantial and sound-thinking businessmen. The unemployed tried hard, as unemployed people usually do, to find jobs; but the situation did not improve. The city fathers had been brought up to believe that there is always enough work for everyone, if you only look for it hard enough. Comforting themselves with this doctrine, the city fathers could have shrugged their shoulders and turned their backs on the problem, except for the fact that they were genuinely kindhearted men. They could not bear to see the unemployed men and their wives and children starving. In order to prevent hardship, they felt that they had to provide these people with some means of sustenance. Their principles told them, nevertheless, that if people were given something for nothing, it would demoralize their character. Naturally this made the city fathers even more unhappy, because they were faced with the horrible choice of (1) letting the unemployed starve, or (2) destroying their moral character.

The solution they finally hit upon, after much debate and soul-searching, was this. They decided to give the unemployed families "relief payments" of two hundred dollars a month. (They considered using the English term "dole," but with their characteristic American penchant for euphemism, they decided on the less offensive term.) To make sure that the unemployed would not take their unearned payments too much for granted, however, they decided that the "relief" was to be accompanied by a moral lesson; to wit: the obtaining of the assistance would be made so difficult, humiliating, and disagreeable that there would be no temptation for anyone to go through the process unless it was absolutely necessary; the moral disapproval of the community would be turned upon the recipients of the money at all times in such a way that they would try hard to get "off relief" and "regain their self-respect." Some even proposed that people on relief be denied the vote, so that the moral lesson would be more deeply impressed upon them. Others suggested that their names be published at regular intervals in the newspapers. The city fathers had enough faith in the goodness of human nature to expect that the recipients

Words forming thought and vice versa

would be grateful, since they were getting something for nothing, something which they hadn't worked for.

When the plan was put into operation, however, the recipients of the relief checks proved to be an ungrateful, ugly bunch. They seemed to resent the cross-examinations and inspections at the hands of the "relief investigators," who, they said, took advantage of a man's misery to snoop into every detail of his private life. In spite of uplifting editorials in A-town *Tribune* telling them how grateful they ought to be, the recipients of the relief refused to learn any moral lessons, declaring that they were "just as good as anybody else." When, for example, they permitted themselves the rare luxury of a movie or an evening of bingo, their neighbors looked at them sourly as if to say, "I work hard and pay my taxes just in order to support loafers like you in idleness and pleasure." This attitude, which was fairly characteristic of those members of the community who still had jobs, further embittered the relief recipients, so that they showed even less gratitude as time went on and were constantly on the lookout for insults, real or imaginary, from people who might think that they weren't as good as anybody else. A number of them took to moping all day long; one or two even committed suicide. Others, feeling that they had failed to provide, found it hard to look their wives and children in the face. Children whose parents were "on relief" felt inferior to classmates whose parents were not "public charges." Some of these children developed inferiority complexes which affected not only their grades at school, but their careers after graduation. Finally, several relief recipients felt they could stand their loss of self-respect no longer and decided, after many efforts to gain honest jobs, that they would earn money by their own efforts even if they had to rob. They did so and were caught and sent to the state penitentiary.

The depression, therefore, hit A-town very hard. The relief policy had averted starvation, no doubt, but suicide, personal quarrels, unhappy homes, the weakening of social organizations, the maladjustment of children, and, finally, crime, had resulted. The town was divided in two, the "haves" and the "have-nots," so that there was class hatred. People shook their heads sadly and declared that it all went to prove over again what they had known from the beginning, that giving people something for nothing inevitably demoralizes their character. The citizens of A-town gloomily waited for prosperity to return, with less and less hope as time went on.

The story of the other community, B-ville, was entirely different. B-ville was a relatively isolated town, too far out of the way to be reached by Rotary Club speakers and other dispensers of conventional wisdom. One of the aldermen, however, who was something of an economist, explained to his fellow aldermen that unemployment, like sickness, accident, fire, tornado, or death, hits unexpectedly in modern society, irrespective of the victim's merits or deserts. He went on to say that B-ville's homes, parks, streets, industries, and everything else B-ville was proud of, had been built in part by the work of these same people who were now unemployed. He then proposed to apply a principle of insurance: if the work these unemployed people had previously done for the community could be regarded as a form of "premium" paid to the community against a time of misfortune, payments now made to them to prevent their starvation could be regarded as "insurance claims." He therefore proposed that all men of good repute who had worked in the community in some line of useful endeavor, whether as machinists, clerks, or bank managers, be regarded as "citizen policyholders," having "claims" against the city in the case of unemployment for two hundred dollars a month until such time as they might again be employed. Naturally, he had to talk very slowly and patiently, since the idea was entirely new to his fellow aldermen. But he described his plan as a "straight business proposition," and finally they were persuaded. They worked out in detail, to everyone's satisfaction, the conditions under which citizens should be regarded as policyholders in the city's social insurance plan, and decided to give checks for two hundred dollars a month to the heads of each of B-ville's indigent families.

B-ville's "claim adjusters," whose duty it was to investigate the claims of the citizen "policyholders," had a much better time than A-town's "relief investigators." While the latter had been resentfully regarded as snoopers, the former, having no moral lesson to teach but simply a business transaction to carry out, treated their clients with businesslike courtesy and got the same amount of information as the relief investigators had, with considerably less difficulty. There were no hard feelings. It further happened, fortunately, that news of B-ville's plans reached a liberal newspaper editor in the big city at the other end of the state. This writer described the plan in a leading feature story headed "B-VILLE LOOKS AHEAD. Adventure in Social Pioneering Launched by Upper Valley Community." As a result of this publicity, inquiries about the plan began to come to the city hall even before the first checks were mailed out. This led, naturally, to a considerable feeling of pride on the part of the aldermen, who, being boosters, felt that this was a wonderful opportunity to put B-ville on the map.

Accordingly, the aldermen decided that instead of simply mailing out the checks as they had originally intended, they would publicly present the first checks at a monster civic ceremony. They invited the governor of the state, who was glad to come to bolster his none-too-enthusiastic support in that locality, the president of the state university, the senator from their district, and other functionaries. They decorated the National Guard armory with flags and got out the American Legion Fife and Drum Corps, the Boy Scouts, and other civic organizations. At the big celebration, each family to receive a "social insurance check" was marched up to the platform to receive it, and the governor and the mayor shook hands with each of them as they came trooping up in their best clothes. Fine speeches were made; there was much cheering and shouting; pictures of the event showing the recipients of the checks shaking hands with the mayor, and the governor patting the heads of the children, were published not only in the local papers but also in several metropolitan picture sections.

Every recipient of these insurance checks had a feeling, therefore, that he had been personally honored, that he lived in a wonderful little town, and that he could face his unemployment with greater courage and assurance since his community was behind him. The men and women found themselves being kidded in a friendly way by their acquaintances for having been "up there with the big shots," shaking hands with the governor, and so on. The children at school found themselves envied for having had their pictures in the papers. All in all, B-ville's unemployed did not commit suicide, were not haunted by a sense of failure, did not turn to crime, did not manifest personal maladjustments, did not develop class hatred as the result of their two hundred dollars a month. . . .

At the conclusion of the Professor's story, the discussion began:

"That just goes to show," said the Advertising Man, who was known among his friends as a realistic thinker, "what good promotional work can do. B-ville's city council had real advertising sense, and that civic ceremony was a masterpiece . . . made everyone happy . . . put over the scheme in a big way. Reminds me of the way we do things in our business: as soon as we called horse-mackerel tuna-fish, we developed a big market for it. I suppose if you called relief 'insurance,' you could actually get people to like it, couldn't you?"

"What do you mean, 'calling' it insurance?" asked the Social Worker. "B-ville's scheme wasn't relief at all. It *was* insurance."

"Good grief, man! Do you realize what you're saying?" cried the Advertising Man in surprise. "Are you implying that those people had any *right* to that money? All I said was that it's a good idea to *disguise* relief as insurance if it's going to make people any happier. But it's still relief, no matter what you *call* it. It's all right to kid the public along to reduce discontent, but we don't need to kid ourselves as well!"

"But they *do* have a right to that money! They're not getting something for nothing. It's insurance. They did something for the community, and that's their prem—"

"Say, are you crazy?"

"Who's crazy?"

"You're crazy. Relief is relief, isn't it? If you'd only call things by their right names. . . ."

"But, confound it, insurance is insurance, isn't it?"

P.S. Those who have concluded that the point of the story is that the Social Worker and the Advertising Man were "only arguing about different names for the same thing," are asked to reread the story and explain what they mean by (1) "only" and (2) "the same thing."

The crucial point to be considered in a study of language behavior is the relationship between language and reality, between words and not-words. Except as we understand this relationship, we run the grave risk of straining the delicate connection between words and facts, of permitting our words to go wild, and so of creating for ourselves fabrications of fantasy and delusion.

Wendell Johnson

An edible: *Good to eat and wholesome to digest, as a worm to a toad, a toad to a snake, a snake to a pig, a pig to a man, and a man to a worm.*

Ambrose Bierce

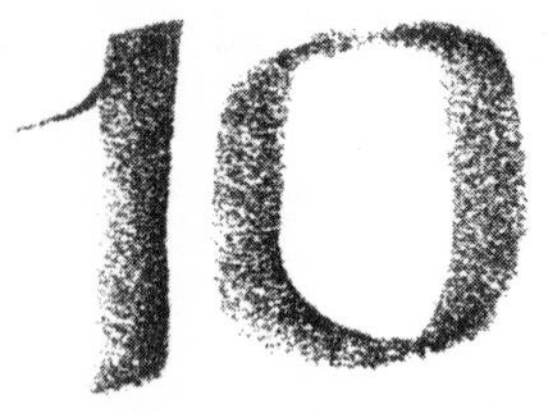

how we know what we know

Bessie, the Cow

The universe is in a perpetual state of flux. The stars are growing, cooling, exploding. The earth itself is not unchanging; mountains are being worn away, rivers are altering their channels, valleys are deepening. All life is also a process of change, through birth, growth, decay, and death. Even what we used to call inert matter—chairs and tables and stones—is not inert, as we now know, for, at the submicroscopic level, it is a whirl of electrons. If a table looks today very much as it did yesterday or as it did a hundred years ago, it is not because it has not changed, but because the changes have been too minute for our coarse perceptions. To modern science there is no "solid matter." If matter looks "solid" to us, it does so only because its motion is too rapid or too minute to be felt. It is "solid" only in the sense that a rapidly rotating color chart is "white" or a rapidly spinning top is "standing still." Our senses are extremely limited, so that we constantly have to use instruments, such as microscopes, telescopes, speedometers, stethoscopes, and seismographs, to detect and record occurrences which our senses are not able to record directly. The way in which we happen to see and feel things is the result of the peculiarities of our nervous systems. There are "sights" we cannot see and, as even children know today with their high-frequency dog whistles, "sounds" we cannot hear. It is absurd, therefore, to imagine that we ever perceive anything "as it really is."

Inadequate as our senses are, with the help of instruments they tell us a great deal. The discovery of microörganisms with the use of the microscope has given us a measure of control over bacteria; we cannot see, hear, or feel electromagnetic waves, but we can create and transform them to useful purpose. Most of our conquest of the external world, in engineering, in chemistry, and in medicine, is due to our use of mechanical contrivances of one kind or another to increase the capacity of our nervous systems. In modern life, our unaided senses are not half enough to get us about in the world. We cannot even obey speed laws or compute our gas and electric bills without mechanical aids to perception.

To return, then, to the relations between words and what they stand for, let us say that there is before us "Bessie," a cow. Bessie is a living organism, constantly changing, constantly ingesting food and air, transforming it, getting rid of it again. Her blood is circulating, her nerves are sending messages. Viewed microscopically, she is a mass of variegated corpuscles, cells, and bacterial organisms; viewed from the point of view of modern physics, she is a perpetual dance of electrons. What she is in her entirety, we can never know; even if we could at any precise moment say what she was, at the next moment she would have changed enough so that our description would no longer be accurate. It is impossible to say completely what Bessie or anything else really *is*. Bessie is not a static "object," but a dynamic process.

The Bessie that we experience, however, is something else again. We experience only a small fraction of the total Bessie: the lights and shadows of her exterior, her motions, her general configuration, the noises she makes, and the sensations she presents to our sense of touch. *And because of our previous experience, we observe resemblances in her to certain other animals to which, in the past, we have applied the word "cow."*

The Process of Abstracting

The "object" of our experience, then, is not the "thing in itself," but *an interaction between our nervous systems (with all their imperfections) and something outside them.* Bessie is unique—there is nothing else in the universe exactly like her in all respects. But we automatically *abstract* or select from the process-Bessie those features of hers in which she resembles other animals of like shape, functions, and habits, and we *classify* her as "cow."

When we say, then, that "Bessie is a cow," we are only noting the process-Bessie's resemblances to other "cows" and *ignoring differences.* What is more, we are leaping a huge chasm: from the dynamic process-Bessie, a whirl of electro-chemico-neural eventfulness, to a relatively static "idea," "concept," or *word,* "cow." In this connection, the reader is referred to the diagram entitled "The Abstraction Ladder," which he will find on page 153.[1]

As the diagram illustrates, the "object" we see is an abstraction of the lowest level; but it is still an abstraction, since it leaves out characteristics of the process that is the real Bessie. The *word* "Bessie" (cow_1) is the lowest *verbal* level of abstraction, leaving out further characteristics —the differences between Bessie yesterday and Bessie today, between Bessie today and Bessie tomorrow—and selecting only the similarities. The word "cow" selects only the similarities between Bessie (cow_1), Daisy (cow_2), Rosie (cow_3), and so on, and therefore leaves out still more about Bessie. The word "livestock" selects or abstracts only the features that Bessie has in common with pigs, chickens, goats, and sheep. The term "farm asset" abstracts only the features Bessie has in common with barns, fences, livestock, furniture, generating plants, and tractors, and is therefore on a very high level of abstraction.

Our concern here with the process of abstracting may seem strange since the study of language is all too often restricted to matters of pronunciation, spelling, vocabulary, grammar, and sentence structure. The methods by which composition and oratory are taught in old-fashioned school systems seem to be largely responsible for this widespread notion that the way to study words is to concentrate one's attention exclusively on words.

But as we know from everyday experience, learning language is not simply a matter of learning words; it is a matter of correctly relating our words to the things and happenings for which they stand. We learn the language of baseball by playing or watching the game *and studying what goes on.* It is not enough for a child to learn to *say* "cookie" or "dog"; he must be able to use these words in their proper relationship to nonverbal cookies and nonverbal dogs before we can grant that he is learning the language. As Wendell Johnson has said, "The study of language begins properly with a study of what language is about."

Once we begin to concern ourselves with what language is about, we are at once thrown into a consideration of how the human nervous system

[1]The "Abstraction Ladder" is based on "The Structural Differential," a diagram originated by Alfred Korzybski to explain the process of abstracting. For a fuller explanation both of the diagram and of the process it illustrates, see his *Science and Sanity: An Introduction to Non-Aristotelian Systems and General Semantics* (1933), especially Chapter 25.

ABSTRACTION LADDER
Start reading from the bottom UP

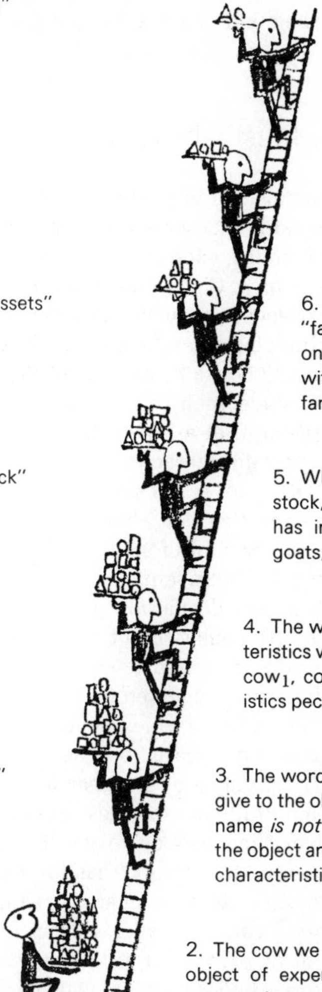

8. "wealth"

8. The word "wealth" is at an extremely high level of abstraction, omitting *almost* all reference to the characteristics of Bessie.

7. "asset"

7. When Bessie is referred to as an "asset," still more of her characteristics are left out.

6. "farm assets"

6. When Bessie is included among "farm assets," reference is made only to what she has in common with all other salable items on the farm.

5. "livestock"

5. When Bessie is referred to as "livestock," only those characteristics she has in common with pigs, chickens, goats, etc., are referred to.

4. "cow"

4. The word "cow" stands for the characteristics we have abstracted as common to cow_1, cow_2, cow_3 . . . cow_n. Characteristics peculiar to specific cows are left out.

3. "Bessie"

3. The word "Bessie" (cow_1) is the *name* we give to the object of perception of level 2. The name *is not* the object; it merely *stands for* the object and omits reference to many of the characteristics of the object.

2.

2. The cow we perceive is not the word, but the object of experience, that which our nervous system abstracts (selects) from the totality that constitutes the process-cow. Many of the characteristics of the process-cow are left out.

1. The cow known to science ultimately consists of atoms, electrons, etc., according to present-day scientific inference. Characteristics (represented by circles) are infinite at this level and ever-changing. This is the *process level.*

works. When we call Beau (the Boston terrier), Pedro (the chihuahua), Snuffles (the English bulldog), and Shane (the Irish wolfhound)—creatures that differ greatly in size, shape, appearance, and behavior—by the same name, "dog," our nervous system has obviously gone to work *abstracting* what is common to them all, ignoring for the time being the differences among them.

Why We Must Abstract

This process of abstracting, of leaving characteristics out, is an indispensable convenience. To illustrate by still another example, suppose that we live in an isolated village of four families, each owning a house. A's house is referred to as *maga;* B's house is *biyo;* C's is *kata;* and D's is *pelel.* This is quite satisfactory for ordinary purposes of communication in the village, unless a discussion arises about building a new house—a spare one, let us say. We cannot refer to the projected house by any one of the four words we have for the existing houses, since each of these has too specific a meaning. We must find a *general* term, at a higher level of abstraction, that means "something that has certain characteristics in common with *maga, biyo, kata,* and *pelel,* and yet is not A's, B's, C's, or D's." Since this is much too complicated to say each time, an *abbreviation* must be invented. So we choose the noise, *house.* Out of such needs do our words come—they are a form of shorthand. The invention of a new abstraction is a great step forward, since it *makes discussion possible*—as, in this case, not only the discussion of a fifth house, but of all future houses we may build or see in our travels or dream about.

A producer of educational films once remarked to me that it is impossible to make a shot of "work." You can shoot Joe hoeing potatoes, Frank greasing a car, Bill spraying paint on a barn, but never just "work." "Work," too, is a shorthand term, standing, at a higher level of abstraction, for a characteristic that a multitude of activities, from dishwashing to navigation to running an advertising agency to governing a nation, have in common. The special meaning that "work" has in physics is also clearly derived from abstracting the common characteristics of many different kinds of work. ("A transference of energy from one body to another, resulting in the motion or displacement of the body acted upon, in the direction of the acting force and against resistance." Funk and Wagnalls' *Standard College Dictionary.*)

The indispensability of this process of abstracting can again be illustrated by what we do when we "calculate." The word "calculate" originates from the Latin word *calculus,* meaning "pebble," and derives its present meaning from such ancient practices as putting a pebble into a box for each sheep as it left the fold, so that one could tell, by checking the sheep returning at night against the pebbles, whether any had been lost. Primitive as this example of calculation is, it will serve to show why mathematics works. Each pebble is, in this example, an abstraction representing the "oneness" of each sheep—its numerical value. And because we are abstracting from extensional events on clearly understood and uniform principles, the numerical facts about the pebbles are also, barring unforeseen circumstances, numerical facts about the sheep. Our *x*'s and *y*'s and other mathematical symbols are abstractions made from numerical abstractions, and are therefore abstractions of still higher level. And they are useful in predicting occurrences and in getting work done because, since they are abstractions properly and uniformly made from starting points in the extensional world, the relations revealed by the symbols will be, again barring unforeseen circumstances, relations existing in the extensional world.

On Definitions

Definitions, contrary to popular opinion, tell us nothing about things. They only describe people's linguistic habits; that is, they tell us what noises people make under what conditions. Definitions should be understood as *statements about language.*

> *House:* This word, at the next higher level of abstraction, can be substituted for the more cumbersome expression, "Something that has characteristics in common with Bill's bungalow, Jordan's cottage, Mrs. Smith's guest home, Dr. Jones's mansion. . . ."
>
> *Red:* A feature that rubies, roses, ripe tomatoes, robins' breasts, uncooked beef, and lipsticks have in common is abstracted, and this word expresses that abstraction.
>
> *Kangaroo:* Where the biologist would say "herbivorous mammal, a marsupial of the family Macropodidae," ordinary people say "kangaroo."

Now it will be observed that while the definitions of "house" and "red" given here point *down* the abstraction ladder (see the charts) to *lower* levels of abstraction, the definition of "kangaroo" remains at the same level. That is to say, in the case of "house," we could if necessary go and *look* at Bill's bungalow, Jordan's cottage, Mrs. Smith's guest home, and Dr. Jones's mansion, and figure out for ourselves what features they seem to have in common; in this way, we might begin to understand under what conditions to use the word "house." But all we know about "kangaroo" from the above is that where some people say one thing, other people say another. That is, when we stay at the *same* level of abstraction in giving a definition, we do not give any information, unless, of course, the listener or reader is already sufficiently familiar with the defining words to work himself down the abstraction ladder. Dictionaries, in order to save space, have to assume in many cases such familiarity with the language on the part of the reader. But where the assumption is unwarranted, definitions at the same level of abstraction are worse than useless. Looking up "indifference" in some cheap pocket dictionaries, we find it defined as "apathy"; we look up "apathy" and find it defined as "indifference."

Even more useless, however, are the definitions that go *up* the abstraction ladder to higher levels of abstraction—the kind most of us tend to make automatically. Try the following experiment on an unsuspecting friend:

> "What is meant by the word *red?*"
> "It's a color."
> "What's a *color?*"
> "Why, it's a quality things have."
> "What's a *quality?*"
> "Say, what are you trying to do, anyway?"

You have pushed him into the clouds. He is lost.

If, on the other hand, we habitually go *down* the abstraction ladder to *lower* levels of abstraction when we are asked the meaning of a word, we are less likely to get lost in verbal mazes; we will tend to "have our feet on the ground" and know what we are talking about. This habit displays itself in an answer such as this:

> "What is meant by the word *red?*"
> "Well, the next time you see some cars stopped at an intersection, look at the traffic light facing them. Also, you might go to the fire department and see how their trucks are painted."

"Let's Define Our Terms"

An extremely widespread instance of an unrealistic (and ultimately superstitious) attitude toward definitions is found in the common academic prescription, "Let's define our terms so that we shall all know what we are talking about." As we have already seen in Chapter 4, the fact that a golfer, for example, cannot define golfing terms is no indication that he cannot understand and use them. Conversely, the fact that a man can define a large number of words is no guarantee that he knows what objects or operations they stand for in concrete situations. Having defined a word, people often believe that some kind of understanding has been established, ignoring the fact that the words in the definition often conceal even more serious confusions and ambiguities than the word defined. If we happen to discover this fact and try to remedy matters by defining the defining words, and then, finding ourselves still confused, we go on to define the words in the definitions of the defining words, and so on, we quickly find ourselves in a hopeless snarl. The only way to avoid this snarl is to keep definitions to a minimum and to point to extensional levels wherever necessary; in writing and speaking, this means giving specific examples of what we are talking about.

Operational Definitions

Another way to keep extensional levels in mind, when definitions are called for, is to use what physicist P. W. Bridgman called "operational definitions." As he says,

> To find the length of an object, we have to perform certain physical operations. The concept of length is therefore fixed when the operations by which length is measured are fixed. . . . In general, we mean by any concept nothing more than a set of operations; *the concept is synonymous with the corresponding set of operations.*[2]

The operational definition, then, as Anatol Rapoport explains, is one that tells you "*what to do* and *what to observe* in order to bring the thing defined or its effects within the range of one's experience." He gives the following simple example of how to define "weight": go to a railroad station or drugstore, look for a scale, stand on it, put in a penny, read the number at which the pointer comes to rest. *That* is your weight. But supposing different scales give different readings? Then your weight can be said to be within the range of, say, 140 to 145 pounds. With more accurate scales you might get closer readings, such as 142 pounds plus-or-minus one. But there is no "property" called weight that exists apart from the operations measuring it. As Rapoport says, "If the only way we can be aware of the amount of weight is by means of the scale, then the very definition of weight has to be in terms of the scale."[3]

Such, then, is the scientific, or "operational," point of view toward definition—one that attempts rigidly to exclude non-extensional, non-sense statements. We can extend this idea from science to the problems of everyday life and thought. Just as there is no such thing as "length" apart from the operations by which length is measured, just as there is no "weight" apart from the operations by which weight is determined, there is likewise no "democracy" apart from the sum-total of democratic *practices*, such as universal franchise, freedom of speech, equality before the law, and so on. Similarly, there is no such thing as "brotherhood" apart from brotherly behavior, nor "charity" apart from charitable actions.

The operational point of view does much to keep our words meaningful. When people say things like, "Let's have no more of *progressive* methods in our schools," "Let's get back to *sound business principles* in running our county government," "Let's try to do the *Christian* thing," "Let's put father back as head of the family," we are entitled to ask, "what do you mean—*extensionally speaking?*" To ask this question often—of ourselves as well as of others—is to do our bit toward reducing the vast amount of non-sense that is written, spoken, and shouted in this incredibly garrulous world.

[2]*The Logic of Modern Physics* (1927), p. 5.
[3]*Operational Philosophy* (1953), p. 25.

The best examples in everyday life of operational definitions are to be found in cookbooks, which describe the *operations* by means of which the entity defined may be extensionally experienced. Thus: "*Steak Diane.* Slice tenderloin beef very thin and give it a few whacks with a meat mallet to flatten it even more; sprinkle with salt and pepper to taste. Have your pan very hot. . . ." *(The Sunset Cook Book.)* Writers and speakers would do well to study cookbooks occasionally to increase the clarity and verifiability of their utterances.

Chasing Oneself in Verbal Circles

In other words, the kind of "thinking" we must be extremely wary of is that which *never* leaves the higher verbal levels of abstraction, the kind that never points *down* the abstraction ladder to lower levels of abstraction and from there to the extensional world:

> "What do you mean by *democracy?*"
> "Democracy means the preservation of human rights."
> "What do you mean by *rights?*"
> "By rights I mean those privileges God grants to all of us—I mean man's inherent privileges."
> "Such as?"
> "Liberty, for example."
> "What do you mean by *liberty?*"
> "Religious and political freedom."
> "And what does that mean?"
> "Religious and political freedom is what we enjoy under a democracy."

Of course it is possible to talk meaningfully about democracy, as Jefferson and Lincoln have done, as Frederick Jackson Turner does in *The Frontier in American History* (1950), as Karl R. Popper does in *The Open Society and Its Enemies* (1950), as T. V. Smith and Eduard Lindeman do in *The Democratic Way of life* (1939)—to name only a few examples that come to mind. The trouble with speakers who never leave the higher levels of abstraction is not only that their audiences fail to

Words defining words

notice when they are saying something and when they are not; but also that they themselves lose their ability to discriminate. Never coming down to earth, they frequently chase themselves around in verbal circles, unaware that they are making meaningless noises.

This is by no means to say that we must never make extensionally meaningless noises. When we use directive language, when we talk about the future, when we utter ritual language or engage in social conversation, we often make utterances that have no extensional verifiability. It must not be overlooked that our highest ratiocinative and imaginative powers are derived from the fact that symbols *are* independent of things symbolized, so that we are free not only to go quickly from low to extremely high levels of abstraction (from "canned peas" to "groceries" to "commodities" to "national wealth") and to manipulate symbols even when the things they stand for cannot be so manipulated ("If all the freight cars in the country were hooked up to each other in one long line . . ."), but we are also free to manufacture symbols at will even if they stand only for abstractions made from other abstractions and not for anything in the extensional world. Mathematicians, for example, often play with symbols that have no extensional content just to find out what can be done with them; this is called "pure mathematics." And pure mathematics is far from being a useless pastime, because mathematical systems that are elaborated with no extensional applications in mind often prove to be applicable later in useful and unforeseen ways. But when mathematicians deal with extensionally meaningless symbols, they usually know what they are doing. *We* likewise must know what we are doing.

Nevertheless, all of us (including mathematicians), when we speak the language of everyday life, often make meaningless noises without knowing that we are doing so. We have already seen what confusions this can lead to. The fundamental purpose of the abstraction ladder, as shown in both this chapter and the next, is to make us aware of the process of abstracting.

The Distrust of Abstractions

We may, using our abstraction ladder, allocate statements as well as words to differing levels of abstraction. "Mrs. Levin makes good potato pancakes" may be regarded as a statement at a fairly low level of abstraction, although, to be sure, it leaves out many elements, such as (1) the meaning of "goodness" in potato pancakes, and (2) the infrequent occasions when her pancakes fail to turn out well. "Mrs. Levin is a good cook" is a statement at a higher level of abstraction, covering Mrs. Levin's skill not only with potato pancakes, but also with roasts, pickles, noodles, strudels, and so on, nevertheless omitting *specific* mention of what she can accomplish. "Chicago women are good cooks" is a statement at a still higher level of abstraction; it can be made (if at all) only from observation of the cooking of a statistically significant number of Chicago women. "The culinary art has reached a high state in America" would be a still more highly abstract statement and, if made at all, would have to be based not only on observation of the Mrs. Levins of Chicago, New York, San Francisco, Denver, Albuquerque, and Chattanooga, but also on observation of the quality of meals served in hotels and restaurants, the quality of training in high school and college departments of home economics, the quality of writings on culinary art in American books and magazines, and many other relevant factors.

Unfortunately, though understandably, there is a tendency in our times to speak with contempt of "mere abstractions." The ability to climb to higher and higher levels of abstraction is a distinctively human trait without which none of our philosophical or scientific insights would be possible. In order to have a science of chemistry, one *has* to be able to think of "H_2O," leaving out of consideration for the time being the wetness of water, the hardness of ice, the pearliness of dew, and the other extensional characteristics of H_2O at the objective level. In order to have a study called "ethics," one has to be able to think of what elements in ethical behavior have in common under different conditions and in different civilizations; one has to abstract that which is common to the behavior of the ethical carpenter, the ethical politician, the ethical businessman, and the ethical soldier—and that which is common to the laws of conduct of the Buddhist, the Orthodox Jew, the Confucian, and the Christian. Thinking that is most abstract can also be that which is most generally useful. The famous injunction of Jesus, "And as ye would that men should do to you, do ye also to them likewise," is, from this point of view, a brilliant generalization of more particular directives—a generalization at so high a level of abstraction that it appears to be applicable to all men in all cultures.

But high-level abstractions acquire a bad reputation because they are so often used, consciously or unconsciously, to confuse and befuddle people. A grab among competing powers for oil resources may be spoken of as "protecting the integrity of small nations." (Remember Japan's "Greater East Asia Co-prosperity Sphere"?) An unwillingness to pay social security taxes may be spoken of as "maintaining the system of free enterprise." Depriving the Negro of his vote in violation of the Constitution of the United States may be spoken of as "preserving states' rights." The consequence of this free, and often irresponsible, use of high-level abstractions in public controversy and special pleading is that a significant portion of the population has grown cynical about *all* abstractions.

But, as the abstraction ladder has shown, *all we know are abstractions.* What you know about the chair you are sitting in is an abstraction from the totality of that chair. When you eat white bread you cannot tell by the taste whether or not it has been "enriched by vitamin B" as it says on the wrapper; you simply have to trust that the process (from which the words "vitamin B" are abstracted) is actually there. What you know about your wife—even if she has been your wife for thirty years—is again an abstraction. Distrusting all abstractions simply does not make sense.

The test of abstractions then is not whether they are "high-level" or "low-level" abstractions, but *whether they are referrable to lower levels.* If one makes a statement about "culinary arts in America," one should be able to refer the statement down the abstraction ladder to particulars of American restaurants, American domestic science, American techniques of food preservation, down to Mrs. Levin in her kitchen. If one makes a statement about "civil rights in Wisconsin," one should know something about national, state, and local statutes; one should also know something about the behavior of policemen, magistrates, judges, academic authorities, hotel managers, and the general public in Wisconsin, all of whose acts and whose decisions affect that minimum of decent treatment in the courts, in politics, and in society that we call "civil rights." A preacher, a professor, a journalist, or a politician whose high-level abstractions can systematically and surely be referred to lower-level abstractions is not only talking, he is saying something. As *Time* would say, no windbag, he.

"Dead-Level Abstracting"

Professor Wendell Johnson of the University of Iowa, in his *People in Quandaries* (1946), discusses a linguistic phenomenon which he calls "dead-level abstracting." Some people, it appears, remain more or less permanently stuck at certain levels of the abstraction ladder, some on the lower levels, some on the very high levels. There are those, for example, who go in for "persistent low-level abstracting":

> Probably all of us know certain people who seem able to talk on and on without ever drawing any very general conclusions. For example, there is the back-fence chatter that is made up of he said and then I said and then she said and I said and then he said, far into the afternoon, ending with, "Well, that's *just* what I told him!" Letters describing vacation trips frequently illustrate this sort of language, detailing places seen, times of arrival and departure, the foods eaten and the prices paid, whether the beds were hard or soft, etc.

A similar inability to get to higher levels of abstraction characterizes certain types of mental patients who suffer, as Johnson says, "a general blocking of the abstracting process." They go on indefinitely, reciting insignificant facts, never able to pull them together to frame a generalization that would give a meaning to the facts.

Other speakers remain stuck at higher levels of abstraction, with little or no contact with lower levels. Such language remains permanently in the clouds. As Johnson says:

> It is characterized especially by vagueness, ambiguity, even utter meaninglessness. Simply by saving various circulars, brochures, free copies of "new thought" magazines, etc . . . it is possible to accumulate in a short time quite a sizable file of illustrative material. Much more, of course, is to be found on library shelves, on newsstands, and in radio programs. Everyday conversation, classroom lectures, political speeches, commencement addresses, and various kinds of group forums and round-table discussions provide a further abundant source of *words cut loose from their moorings.* [Italics supplied.]

(I once heard of a course in esthetics given at a large Middle Western university in which an entire semester was devoted to Art and Beauty and the principles underlying them, and during which the professor, even when asked by students, persistently declined to name specific paintings, symphonies, sculptures, or objects of beauty to which his principles might apply. "We are interested," he would say, "in principles, not in particulars.")

There are psychiatric implications to dead-level abstracting on higher levels, too, because when maps proliferate wildly without any reference to a territory, the result can only be delusion. But whether at higher or lower levels, dead-level abstracting is, as Johnson says, always dull:

> The low-level speaker frustrates you because he leaves you with no directions as to what to do with the basketful of information he has given you. The high-level speaker frustrates you because he simply doesn't tell you what he is talking about. . . . Being thus frustrated, and being further blocked because the rules of courtesy (or of attendance at class lectures) require that one remain quietly seated until the speaker has finished, there is little for one to do but daydream, doodle, or simply fall asleep.

It is obvious, then, that interesting speech and interesting writing, as well as clear thinking and psychological well-being, require the constant interplay of higher-level and lower-level abstractions, and the constant interplay of the verbal levels with the nonverbal ("object") levels. In science, this interplay goes on constantly, hypotheses being checked against observations, predictions against extensional results. (Scientific *writing,* however, as exemplified in technical journals, offers some appalling examples of *almost* dead-leval abstracting, which is the reason so much of it is hard to read. Nevertheless, the interplay between verbal and nonverbal experimental levels does continue, or else we would not have science.) The work of good novelists and poets also represents this constant interplay between higher and lower levels of abstraction. A "significant" novelist or poet is one whose message has a high level of *general* usefulness in providing insight into life; but he gives his generalizations an impact and a persuasiveness through his ability to observe and describe actual social situations and states of mind. A memorable literary character, such as Sinclair Lewis' George F. Babbitt, has *descriptive* validity (at a low level of abstraction) as the picture of an individual, as well as a *general* validity as a picture of a "typical" American businessman of his time. The great political leader is also one in whom there is interplay between higher and lower levels of abstraction. The ward heeler knows politics only at lower levels of abstraction: what promises or what acts will cause what people to vote as desired; his loyalties are not to principles (high-level abstractions) but to persons (e.g., political bosses) and immediate advantages (low-level abstractions). The so-called impractical political theorist knows the high-level abstractions ("democracy," "civil rights," "social justice") but is not well enough acquainted with facts at lower levels of abstraction to get himself elected county register of deeds. But the political leaders to whom states and nations remain permanently grateful are those who were able, somehow or other, to achieve simultaneously higher-level aims ("freedom," "national unity," "justice") *and* lower-level aims ("better prices for potato farmers," "higher wages for textile workers," "judicial reform," "soil conservation").

The interesting writer, the informative speaker, the accurate thinker, and the sane individual operate on all levels of the abstraction ladder, moving quickly and gracefully and in orderly fashion from higher to lower, from lower to higher, with minds as lithe and deft and beautiful as monkeys in a tree.

APPLICATIONS

I. Starting with the one at the lowest level of abstraction, arrange the following statements in order of increasing abstraction.

A. **1.** Joe keeps all our household appliances in working condition.
2. Joe is a mechanical genius.
3. Joe is very handy with tools.
4. Joe is a 100 percent real American boy.
5. Yesterday Joe replaced a burned-out condenser in the radio.
6. Joe is an awfully useful person to have around.
7. Joe keeps that radio in working condition.

B. **1.** Children are just a lot of trouble.
2. Little Johnny is a darling child.
3. The population of this country will double in thirty-five years.
4. All of my boys will get the best education possible.
5. The period of dependency on parents is longer for human infants than for any other life forms.

II. Try to apply the following terms to the extensional world by going down the ladder of abstraction and offering operational definitions for guidance. Try to translate the accompanying quotations into operational definitions. If you cannot, explain why and make up your own operational definitions. Do you find any circularity, dead-level abstracting, or verbal circularity in these quotations?

1. *Alimony:* When two people make a mistake and one of them continues to pay for it.
2. *Radical:* "In short, liberalism must now become radical, meaning by 'radical' perception of the necessity of thoroughgoing changes in the set-up of institutions and corresponding activity to bring the changes to pass."

   JOHN DEWEY, *Liberalism and Social Action*
3. *Democracy:* "We seek the establishment of a democracy of individual participation governed by two central aims: That the individual share in those social decisions determining the quality and direction of his life; that society be organized to encourage independence in men and provide the media for their common participation."

   Founding Manifesto of SDS
4. *Beauty:* "Beauty is in the eye of the beholder."
5. *Mahayuga:* "A complete cycle, a mahayuga, comprises 12,000 years. It ends with a dissolution, a *pralaya,* which is repeated more drastically (*mahapralaya,* the Great Dissolution) at the end of the thousandth cycle. . . . The 12,000 years of a mahayuga were regarded as divine years, each with a duration of 360 years, which gives a total of 4,320,000 years for a single cosmic cycle."

   MIRCEA ELIADE, *The Sacred and the Profane*
6. *Power:* "Power to the People."

   Black Panther slogan.
7. *Scapegoat:* ". . . just as society must have a scapegoat, so hatred must have a symbol. Georgia has the Negro and Harlem has the Jews."

   JAMES BALDWIN

III. Analyze the following passages in terms of levels of abstraction:

1. A *phobia* is a recurrent and persistent fear of a particular object or situation which in "objective" reality presents no actual danger to the subject—although (cf. Case 1) in his unconsciously equated experience the patient may conceive the symbolized danger to be overwhelming. Phobias, indeed, are originally derived from situation-related fears, and differ from the latter only in their "rationality," symbolic spread, and generalization to remote aspects of the situation. For instance, fear of a rampant tiger is directly understandable, but it is justifiable to consider abnormal the reactions of a severely ailurophobic patient who exhibits fear within a mile of a well-protected zoo, cannot bear the approach of a kitten, and experiences anxiety when any animal of the genus *Felis* is shown on a motion picture screen. In neither the "normal" or "abnormal" instance, be it noted, need the fear be based on a direct experience with the "object" feared, although in both the tiger is, of course, symbolically equated with physical danger. The difference lies in this: that the phobia, unlike the fear, is based on no rational conscious reasons whatever, but springs from experiences deeply repressed

and not necessarily related to a direct attack by a big or little cat at any time in the patient's life. To illustrate:

Case 7: Anne A——, an eighteen-year-old girl was brought to the psychiatric out-patient clinic by her . . .

JULES MASSERMAN, *Principles of Dynamic Psychiatry*

SAMPLE ANALYSIS: The author starts with a definition of phobia that names the general conditions under which a fear may be called a phobia. The second sentence is also general and adds information about the origin of a phobia and shows how it differs from "situation-related fears." So far the author seems to be writing at a high level of abstraction without much progress up or down the abstraction ladder. The third sentence goes, however, down the abstraction ladder to a specific example, capable of being visualized by the reader ("rampant tiger") and also gives examples of specific situations (zoo, kitten, moving pictures) where fear may be termed a phobia. After more general explanations, there is a case history of a specific patient, Anne A——, reporting facts at still lower (descriptive) levels of abstraction. Whether or not other scientists agree with Dr. Masserman in calling this case a phobia, we at least know that, when *he* uses the word, this is the kind of case *he* is talking about. So far as relationships between higher and lower levels of abstraction are concerned, this passage is a good extensionally-directed definition of phobia.

2. A function . . . is a table giving the relation between two variable quantities, where a change in one implies some change in the other. The cost of a quantity of meat is a function of its weight; the speed of a train, a function of the quantity of coal consumed; the amount of perspiration given off, a function of the temperature. In each of these illustrations, a change in the second variable: weight, quantity of coal consumed, and temperature, is correlated with a change in the first variable: cost, speed, and volume of perspiration. The symbolism of mathematics permits functional relationships to be simply and concisely expressed. Thus $y = x$, $y = x^2$, $y = \sin x$, $y = \operatorname{csch} x$, $y = e^x$ are examples of functions.

EDWARD KASNER and J. R. NEWMAN, *Mathematics and the Imagination*

3. The family, to begin with, is a marriage. Dr. Paul C. Glick, the Census Bureau's expert on marriage, says: "The more I study the subject, the more apparent it becomes: marriage is regarded as—and is—the happiest, healthiest and most desired state of human existence. We get divorced not because we don't like marriage, but to find a better partner. We live longer and are healthier if we are married. More of us are getting married, more of us are staying married longer and we are getting married younger. Marriage is the central fact of our lives." The Bible, Proverbs XVIII:22 says much the same thing, but more succinctly: "Who so findeth a wife, findeth a good thing."

BEN J. WATTENBERG and RICHARD M. SCAMMON, *This U.S.A.*

IV. In order to avoid making errors due to dead-level abstracting it is important to keep this process in mind. The following selection deals with this and several other matters worth noting:

Consider this, which purports to *make clearer* one of Shakespeare's plays:

The creation of character, indeed, is not to be regarded as the unique, or even principal, end of Shakespeare's dramatic creations, in which plot and motive, themselves handled with greater flexibility and insight, tend increasingly to find their proper context in a more ample artistic unity which embraces and illuminates them; but in the delineation of personality beyond the limits of convention his language first attained some sense of its full possibilities.

No mind, including the author's, can take in at one scoop the message of this clumsy compound. Therefore he had no excuse for printing it, even if when he writes his mind does work on the rocket principle, shooting out fresh phrases at intervals as he proceeds where we cannot follow. He should make a first stop after "creations"; and a second after "unity." Rereading this, the author would see that the portion beginning with "but" is so flabbily contrasted with what went before that he should ask himself what, in fact, he did have in mind.

Nor is sprawling his only sin against sense. He gives us an anthology of faults: (1) Awkward repetition: "creation" in line 1, "creations" in line 2. (2) Tautology: "themselves" in line 3 and the whole phrase beginning "find their proper context . . ." down to "embraces" ("context," "unity," and "embraces" say the same thing three times). (3) Illogic: how are we to interpret the comparison in "greater" and "more ample"? Than what? "Increasingly" suggests "as time went on, " but we must guess this. (4) Pronouns adrift: "their" in line 4 and "them" in line 5 have two possible antecedents—"dramatic creations," on the one hand, and "plot and motive," on the other. (5) The vagueness of perpetual abstraction: what does it *mean* "to handle plot and motive with greater flexibility and insight"? "to find a proper context"? "to be embraced and illuminated by a more ample artistic unity"? "to delineate personality beyond the limits of convention"? And how in the name of heaven does a writer's *language* "attain some sense of its full possibilities"?

JACQUES BARZUN and HENRY F. GRAFF, *The Modern Researcher*

Find some passages in a newspaper or magazine (or one of your textbooks) and make the same kind of an analysis as Barzun and Graff have made here. Try choosing some paragraphs, at random, from newspaper editorials. Do you find a great deal of dead-level abstracting? If so, why?

As I was going up the stair
I met a man who wasn't there.
He wasn't there again to-day.
I wish, I wish he'd stay away.
Hughes Mearns

Everybody is familiar with the fact that the ordinary man does not see things as they are, but only sees certain fixed types. . . . Mr. Walter Sickert is in the habit of telling his pupils that they are unable to draw any individual arm because they think of it as an arm; and because they think of it as an arm they think they know what it ought to be.
T. E. Hulme

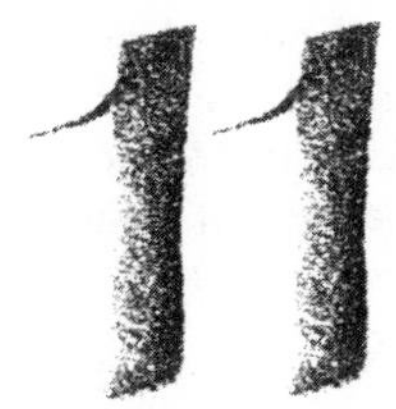

the little man who wasn't there

How Not to Start a Car

The following newspaper story is presented in the hope that the reader will find it as instructive (and as depressing) as I did:

> More than one motorist has secretly wished he could do what Samuel Rios, 30, was accused of doing yesterday. Driving at 12:30 A.M. through Williamsburg, he swung around a corner and accidentally sideswiped a sedan parked at the curb in front of 141 Hopkins Street. Furious, police charged, Rios stopped, took the jack handle from his car trunk, and slam-banged the offending obstacle from windshield to tail-lights.
>
> New York *Post*

Let us examine the mechanism of this man's reaction. He got angry at the parked car just as he might have gotten angry at a person, horse, or mule that got in his way. He thereupon proceeded to "teach" that car a "lesson." Although the reaction was unreflecting and automatic, it is nevertheless a complicated one, since it involves (1) his making up an abstraction about the car (which is seen as maliciously obstructive) and then (2) his reacting to his own abstraction rather than to the actual car itself.

People in primitive societies often act in similar ways. When crops fail or rocks fall upon them, they make a deal with—offer sacrifices to—the "spirits" of vegetation or of the rocks, in order to obtain better treatment from them in the future. We too have certain reactions of similar kinds: sometimes, tripping over a chair, we kick it and call it names; some people, indeed, when they fail to get letters, get angry at the postman. In all such behavior, we *confuse* the abstraction which is *inside* our heads with that which is *outside,* and act as if the abstraction *were* the event in the outside world. We create in our heads an imaginary chair that maliciously trips us and then "punish" the extensional chair that bears ill will to nobody; we create an imaginary, inferential postman who is "holding back our mail" and then we bawl out the extensional postman who would gladly bring us letters if he had any to bring.

It is in these terms that Sigmund Freud sought to explain the origin of religion: our primitive ancestors, frightened by natural events they could not understand, projected their fears and anxieties upon the world, personalized them into a malevolent Being, and then tried to propitiate this Being through sacrifices of one kind or another. They mistook their abstractions for reality.

Confusion of Levels of Abstraction

In a wider sense, however, we are confusing levels of abstraction—confusing what is inside our heads with what is outside—all the time. For example, we talk about the yellowness of a pencil as if the yellowness were a "property" of the pencil and not a product, as we have seen, of the *interaction* of something outside our skins with our nervous systems. We confuse, that is to say, the two lowest levels of the abstraction ladder (see p. 153) and treat them as one. Properly speaking, we should not say, "The pencil is yellow," which is a statement that places the yellowness in the pencil; we should say instead, "That which has an effect on me which leads me to say 'pencil' also has an effect on me which leads me to say 'yellow.'" We don't have to be that precise, of course, in the language of everyday life, but it should be observed that the latter statement takes into consideration the part our nervous systems play in creating whatever pictures of reality we may have in our heads while the former statement does not.

Now this habit of confusing what is inside our skins and what is outside is essentially a relic of prescientific patterns of thinking. The more advanced civilization becomes, the more conscious we must be that our nervous systems *automatically leave out characteristics* of the events before us. If we are not aware of characteristics left out, if we are not conscious of the process of abstracting, we make *seeing and believing a single process.* If, for example, you react to the twenty-second rattlesnake you have seen in your life as if it were identical with the abstraction you have in your head as the result of the last twenty-one rattlesnakes you have seen, you may not be far out in your reactions. But civilized life provides our nervous systems with more complicated problems than rattlesnakes to deal with.

There is a case cited by Korzybski in *Science and Sanity* of a man who suffered from hay fever whenever there were roses in the room. In an experiment, a bunch of roses was produced unexpectedly in front of him, and he immediately had a violent attack of hay fever, despite the fact that the "roses" in this case were *made of paper.* That is, his nervous system saw-and-believed in one operation.

But words, as we have seen by means of the abstraction ladder, are still higher levels of abstraction than the "objects" of experience. The more words at extremely high levels of abstraction we have, the more conscious we must be of this process of abstracting. For example, the word "rattlesnake" leaves out every important feature of the actual rattlesnake. But if the word is vividly remembered as part of a whole complex of terrifying experiences with an actual rattlesnake, the word itself is capable of arousing the same feelings as an actual rattlesnake. There are people, therefore, who turn pale at the *word.*

A once popular musical comedy *(High-Button Shoes)* contains a routine in which a comedian gets an attack of sneezing at the mention of the words "fresh country air" and "ragweed." The fact that this theme of reacting to words as things is extremely common in the humor of comic strips, movies, and radio demonstrates, I believe, not only that such reactions are widespread, but also that most people in the audience have enough of a tendency in this direction to recognize in the comedy characterization *an exaggeration of their own reactions.*

Professor Leo Hamalian adds the following anecdote:

> Another interesting example of reactions to words took place when I was officer in charge of a group of men preparing a ship for embarkation at Port Newark. When we finished our work, we were told to go below and stay there until the following morning, when we could expect to be miles at sea. We did so, and the next morning a number of the men declared that the ship's motion was making them seasick. They vomited and showed all the symptoms. I decided to go above for some fresh air. When I got to the deck, I saw that we were still tied up at our berth in Port Newark!

This, then, is the origin of word-magic. The word "rattlesnake" and the actual creature are felt to be *one and the same thing,* because they arouse the same reactions. This sounds like nonsense, of course, and it is nonsense. But from the point of view of a prescientific logic, it has its justification. As Lévy-Bruhl explains in his *How Natives Think* (1926), primitive "logic" works on such a principle. The creature frightens us; the word frightens us; therefore the creature and the word are "the same"—not actually the same, perhaps, but there is a "mystic connection" between the two. This sense of "mystic connection" is Lévy-Bruhl's term for what we have called "necessary connection" in our discussion in Chapter 2 of naive attitudes toward symbols. As a consequence of this naiveté, "mystical power" is attributed to words. There come to be "fearful words," "forbidden words," "unspeakable words"—words taking on the characteristics of the things they stand for. The word "grammarian" once referred to a person who had magical power—one who was versed in "gramarye" and therefore could manipulate to advantage the mystical power of words.

The feeling that a repetition of the right *words* will somehow or other bring about the desired *events* remains with us, in spite of the pride we take in our allegedly advanced scientific culture. In the 1930's, politicians and business leaders and newspapers repeated like an incantation the words, "Prosperity is just around the corner!" Cheering squads at football games urge their teams to "Go! Go! Go!" reiterating the word as if it had magical power. In craps, the dice-thrower will call for "Little Ada from Decatur," and if he rolls a seven before an eight, he attributes his failure to "the wrong kind of call." Crapshooters are especially given to talking to their dice in order to influence outcomes; in this they behave very much like commentators on the stock market. The very intensity with which a player will hiss, "Snake eyes! you son-of-a-bitch!" reveals the degree to which he believes in the power of his words over the dice.

However, the commonest form of this confusion of levels of abstraction is illustrated by our reacting to the "conservative" to whom we are just being introduced ("I want you to meet Mr. Lee Buck, who is active in our new conservative movement on campus") as if he were identical with the abstraction "conservative" inside our heads. "If he is a conservative, he is OK"—or "he is a Bircher"— we are likely to say, confusing the extensional conservative with our abstraction, "conservative," which is the product not only of the previous "conservatives" we have met, but also of all that we have been *told* about "conservatives."

"Jews"

To make the principles clearer, we shall use an example that is loaded with prejudices for many people: "Mr. Miller is a *Jew.*" On hearing this, some "Christians" have marked hostile reactions instantaneously; they will, for example, put themselves on guard against Mr. Miller's expected sharp financial practices. That is to say, a "Christian" of this kind confuses his high-level abstraction, "Jew," with the extensional Mr. Miller and behaves toward Mr. Miller as if he were identical with that abstraction. (See the abstraction ladder, p. 153.) "Jew" is only *one* of thousands upon thousands of abstractions which may be applied to Mr. Miller, to whom such terms as "left-hander," "parent," "amateur golfer," "history teacher," "teetotaler," "Bostonian," and so on may possibly be equally applied. But the prejudiced person is unaware of all but the one abstraction—perhaps in most contexts the least relevant one—"Jew."

Moreover, the word "Jew" is perhaps one of the most sloppily constructed abstractions in the language—that is, one of the most difficult to refer systematically down the abstraction ladder to lower levels. Does "Jew" refer to a race, a religion, a nationality, a physical type, a state of mind, a caste? If not these, what? Major conferences and conventions of American Jews in recent years have included sessions on the question, "What is a Jew?" The prime minister of Israel and most members of his cabinet do not set foot in a synagogue except on special state occasions. Are they Jews? What about the fanatical Neturai Karta sect of Jerusalem, who in addition to three regular daily services also hold a midnight prayer and vigil for the coming of the Messiah—and refuse to recognize the Jewish state or to bear arms for it? The government of Israel, confronted with a flood of "Jewish" refugees from many parts of Europe, the Middle East, and Asia, was compelled long ago to give up the attempt to define a "Jew"; the rule now is that *anyone who calls himself a "Jew" is a Jew*—an operational definition that is difficult to improve upon.

Now it happens that the word "Jew" has powerful affective connotations in Christian culture as the result of a number of historical accidents associating "Jews" with money. These affective connotations create such expressions as, "He *jewed* me out of ten dollars," "I *jewed* down the price." In parts of rural America where itinerant Jewish peddlers used to

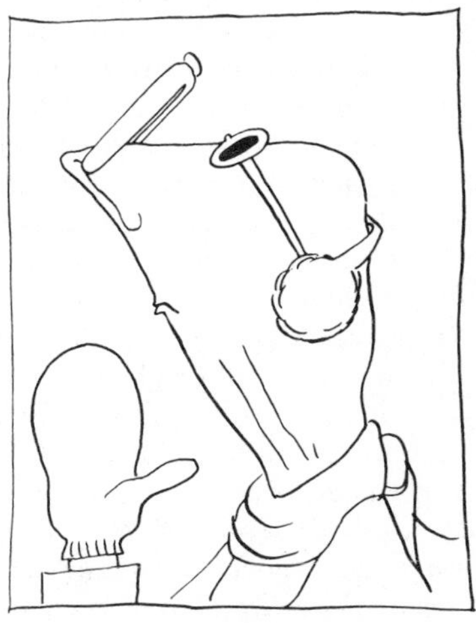

Intolerance listening to reason

roam, some mothers disciplined their children with, "If you don't behave, I'll sell you to the old Jew man."

Let us return to our hypothetical Mr. Miller, who has been introduced as a "Jew." To a person for whom these affective connotations are very much alive, and who habitually confuses what is inside his head with what is outside, Mr. Miller is a man "not to be trusted." If Mr. Miller succeeds in business, that "proves" that "Jews are smart"; if Mr. Johansen succeeds in business, it only proves that Mr. Johansen is smart. If Mr. Miller fails in business, it is alleged that he nevertheless has "money salted away somewhere." If Mr. Miller is strange or foreign in his habits, that "proves" that "Jews don't assimilate." If he is thoroughly American—i.e., indistinguishable from other natives—he is "trying to pass himself off as one of us." If Mr. Miller fails to give to charity, that is because "Jews are tight"; if he gives generously, he is "trying to buy his way into society." If Mr. Miller lives in the Jewish section of town, that is because "Jews are so clannish"; if he moves to a locality where there are no other Jews, that is because "they try to horn in everywhere." In short, Mr. Miller is automatically condemned, no matter who he is or what he does.

But Mr. Miller may be, for all we know, rich or poor, a wife-beater or a saint, a stamp collector or a violinist, a farmer or a physicist, a lens grinder or an orchestra leader. If, as the result of our automatic reactions, we put ourselves on guard about our *money* immediately upon meeting Mr. Miller, we may offend a man from whom we might have profited financially, morally, or spiritually, or we may fail to notice his attempts to run off with our wife—that is, we shall act with complete inappropriateness to the *actual* situation at hand. Mr. Miller is not identical with our notion of "Jew," *whatever our notion of "Jew" may be.* The "Jew," created by intensional definition of the *word, simply is not there.*

Indeed, to say that some people are blinded by prejudice seems to be more than a metaphor. Ralph Ellison calls his central character, a Negro, "The Invisible Man," in his novel of that name. This is to suggest that most white people, on encountering a Negro, see only the abstraction "Negro" that they carry in their heads; busy with this "little man that isn't there," they never notice the actual Negro individual.

Something similar may be said about the typical Western attitude toward the "Arab." Many people would be surprised to know that not all Arabs are Moslems (there are thousands of Christian Arabs living in Lebanon and Syria), that the Arabs of Syria hate the Arabs of Egypt, that the Arabs of Lebanon want little to do with the Arabs of Syria or Iraq, and that not infrequently Arabs are tall, blond, and blue-eyed. The term "Arab" as it is often used by the Westerner must be regarded as brother to the term "Jew" as it is used by the prejudiced or the ignorant. This does not mean that the term "Arab" should be discarded; it should be used more accurately. According to Edward Atiyah, an expert on the Arab world, the term may have three meanings. (1) It may designate the nomadic people who inhabit the Jordanian, Arabian, Syrian, and North African deserts, known as the *Bedu* or *Bedouin*. (2) It may designate the people of the Arabian peninsula (often referred to as "the Arabians"), both the nomads and the city-dwellers; in this sense, the word denotes an ethnic group—the present-day Saudis, Yemenites, Kuwaitis, and other descendants of the original Arab homeland. (3) Finally, the word "Arab" may mean a culture group—a *bloc* of Arab-speaking communities stretching continuously from the Persian Gulf in the east to the Atlantic in the west. In this vast area, the proportion of nomads to sedentary population is very small, the majority of people being *fellahin* (farmers) and inhabitants of the ancient and famous cities—Aleppo, Damascus, Beirut, Latakia, Cairo, Alexandria, Baghdad, Jerusalem, Tunis, Algiers—once the centers of world civilization. Hence, if we wish to speak with some precision and without giving offense to a group of people whose importance in the world is growing daily, we should learn at least to distinguish among these different abstractions and to avoid applying the word "Arab" as if it corresponded to the stereotype many of us know from adventure movies about the Foreign Legion.

John Doe, the "Criminal"

Another instance of the confusion of levels of abstraction is to be found in cases like this: Let us say that a man, John Doe, is introduced as one "who has just been released after three years in the penitentiary." This statement is already on a fairly high level of abstraction, but it is nevertheless a *report*. From this point, however, many people *immediately and unconsciously* climb to still higher levels of abstraction: "John Doe is an *ex-convict* . . . he's a criminal!" But the word "criminal" is not only on a much higher level of abstraction than "the man who spent three years in the penitentiary," but it is also, as we have seen before in Chapter 3, a *judgment*, with the implied prediction, "He has committed a crime in the past and will probably commit more crimes in the future." The result is that when John Doe applies for a job and is forced to state that he has spent three years in the penitentiary, prospective employers, automatically confusing levels of abstraction, may say *without bothering to learn any more about him*, "You can't expect me to give jobs to criminals!"

John Doe, for all we know from the report, may have undergone a complete reformation or, for that matter, may have been unjustly imprisoned in the first place; nevertheless, he may wander in vain, looking for a job. If, in desperation, he finally says to himself, "If everybody is going to treat me like a criminal, I might as well become one," and goes out and commits a robbery, the blame can hardly be said to be entirely his.

The reader is familiar with the way in which rumor grows as it spreads. Much of the exaggeration is again due to this tendency on the part of some people to climb to higher levels of abstraction—from reports to inferences to judgments—and then to confuse the levels. According to this kind of "reasoning":

> *Report.* "Mary Smith didn't get in until three last Saturday night."
> *Inference.* "I bet she was out tearing around!"
> *Judgment.* "She's nothing but a tramp. I never did like her looks. I knew it the moment I first laid eyes on her."

When we base our actions toward our fellow human beings on such hastily abstracted judgments it is no wonder that we frequently make life miserable not only for others, but for ourselves.

As a final example of this type of confusion, *notice the difference between what happens when a man says to himself, "I have failed three times," and what happens when he says, "I am a failure!"*

Delusional Worlds

Consciousness of abstracting prepares us in advance for the fact that (1) things that look alike may *not* be alike; (2) things that have the same name are *not* necessarily the same; and (3) judgments which may be based on reports are *not* reports. In short, it prevents us from acting like fools. Without consciousness of abstracting—or rather, without the habit of *delaying reactions,* which is the product of a deep awareness that seeing is not believing—we are completely unprepared for the differences between roses and paper roses, between the intensional "Jew" and the extensional Mr. Miller, between the intensional "criminal" and the extensional John Doe.

Such delayed reactions are a sign of adulthood. It happens, however, that as the result of miseducation, bad training, frightening experiences in childhood, traditional beliefs, propaganda, and other influences in our lives, all of us have what might be termed "areas of insanity" or, perhaps better, "areas of infantilism," in which we are at the mercy of ingrained, inappropriate semantic reactions. Some people, as the result of childhood experience, cannot help being frightened by the mere sight of a policeman—any policeman; the terrifying "policeman" inside their heads "is" the extensional policeman outside, who probably has no designs that anyone could regard as terrifying. Some people turn pale at the sight of a spider—any spider—even a nice, harmless one safely enclosed in a bottle. Some people automatically become hostile at the *words* "un-American," "communist," "reactionary," "liberal," and "welfare."

Dr. G. Brock Chisholm, former director general of the World Health Organization (1948–53) and president of the World Federation for Mental Health, has commented eloquently on the tyranny of prejudice-laden words:

> The power these words have over much of the race is astonishing. They . . . are the chains that bind man to his miserable past and his discouraging present. They are the premises which were incorporated . . . when each human was too young and dependent to defend himself by using his intelligence. We find that rarely is it possible to discuss intelligently, without striking prejudices which have been inculcated in childhood, such ordinary commonplace subjects as health, clothes, Negroes, politics, patriotism, conscience, Jews, superstitions, war and peace, money, sex, property, marriage, religions, some diseases, India, wage scales, socialism, communism, trade unions, political parties, and so on through a long list which varies from place to place, time to time, and family to family. Very few people can think clearly and honestly about many of these things; and yet these, and such as these, are the things which make up the life of man and which, misunderstood, mishandled, and fought over, have caused most of the fear and misery of the world.[1]

Dr. Chisholm does not mean, of course, that we must not learn from our elders. We learn two kinds of things from those who teach us: (1) a body of ideas and beliefs, and (2) a *way of holding them.* If our ideas and beliefs are held with consciousness of abstracting, they can be changed if found to be inadequate or erroneous. But if they are held without consciousness of abstracting—if our mental maps are believed *to be* the territory—they are prejudices. As teachers and parents, we cannot help passing on to the young a certain amount of misinformation and error, however hard we may try not to. But if we also teach them to be habitually conscious of the process of abstraction, we give them the means with which to free themselves from whatever erroneous notions we may have taught them. Our educational efforts will then not "bind them to a miserable past," but enable them to grow with advancing years and experience.

The picture of reality created inside our heads by the lack of consciousness of abstracting is not a "map" of any existing "territory." It is a delusional world. In this never-never land, all "Jews" are out to cheat you; all "capitalists" are overfed tyrants, smoking expensive cigars and gnashing their teeth at labor unions. In this world, too, all snakes are poisonous, all widows and orphans are meritorious, automobiles can be disciplined by being beaten with a tire-iron, and every stranger with a foreign accent is a communist spy. Some of the people who spend too much of their time in such delusional worlds eventually get locked up but, needless to say, there are many still at large.

How do we reduce such areas of infantilism in our thought? One way is to know deeply that there is no "necessary connection" between words and what they stand for. For this reason, the study of a foreign language is always good for us, even if it has no other uses. Other ways have already been suggested: to be aware of the process of abstracting and *to realize fully that words never "say all" about anything.* The abstrac-

[1] "Can Man Survive?" *ETC.*, IV (1947), p. 107.

tion ladder—an adaptation of a diagram originated by Alfred Korzybski to illustrate visually the relationship between words, "objects," and events—is designed to help us understand and remain conscious of the process of abstracting.

APPLICATIONS

I. For your scrapbook or card index—see page 30—take some of the basic principles dealing with the relationship between language and behavior and find some clippings and quotations that illustrate them. The following sample headings are some of the topics you might choose:

Straight reports.
Stories featuring inferences, with full awareness that they are inferences.
Stories featuring inferences in such a way that they may be mistaken for reports.
Reacting to judgments as if they were reports.
Shifts of meaning resulting from changes in context.
Snarl-words and purr-words mistaken for reports.
Slanting.
Quarrels over nonsense questions.
Social conversation.
Over-reacting to affective connotations of words.
Directives mistaken for reports.
Disillusionment caused by directives imperfectly understood.
Dead-level abstracting.
Meaningless use of high-level abstractions.
Higher- and lower-level abstractions properly related.
Seeing-and-believing.
The little man who wasn't there.

Other headings will occur to you as you review the chapters to follow. The study of the relationships between language and behavior is one that can be pursued at any time anywhere—in an office, at school, at church, behind (or in front of) a hosiery counter, at parties, at meetings, in all one's reading, and in the course of intimate family or personal relationships. Even a desultory collection of examples of language-in-action, if carefully noted and pasted down and pondered over, will help you understand what the writer of this book is saying *and why he wants to say it.* Collectors of such examples will no doubt find reasons for wishing to refine, expand, or correct some of the statements made in this book. Further progress in the scientific study of the relationships between language and behavior depends upon such corrections and improvements of the present generalizations. Your cooperation is earnestly invited.

II. We often hear about "cleaning the gooks out" of Vietnam, or "flushing the VC's out." What does this reveal about the thought processes of people using this language? Is a "gook" a "little man who isn't there"? Write a 500-word essay analyzing the two quotations from a semantic point of view.

III. The continual confusion of abstractions with reality is one of the most apparent errors of human thought, regardless of time or place. Very often, this confusion results from our apparent inability or unwillingness to understand the processes of reality. Oliver Wendell Holmes recognized this failing when he noted that "men heap together all the mistakes of their lives and create a monster called Destiny." The following sentences contain words especially liable to become separated from what they represent. Take each sentence and give the key abstraction in the real world, following the process of this chapter dealing with the word "Jew." Do you find that some of the words are too general or abstract to contain substantial meaning?

1. The *Establishment* is rotten to the core, and must be destroyed.
2. *Free enterprise* is the only means of ensuring high productivity and financial incentive.
3. *The Church* has impeded progress for centuries.
4. The *system* keeps people from developing their true personalities.
5. *Revolution* is the only way!

IV. One way to avoid the dangers of confusing levels of abstraction would be to follow the method of the Academy of Lagado, as described in Swift's *Gulliver's Travels:*

> The first project was to shorten discourse by cutting polysyllables into one, and leaving out verbs and participles, because in reality all things imaginable are but nouns. The other was a scheme for entirely abolishing all words whatsoever; and this was urged as a great advantage in point of health as well as brevity. For it is plain, that every word we speak is in some degree a diminution of our lungs by corrosion, and consequently contributes to the shortening of our lives. An expedient was therefore offered, that since words are only names for *things,* it would be more convenient for all men to carry about them such *things* as were necessary to express the particular business they are to discourse on. . . . I have often beheld two of those sages almost sinking under the weight of their packs, like pedlars among us; who when they meet in the streets would lay down their loads, open their sacks and hold conversation for an hour together. . . .
>
> Another great advantage proposed by this invention was that it would serve as a universal language to be understood in all civilized nations, whose goods and utensils are generally of the same kind, or nearly resembling, so that their uses might easily be comprehended.

What, if anything, is wrong with this scheme? Is there any element of sense or truth in what these proto-linguists are trying to accomplish? At what level of abstraction would their conversations take place?

V. Racism and religious prejudice, two of the major problems confronting American society today, are relevant to the subjects discussed in this chapter. It is hoped these problems can be better understood by recognizing the various semantic errors made by people who are racist and prejudiced. For further information of a historical, sociological, and political nature, the following books are suggested:

Gunnar Myrdal, *An American Dilemma: The Negro Problem and Modern Democracy* (1944), a classic study by a Swedish social scientist, brought to America as an "impartial observer," which suggests that social engineering is the best way to solve the Negro problem and integrate Negroes into the mainstream of American life.

Lee Rainwater, editor, *Soul* (1970), an excellent collection of articles from *Trans-Action* on the Black experience.

Lewis M. Killian, *The Impossible Revolution?* (1968), a discussion of Black Power and its relation to the American Dream.

C. Vann Woodward, *The Strange Career of Jim Crow* (1966), a treatment of segregation from an historical stance.

Albert B. Cleage, Jr., *The Black Messiah* (1968), a collection of Cleage's sermons dealing with the "theology" of black power.

James Robert Ross, editor, *The War Within* (1971), an anthology that examines the question of violence or nonviolence as a tactic for blacks seeking justice in American society.

Some of the many available books written by Negroes are: Malcolm X and Alex Haley, *The Autobiography of Malcolm X* (1966); Franz Fanon, *The Wretched of the Earth* (1963); and novels and plays by such authors as LeRoi Jones, James Baldwin, Ralph Ellison, and Richard Wright.

Some books dealing with religion and problems of religious discrimination are:

E. Digby Baltzell, *The Protestant Establishment* (1964), a book that deals with anti-Semitism and with the development of our "WASP" (White Anglo-Saxon Protestant) culture.

Reinhold Niebuhr, *Pious and Secular America* (1958), an explanation of some of the theological forces behind racism and anti-Semitism.

Will Herberg, *Protestant-Catholic-Jew* (1955), a study in religious sociology.

Also important are: H. Richard Niebuhr, *The Kingdom of God in America* (1937); Stuart E. Rosenberg, *The Search for Jewish Identity in America* (1964); William James, *The Varieties of Religious Experience* (1907), a classic study of the psychology of religion.

For an encylopedic treatment of American culture in general, as well as the above-mentioned topics in particular, Max Lerner's monumental *America as a Civilization* (1957) is recommended, though it is somewhat dated now.

When a legal distinction is determined . . . between night and day, childhood and maturity, or any other extremes, a point has to be fixed or a line has to be drawn, or gradually picked out by successive decisions, to mark where the change takes place. Looked at by itself without regard to the necessity behind it, the line or point seems arbitrary. It might as well be a little more to the one side or the other. But when it is seen that a line or point there must be, and that there is no mathematical or logical way of fixing it precisely, the decision of the legislature must be accepted unless we can say that it is very wide of any reasonable mark.

Oliver Wendell Holmes

For of course the true meaning of a term is to be found by observing what a man does with it, not by what he says about it.

P. W. Bridgman

classification

Giving Things Names

The figure below shows eight objects, let us say animals, four large and four small, a different four with round heads and another four with square heads, and still another four with curly tails and another four with straight tails. These animals, let us say, are scampering about your village, but since at first they are of no importance to you, you ignore them. You do not even give them a name.

One day, however, you discover that the little ones eat up your grain, while the big ones do not. A differentiation sets itself up, and abstracting the common characteristics of A, B, C, and D, you decide to call these *gogo*; E, F, G, and H you decide to call *gigi*. You chase away the

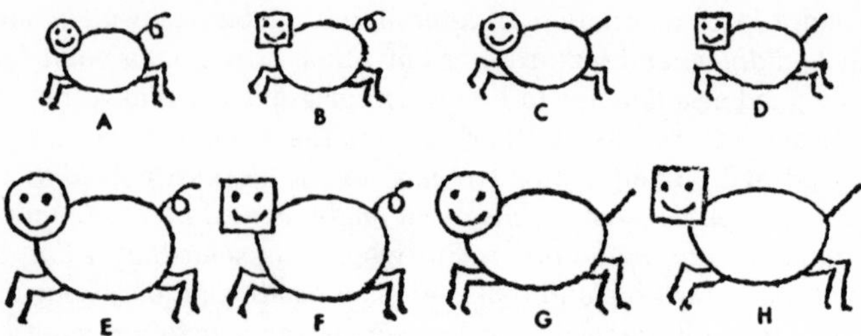

gogo, but leave the *gigi* alone. Your neighbor, however, has had a different experience; he finds that those with square heads bite, while those with round heads do not. Abstracting the common characteristics of B, D, F, and H, he calls them *daba,* and A, C, E, and G he calls *dobo.* Still another neighbor discovers, on the other hand, that those with curly tails kill snakes, while those with straight tails do not. He differentiates them, abstracting still another set of common characteristics: A, B, E, and F are *busa,* while C, D, G, and H are *busana.*

Now imagine that the three of you are together when E runs by. You say, "There goes the *gigi*"; your first neighbor says, "There goes the *dobo*"; your other neighbor says, "There goes the *busa.*" Here immediately a great controversy arises. What is it really, a *gigi,* a *dobo,* or a *busa?* What is its *right name?* You are quarreling violently when along comes a fourth person from another village who calls it a *muglock,* an edible animal, as opposed to *uglock,* an inedible animal—which doesn't help matters a bit.

Of course, the question, "What is it *really?* What is its *right name?*" is a nonsense question. By a nonsense question is meant one that is not capable of being answered. Things can have "right names" only if there is a necessary connection between symbols and things symbolized, and we have seen that there is not. That is to say, in the light of your interest in protecting your grain, it may be necessary for you to distinguish the animal E as a *gigi;* your neighbor, who doesn't like to be bitten, finds it practical to distinguish it as a *dobo;* your other neighbor, who likes to see snakes killed, distinguishes it as a *busa.* What we call things and where we draw the line between one class of things and another depend upon the interests we have and the purposes of the classification. For example, animals are classified in one way by the meat industry, in a different way by the leather industry, in another different way by the fur industry, and in a still different way by the biologist. None of these classifications is any more final than any of the others; each of them is useful for its purpose.

This holds, of course, for everything we perceive. A table "is" a table to us, because we can understand its relationship to our conduct and interests; we eat at it, work on it, lay things on it. But to a person living in a culture where no tables are used, it may be a very big stool, a small platform, or a meaningless structure. If our culture and upbringing were different, that is to say, our world would not even look the same to us.

Many of us, for example, cannot distinguish between pickerel, pike, salmon, smelts, perch, crappies, halibut, and mackerel; we say that they are "just fish, and I don't like fish." To a seafood connoisseur, however, these distinctions are real, since they mean the difference to him between one kind of good meal, a very different kind of good meal, or a poor meal. To a zoologist, even finer distinctions become of great importance, since he has other and more general ends in view. When we hear the statement, then, "This fish is a specimen of the pompano, *Trachinotus carolinus,*" we accept this as being "true," even if we don't care, not because that is its "right name," but because that is how it is *classified* in the most complete and most general system of classification which people most deeply interested in fish have evolved.

When we name something, then, we are classifying. *The individual object or event we are naming, of course, has no name and belongs to no class until we put it in one.* To illustrate again, suppose that we were to give the *extensional* meaning of the word "Korean." We would have to point to all "Koreans" living at a particular moment and say, "The word 'Korean' denotes at the present moment these persons: A_1, A_2, A_3 . . . A_n." Now, let us say, a child, whom we shall designate as Z, is born among these "Koreans." *The extensional meaning of the word "Korean," determined prior to the existence of Z, does not include Z.* Z is a new individual belonging to no classification, since all classifications were made without taking Z into account. Why, then, is Z also a "Korean"? *Because we say so.* And, saying so—fixing the classification—we have determined to a considerable extent future attitudes toward Z. For example, Z will always have certain rights in Korea; he will always

Labeling "I don't see it real clear till I label it"

be regarded in other nations as an "alien" and will be subject to laws applicable to "aliens."

In matters of "race" and "nationality," the way in which classifications work is especially apparent. For example, I am by birth a "Canadian," by "race" a "Japanese," and am now an "American." Although I was legally admitted to the United States on a Canadian passport as a "non-quota immigrant," I was unable to apply for American citizenship until after 1952. According to American immigration law (since 1952 as well as before), a Canadian entering the United States as a permanent resident has no trouble getting in, unless he happens to be of Oriental extraction, in which case his "nationality" becomes irrelevant and he is classified by "race." If the quota for his "race"—for example, Japanese—is filled (and it usually is), and if he cannot get himself classified as a non-quota immigrant, he is not able to get in at all. Are all these classifications "real"? Of course they are, and *the effect that each of them has upon what he may and may not do constitutes their "reality."*

I have spent my entire life, except for short visits abroad, in Canada and the United States. I speak Japanese haltingly, with a child's vocabulary and an American accent; I do not read or write it. Nevertheless, because classifications seem to have a kind of hypnotic power over some people, I am occasionally credited with (or accused of) having an "Oriental mind." Since Buddha, Confucius, General Tojo, Mao Tse-tung, Pandit Nehru, Syngman Rhee, and the proprietor of the Golden Pheasant Chop Suey House all have "Oriental minds," it is difficult to know whether to feel complimented or insulted.

When is a person a "Negro"? By the definition accepted in the United States, any person with even a small amount of "Negro blood"—that is, whose parents or ancestors were classified as "Negroes"—is a "Negro." *It would be exactly as justifiable to say that any person with even a small amount of "white blood" is "white."* Why do they say one rather than the other? Because the former system of classification *suits the purposes of those making the classification.* Classification is not a matter of identifying "essences," as is widely believed. It is simply a reflection of social convenience and necessity—and different necessities are always producing different classifications.

There are few complexities about classifications at the level of dogs and cats, knives and forks, cigarettes and candy, but when it comes to classifications at high levels of abstraction—for example, those describing conduct, social institutions, philosophical and moral problems—serious difficulties occur. When one person kills another, is it an act of murder, an act of temporary insanity, an act of homicide, an accident, or an act of heroism? As soon as the process of classification is completed, our attitudes and our conduct are to a considerable degree determined. We hang the murderer, we lock up the insane man, we free the victim of circumstances, we pin a medal on the hero.

The Blocked Mind

Unfortunately, people are not always aware of the way in which they arrive at their classifications. Unaware of those characteristics of the extensional Mr. Miller not covered by classifying him as "a Jew," and attributing to Mr. Miller all the characteristics *suggested* by the affective connotations of the term with which he has been classified, they pass final judgment on Mr. Miller by saying, "Well, a Jew's a Jew. There's no getting around that!"

We need not concern ourselves here with the injustices done to "Jews," "Roman Catholics," "Republicans," "red-heads," "chorus girls," "sailors," "brass-hats," "Southerners," "Yankees," "school teachers," "government regulations," "socialistic proposals," and so on by such hasty judgments or, as it is better to call them, fixed reactions. "Hasty judgments" suggests that such errors can be avoided by thinking more slowly; this, of course, is not the case, for some people think very slowly with no better results. What we are concerned with is the way in which we block the development of our own minds by such automatic reactions.

To continue with our example of the people who say, "A Jew's a Jew. There's no getting around that!"—they are, as we have seen, confusing the denoted, extensional Jew with the fictitious "Jew" inside their heads. Such persons, the reader will have observed, can usually be made to admit, on being reminded of certain "Jews" whom they admire—perhaps Albert Einstein, perhaps former Associate Justice Arthur Goldberg, perhaps Jascha Heifetz, perhaps Sandy Koufax—that "there are exceptions, of course." They have been compelled by experience, that is to say, to take cognizance of at least a few of the multitude of "Jews" who do not fit their preconceptions. At this point, however, they continue triumphantly, "But exceptions only prove the rule!"[1]—which is another way of saying, "Facts don't count."

In Marin County, California, I once attended hearings at the county courthouse concerning a proposed ordinance to forbid racial discrimination in the rental and sale of housing. (Such discrimination in Marin is chiefly directed against Negroes.) I was impressed by the fact that a large majority of those who rose to speak were in favor of the ordinance; but I was also impressed by the number who, though maintaining that they counted Negroes among their best and most admired friends, still spoke heatedly against a law that would, by forbidding racial discrimination in the sale and rental of housing, enable Negroes to live anywhere in the county. Presumably, all the Negroes whom they loved and admired

[1]This extraordinarily fatuous saying originally meant, "The exception *tests* the rule"—*Exceptio probat regulam.* This older meaning of the word "prove" survives in such an expression as "automobile proving ground."

were "exceptions," and the stereotyped "Negro" remained in their heads in spite of their experience.

People like this may be said to be impervious to new information. They continue to vote for their party *label*, no matter what mistakes their party makes. They continue to object to "socialists," no matter what the socialists propose. They continue to regard "mothers" as sacred, no matter which mother. A woman who had been given up both by physicians and psychiatrists as hopelessly insane was being considered by a committee whose task it was to decide whether or not she should be committed to an asylum. One member of the committee doggedly refused to vote for commitment. "Gentlemen," he said in tones of deepest reverence, "you must remember that this woman is, after all, a mother."[2] Similarly such people continue to hate "Protestants," no matter which Protestant. Unaware of characteristics left out in the process of classification, they overlook, when the term "Republican" is applied to the party of Abraham Lincoln, the party of Warren Harding, the party of Herbert Hoover, the party of Dwight Eisenhower, and the party of Richard M. Nixon, the rather important differences between them.

Cow_1 Is Not Cow_2

How do we prevent ourselves from getting into such intellectual blind alleys, or, finding we are in one, how do we get out again? One way is to remember that practically all statements in ordinary conversation, debate, and public controversy taking the form, "Republicans are Republicans," "Business is business," "Boys will be boys," "Women drivers are women drivers," and so on, are *not true*. Let us put one of these back into a context in life.

> "I don't think we should go through with this deal, Bill. Is it altogether fair to the railroad company?"
>
> "Aw, forget it! *Business is business*, after all."

Such an assertion, although it looks like a "simple statement of fact," is not simple and is not a statement of fact. The first "business" *denotes* the transaction under discussion; the second "business" invokes the *connotations* of the word. The sentence is a *directive*, saying, "Let us treat this transaction with complete disregard for considerations other than profit, as the word 'business' suggests." Similarly, when a father tries to excuse the mischief done by his sons, he says, "Boys will be boys"; in other words, "Let us regard the actions of my sons with that indulgent amusement customarily extended toward those whom we call

[2]One wonders how this committee member would have felt about Elizabeth Duncan, executed for murder in San Quentin in 1962, whose possessive love of her son led her to hire assassins to kill her pregnant daughter-in-law.

'boys,'" though the angry neighbor will say, of course, "Boys, my eye! They're little hoodlums; that's what they are!" These too are not informative statements but directives, directing us to classify the object or event under discussion in given ways, in order that we may feel or act in the ways suggested by the terms of the classification.

There is a simple technique for preventing such directives from having their harmful effect on our thinking. It is the suggestion made by Korzybski that we add "index numbers" to our terms, thus: Englishman_1, Englishman_2, Englishman_3, . . . ; cow_1, cow_2, cow_3, . . . ; Frenchman_1, Frenchman_2, Frenchman_3, . . . ; communist_1, communist_2, communist_3, . . . The terms of the classification tell us what the individuals in that class have in common; *the index numbers remind us of the characteristics left out.* A rule can then be formulated as a general guide in all our thinking and reading: *Cow_1 is not cow_2; Jew_1 is not Jew_2; politician_1 is not politician_2; and so on.* This rule, if remembered, prevents us from confusing levels of abstraction and forces us to consider the facts on those occasions when we might otherwise find ourselves leaping to conclusions which we might later have cause to regret.

"Truth"

Most intellectual problems are ultimately problems of classification and nomenclature. Some years ago there was a dispute between the American Medical Association and the Antitrust Division of the Department of Justice as to whether the practice of medicine was a "profession" or "trade." The American Medical Association *wanted* immunity from laws prohibiting "restraint of trade"; therefore, it insisted that medicine *is* a "profession." The Antitrust Division *wanted* to stop certain economic practices connected with medicine, and therefore it insisted that medicine *is* a "trade." Partisans of either side accused the other of perverting the meanings of words and of not being able to understand plain English.

Can farmers operate oil wells and still be "farmers"? In 1947 the attorney general of the state of Kansas sued to dissolve a large agricultural cooperative, Consumers Cooperative Association, charging that the corporation, in owning oil wells, refineries, and pipe-lines, was exceeding the statutory privileges of purchasing cooperatives under the Cooperative Marketing Act, which permits such organizations to "engage in any activity in connection with manufacturing, selling, or supplying to its members machinery, equipment or supplies." The attorney general held that the cooperative, under the Act, could not handle, let alone process and manufacture, general farm supplies, but only those supplies used in the marketing operation. The Kansas Supreme Court decided unanimously in favor of the defendant (CCA). In so deciding, the court held that gasoline and oil *are* "farm supplies," and producing crude oil *is* "part of the business of farming." The decision which thus enlarged the definition of "farming" read,

> This court will take judicial notice of the fact that in the present state of the art of farming, gasoline . . . is one of the costliest items in the production of agricultural commodities. . . . Anyway, gasoline and tractors are here, and this court is not going to say that motor fuel is not a supply necessary to carrying on of farm operations. . . . Indeed it is about as well put as can be on Page 18 of the state's Exhibit C where the defendant (CCA) says: "*Producing crude oil, operating pipe-lines and refineries, are also part of the business of farming. It is merely producing synthetic hay for iron horses. It is 'off-the-farm farming' which the farmer, in concert with his neighbors, is carrying on. . . .* Production of power farming equipment, then, is logically an extension of the farmers' own farming operations." (Italics supplied.)

Is a harmonica player a "musician"? Until 1948, the American Federation of Musicians had ruled that the harmonica was a "toy." Professional harmonica players usually belonged, therefore, to the American Guild of Variety Artists. Even as distinguished a musician as Larry Adler, who has often played the harmonica as a solo instrument with symphony orchestras, was by the union's definition "not a musician." In 1948, however, the AFM, finding that harmonica players were getting popular and competing with members of the union, decided that they were "musicians" after all—a decision that did not sit well with the president of AGVA, who promptly declared jurisdictional war on the AFM.[3]

Thurman Arnold tells of another instance of a problem in classification:

> A plaster company was scraping gypsum from the surface of the ground. If it was a mine, it paid one tax; if a manufacturing company, it paid another. Expert witnesses were called who almost came to blows, such was their disgust at the stupidity of those who could not see that the process was essentially mining, or manufacturing. A great record was built up to be reviewed by the State Supreme Court on this important question of "fact."[4]

Is aspirin a "drug" or not? In some states, it is legally classified as a "drug," and therefore it can be sold only by licensed pharmacists. If people want to be able to buy aspirin in groceries, lunchrooms, and pool halls (as they can in other states), they must have it reclassified as "not a drug."

Is medicine a "profession" or a "trade"? Is the production of crude oil "a part of farming"? Is a harmonica player a "musician"? Is aspirin a "drug"? Such questions are commonly settled by appeals to dictionaries

[3] "The S.F. Police Dept. Bagpipe Band . . . will soon be decked out in the traditional finery of bagpipers. Pan-Am is flying over from Scotland 21 uniforms. . . . The pipers, by the way, don't have to belong to the Musicians Union since the bagpipe is classified as 'an instrument of war.' Has there ever been any doubt?" Herb Caen in the San Francisco *Chronicle*.

[4] *The Folklore of Capitalism* (1938), p. 182.

to discover the "real meanings" of the words involved. It is also common practice to consult past legal decisions and all kinds of learned treatises bearing on the subject. The decision finally rests, however, not upon appeals to past authority, but upon *what people want.* If they want the AMA to be immune from antitrust action, they will go to the Supreme Court if necessary to get medicine "defined" as a "profession." If they want the AMA prosecuted, they will get a decision that it is a "trade." (They got, in this case, a decision from the Court that it did not matter whether the practice of medicine was a "trade" or not; what mattered was that the AMA had, as charged, *restrained* the trade of Group Health Association, Inc., a cooperative which procured medical services for its members. The antitrust action was upheld.)

If people want agricultural cooperatives to operate oil wells, they will get the courts to define the activity in such a way as to make it possible. If the public doesn't care, the decision whether a harmonica player is or is not a "musician" will be made by the stronger trade union. The question whether aspirin is or is not a "drug" will be decided neither by finding the dictionary definition of "drug" nor by staring long and hard at an aspirin tablet. It will be decided on the basis of where and under what conditions people want to buy their aspirin.

In any case, society as a whole ultimately gets, on all issues of wide public importance, the classifications it wants, even if it has to wait until all the members of the Supreme Court are dead and an entirely new court is appointed. When the desired decision is handed down, people say, "Truth has triumphed." *In short, society regards as "true" those systems of classification that produce the desired results.*

The scientific test of "truth," like the social test, is strictly practical, except for the fact that the "desired results" are more severely limited. The results desired by society may be irrational, superstitious, selfish, or humane, but the results desired by scientists are only that our systems of classification produce predictable results. Classifications, as amply indicated already, determine our attitudes and behavior toward the object or event classified. When lightning was classified as "evidence of divine wrath," no courses of action other than prayer were suggested to prevent one's being struck by lightning. As soon, however, as it was classified as "electricity," Benjamin Franklin achieved a measure of control over it by his invention of the lightning rod. Certain physical disorders were formerly classified as "demonic possession," and this suggested that we "drive the demons out" by whatever spells or incantations we could think of. The results were uncertain. But when those disorders were classified as "bacillus infections," courses of action were suggested that led to more predictable results.

Science seeks only the *most generally useful* systems of classification; these it regards for the time being, until more useful classifications are invented, as "true."

APPLICATIONS

I. One of the basic techniques for producing humor involves unexpected shifts of classification leading to incongruities that strike us as funny. Examine the cartoons or joke page of a magazine, or think about what happened in a television comedy and you will notice how frequently classification shifts are at work. Thus, one reason we laugh when someone is hit with a cream pie in a slapstick skit is because the recipient of the pie, in effect, is reclassified as a "messy baby" who gets himself all dirty when he eats.

Some other examples which use reclassification or uncritical classification (stereotypes) follow:

1. "Billy," said the teacher, "why are you late?"
"I had to take the bull to the cows," he replied.
"Couldn't your father do that?" she asked?
"No," said Billy, "you have to have a bull."

2. During a rain storm in Boston a man looked out of his office and said, "It's raining cats and dogs today."
"I know," said a co-worker, "I just stepped on a poodle."

3. Said a monk as he swung by his tail
To the little monks, male and female,
  "From your offspring, my dears,
  In a few million years,
May evolve a professor at Yale."

4. A woman of the world was speaking to her social worker.
"For ten years I led a life of shame. . . ."
"Yes," replied the eager social worker. "Then what?"
"Then I got over being ashamed!"

5. A priest was walking down the street and two hippies who knew him came over to say hello. He was heavily bandaged so one hippie asked, "How did you get hurt bad enough to require such a bandage?" "Oh, it was nothing," said the priest, "I slipped in my bath. But it is fine now and no trouble." The hippies said they were sorry he was injured and were glad he was better, and then walked away. A half block down the street the first hippie turned to the second and asked, "What's a bath?" A block later the second hippie turned to the first and said, "How should I know? . . . I'm not a Catholic."

II. Discuss the following passages in terms of the ideas presented in this chapter:

1. In one of G. K. Chesterton's delightful Father Brown stories, a crime is successfully committed by a waiter in an exclusive private club—because the guests and the waiters are both dressed in tuxedos and cannot be told apart except by their actions and attitudes.

Chesterton is making the point that people who dress the same are looked upon the same, until they begin to function. I thought of this story in relation to the hippie costume that is so popular among the young today.

The hippie costume has been a blessing to a whole generation of misfits, losers, and rotten eggs. For the first time, they are now able to disguise themselves as hippies, permitting the hippie movement to take the blame (in the public eye) for all their neurotic misconduct.

Until the adoption of this regulation uniform a few years ago, the losers had nothing to identify with and no place to hide. They were forced to take individual responsibility for their behavior and were not condemned as part of a youth bloc.

Now, by the simple subterfuge of adorning themselves with a few belts of beads, they can be their old noxious selves and pass the onus along to the movement they pretend to belong to.

Simply by masquerading as hippies, they feel they can get away with the most outrageous conduct, in violation of all genuine hippie beliefs—knowing that the public cannot discriminate between them and the real thing. The public always mistakes mere form for substance.

SYDNEY J. HARRIS, *San Francisco Sunday Examiner and Chronicle*, Aug. 2, 1970

2. You begin the interview [with Malcolm X, leader of the Black Muslim movement] by asking why his second name is "X." He grins and replies, "During slavery days black men were given the names of their masters—like the branding of cattle. Smith, Jones, and Williams are not African names; they're Anglo-Saxon names that were forced upon the so-called Negro. Rather than bear the brand of a slavemaster, we Muslims change our second names to X—which is the Arabic symbol for the unknown. It removes the white man's stigma."

Why does he use the expression, "so-called Negro"?

"Not content with stripping us of our names," states Malcolm, "the white man, in his evilness, stripped us of our humanity. . . . So the white man made up a special name for his slave-animal—'Negro.' It's a synthetic name that means low, filthy beast. We want no part of it."

Saga

III. It is possible to make a fascinating experiment based on classification. Collect several dozen different objects (such as you might find in various rooms in a house) and ask someone to divide the objects into two piles. Ask them to perform this operation four or five times, using different systems of classification each time, but do not give them any suggestions or hints as to which classifications to use. Record the systems of classifications used and the order of classifications. What problems arose with what particular objects? (Were these problems usually related to some difficulty in determining a class for the object?) If someone makes a classification that you do not understand, find out why he made it. If some persons need more than two categories and want to make more than two piles of objects, find out why. After a few people have participated in this experiment, write up your findings and see what conclusions you can reach.

You can try something similar with books. Should a book that deals with political decision making amongst the poor from a social-psychological standpoint be classified as political science, sociology, or psychology?

Salvatore Russo and Howard Jaques have written an article, "Semantic Play Therapy,"* dealing with an emotionally disturbed eleven-year-old boy who "clung so rigidly to his categories that he was enslaved by them. . . . When his stubborn use of categories became frustrating or painful, he . . . resorted to sulking, crying, or temper tantrums." The treatment given the boy involved having him play a sorting game much like the one described above, that forced him to recognize that classifications are made on the basis of interest and use and are not "absolute" or "eternally true." The paper is instructive to read in connection with the Application above.

IV. One of the serious problems in this country today is how to classify marijuana. Should it be classified as a "dangerous drug" as are heroin and LSD, or should it be considered legally in the same class with alcohol? Recently the courts of several states have held that a judge may, at his discretion, rule the possession or use of this drug a misdemeanor rather than a felony—a difference of classification which could mean the difference between a stiff prison sentence and a small fine with probation. Write an essay defending or attacking a hypothetical law that would classify marijuana as a harmless stimulant and would make any possessor of it subject to a light fine. How would you classify the drug medically? Morally? Do your classifications have extensional validity founded on reports?

V. Does this chapter imply that "Cow_1 is not Cow_2" excludes all possibility of generalization? Could the principle of "Enemy_1 is not Enemy_2" hinder necessary action? With reference to this chapter, comment on the following passage:

> One can imagine a semanticist in Poland, France, Norway, Greece, or any other country occupied by the Nazis. . . . Here, where revolutionary resistance to alien oppression was the only constructive therapy, the treacherous effects of the cult [of semantics] would have been clear. Nazi_1 was not the same as Nazi_2 or Nazi_3 to be sure, but more important for the victims was the functioning of all Nazis in a single pattern of destructive, anti-human behavior. In the coming period, with its sharpened imperialist rivalries so dreadfully jeopardizing our efforts toward world peace, there will no doubt be further destructive group actions which must be countered by positive and heroic struggles toward constructive ends. The alternatives are critical as never before in human history. In these times, harkening to the semantic cult is . . . rendering ourselves completely defenseless while

*ETC., XIII (1956), pp. 265–71; reprinted in S. I. Hayakawa, editor, *Our Language and Our World* (1959), pp. 133–40.

we indulge in private games. For this reason I believe the vogue must not be dismissed as another curious but unimportant preoccupation of quasi-intellectuals. It must be clearly revealed as a menace to the constructive social action so sorely needed today, and vigorously opposed.

MARGARET SCHLAUCH, *"The Cult of the Proper Word," New Masses*

People with college educations, the student said, know more, and hence are better judges of people. But aren't you assuming, I asked, that a college education gives not only what we usually call "knowledge" but also what we usually call "shrewdness" or "wisdom"? Oh, he said, you mean that there isn't any use in going to college!

Francis P. Chisholm

Once we have cast another group in the role of the enemy, we know that they are to be distrusted—that they are evil incarnate. We then twist all their communications to fit our belief.

Jerome D. Frank

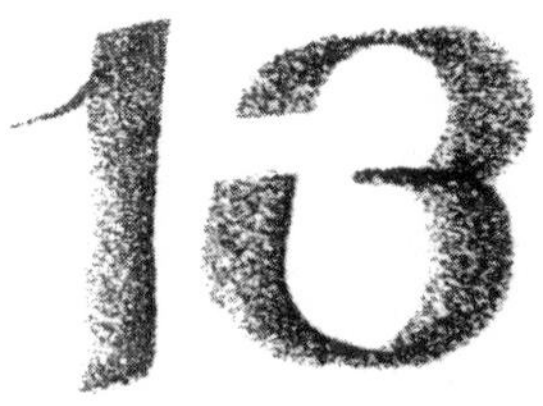

the two-valued orientation

In the expression, "We must listen to both sides of every question," there is an assumption, frequently unexamined, that every question has two sides—and only two sides. We tend to think in opposites, to feel that what is not good must be bad and that what is not bad must be good. When children are taught English history, for example, the first thing they want to know about every ruler is whether he was a "good king" or a "bad king." Much popular political thought, like the plots of television westerns, views the world as divided into "good guys" and "bad guys"—those who believe in "one-hundred-per-cent Americanism" as opposed to those who harbor "un-American ideas." The same tendency is clearly discernible in those who do not believe in the existence of "neutralist" nations; any nation that is not fully committed to "our side" in the cold war is believed to be on the Russian side. This penchant to divide the world into two opposing forces—"right" versus "wrong," "good" versus

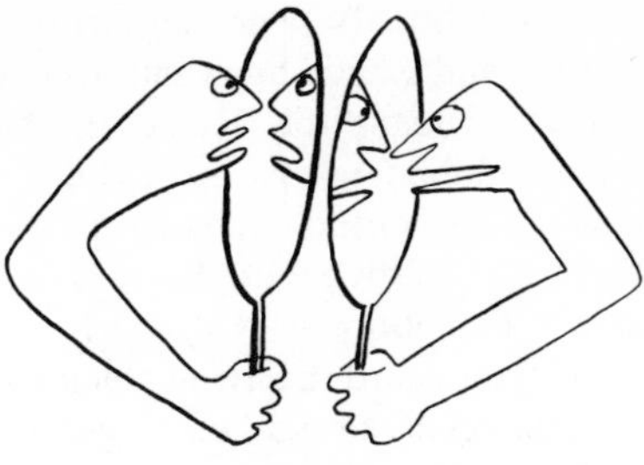

Argument

"evil"—and to ignore or deny the existence of any middle ground, may be termed the *two-valued orientation.*

In a situation of actual physical combat, the two-valued orientation is inevitable—and necessary. Total absorption in the fight reduces reality for the time being into two, and only two, objects of concern—myself and the enemy. This narrowed view of the world is accompanied by accelerated heart-beat and circulation, increased muscular tension, and the release by the adrenal glands of hormones into the blood to contract the arteries and thus slow down the flow of blood in case of injury. This ability to direct and mobilize one's entire mental and physical resources in the face of physical danger—which the physiologist Walter B. Cannon described as the "fight or flight" mechanism—has been necessary to survival through most of the long history of the human race, and probably remains so.

However, for the symbol-using class of life at a high level of cultural development, fighting and fleeing, the primitive outlets for fear, hatred, and anger, are not available. Although we may sometimes get angry enough at our rivals and enemies to *want* to strike them down, or even to kill them, we have to content ourselves most of the time with *verbal* assault: calling them names, criticizing them, reporting them to the boss, writing letters of complaint or accusation, outmaneuvering them in social or business competition, or in rare cases instituting lawsuits against them. Words are not blows, name-calling breaks no bones, and even a smashing insult results in no loss of blood. Hence, some individuals—especially those who are quick to lose their tempers and slow to regain them—are in an almost constant state of overstimulation under the influence of a higher-than-necessary concentration of adrenal hormones in their systems. For such people, the two-valued orientation is a way of life.

The Two-Valued Orientation in Politics

Under a two-party political system such as we have in the United States, there is abundant occasion for uttering two-valued pronouncements.

I have often listened to political speeches carried by sound-trucks in crowded Chicago streets and I have been impressed with the thoroughness with which the Republicans (or Democrats) have been castigated and the Democrats (or Republicans) praised. Not a shadow of praise or even of extenuation is offered to the opposing party. When I once asked a candidate for state representative why this was so, I was told, "Among our folks, it don't pay to be subtle."

Fortunately, most voters regard this two-valuedness of political debate as "part of the game," especially around election time, so that it does not appear to have uniformly harmful consequences; overstatements on either side are at least partially canceled out by overstatements on the other. Nevertheless, there remains a portion of the electorate—*and this portion is by no means confined to the uneducated*—who take the two-valued orientation seriously. These are the people (and the newspapers) who speak of their opponents as if they were enemies of the nation rather than fellow-Americans with differing views as to what is good for the nation.

On the whole, however, a two-valued *orientation* in politics is difficult to maintain in a two-party system of government. The parties have to cooperate with each other between elections and therefore have to assume that members of the opposition are something short of fiends in human form. The public, too, in a two-party system, sees that the dire predictions of Republicans regarding the probable results of Democratic rule, and the equally dire predictions of the Democrats regarding Republican rule, are never more than partially fulfilled. Furthermore, criticism of the administration is not only possible, it is energetically encouraged by the opposition. Hence the majority of people can never quite be convinced that one party is "wholly good" and the other "wholly bad."

But when a nation's traditions (or its lack of traditions) permit a political party to feel that it is *so good for the country that no other party has any business existing*—and such a party gets control—there is immediate silencing of opposition. In such a case the party declares its philosophy to be the official philosophy of the nation and its interest to be the interests of the people as a whole. "Whoever is an enemy of the National Socialist party," as the Nazis said, "is an enemy of Germany." Even if you loved Germany greatly, but still didn't agree with the National Socialists as to what was good for Germany, you were liquidated. *Under the one-party system, the two-valued orientation, in its most primitive form, becomes the official national outlook.*

Because the Nazis carried the two-valued orientation to extremes never before reached by a political party—extremes of ridiculousness as well as extremes of barbarity—it is worth while recalling, in the context of semantic study, some of the techniques they used. First of all, the two-valued assumption was explicitly stated over and over again:

Discussion of matters affecting our existence and that of the nation must cease altogether. Anyone who dares to question the rightness of the National Socialist outlook will be branded as a traitor.

HERR SAUCKEL, Nazi Governor of Thuringia, June 20, 1933

Everyone in Germany is a National Socialist—the few outside the party are either lunatics or idiots.

ADOLF HITLER, Klagenfurt, Austria, on April 4, 1938
Quoted by *The New York Times*, April 5, 1938

Everyone not using the greeting "Heil Hitler" or using it only occasionally and unwillingly, shows he is an opponent of the Fuehrer or a pathetic turn-coat . . . The German people's only greeting is "Heil Hitler." Whoever does not use it must recognize that he will be regarded as outside the community of the German nation.

Labor Front chiefs in Saxony, December 5, 1937

National Socialists say: Legality is that which does the German people good; illegality is that which harms the German people.

DR. FRICK, Minister of the Interior

Anyone or anything that stood in the way of Hitler's wishes was "Jewish," "degenerate," "corrupt," "democratic," "internationalist," and, as a crowning insult, "non-Aryan." On the other hand, everything that Hitler chose to call "Aryan" was by definition noble, virtuous, heroic, and altogether glorious. Courage, self-discipline, honor, beauty, health, and joy were "Aryan." Whatever he called upon people to do, he told them to do "to fulfill their Aryan heritage."

An incredible number of areas were examined in terms of this two-valued orientation: art, books, people, calisthenics, mathematics, physics, dogs, cats, architecture, morals, cookery, religion. If Hitler approved, it was "Aryan"; if he disapproved, it was "non-Aryan" or "Jewish-dominated."

We request that every hen lay 130 to 140 eggs a year. The increase can not be achieved by the bastard hens (non-Aryan) which now populate German farm yards. Slaughter these undesirables and replace them. . . .

Nazi Party News Agency, April 3, 1937

The rabbit, it is certain, is no German animal, if only for its painful timidity. It is an immigrant who enjoys a guest's privilege. As for the lion, one sees in him indisputably German fundamental characteristics. Thus one could call him a German abroad.

GENERAL LUDENDORFF, in *Am Quell Deutscher Kraft*

Proper breathing is a means of acquiring heroic national mentality. The art of breathing was formerly characteristic of true Aryanism and known to all Aryan leaders. . . . Let the people again practice the old Aryan wisdom.

Berlin *Weltpolitische Rundschau*, quoted in *The Nation*

Cows or cattle which were brought from Jews directly or indirectly may not be bred with the community bull.

Mayor of the Community of Koenigsdorf, Bavaria.
Tegernseerzeitung, Nazi Party organ, October 1, 1935

> There is no place for Heinrich Heine in any collection of works of German poets. . . . When we reject Heine, it is not because we consider every line he wrote bad. The decisive factor is that this man was a Jew. Therefore, there is no place for him in German literature.
>
> *Schwarze Korps*

Because the Japanese were, before and during World War II, on friendly terms with Hitler's Germany, they were classified as "Aryans." At one point in the war, when Germany was hoping for Mexico as an ally, the German ambassador in Mexico City announced that Mexicans were members of the Nordic race who had emigrated by way of the Bering Straits and come south! But the greatest error in classification that the Nazis made was when they labeled certain theories in physics as "non-Aryan," and deprived of his property, position, and citizenship the originator of those theories, Albert Einstein. Hitler could hardly have guessed then that those same theories would have military consequences beyond his wildest dreams.

The connection between the two-valued orientation and combat is clearly apparent in the history of Nazism. From the moment Hitler achieved power, he told the German people that they were surrounded by enemies. Long before World War II started, the German people were called upon to act as if a war were already in progress. Everyone, including women and children, was pressed into "war" service of one kind or another. In order to keep the combative sense from fizzling out for want of tangible enemies before the start of actual warfare, the people were kept fighting at home against alleged enemies within the gates: principally the Jews, but also anyone else whom the Nazis happened to dislike. Education, too, was made to serve the purposes of war and to create a warlike spirit:

> There is no such thing as knowledge for its own sake. Science can only be the soldierly training of our minds for service to the nation. The university must be a battleground for the organization of the intellect. Heil Adolf Hitler and his eternal Reich!
>
> Rector of Jena University

> The task of universities is not to teach objective science, but the militant, the warlike, the heroic.
>
> DR. DRIECK, headmaster of the Mannheim public schools[1]

The official National Socialist orientation never permitted a relaxation of the two-valued conviction that nothing is too good for the "good," and nothing is too bad for the "bad," and *that there is no middle ground.* "Whoever is not for us is against us!" This is the cry of intolerance armed with certainty.

[1]The National Socialist pronouncements quoted in this chapter are from a collection of such utterances by Adolf Hitler and his associates, compiled by Clara Leiser and published under the title *Lunacy Becomes Us* (1939).

Man's Inhumanity to Man

The cruelties of the Nazi treatment of Jews and other "enemies"—the wholesale executions, the gas chambers, the "scientific" experiments in torture, starvation, and vivisection performed on political prisoners—have often taxed the credulity of the outside world. Stories of Nazi prison camps and death chambers are still regarded in some quarters as wartime anti-Nazi fabrications.

To the student of two-valued orientations, however, these stories are credible. If good is "absolutely good" and evil is "absolutely evil," the logic of a primitive, two-valued orientation demands that "evil" be exterminated by every means available. Murdering Jews becomes, under this orientation, a moral duty—to be carried out systematically and conscientiously. Judging from the evidence produced at the Nuremberg trials as well as at the Eichmann trial, this appears to be how the task was regarded. Nazi prison guards and executioners carried out their ghastly tasks, not in rage or in fiendish glee, but simply as matters of duty. So completely had the abstraction "Jew" blotted out all other perceptions, that killing Jews became pretty much a matter of course. Aldous Huxley has said that it is the function of propaganda to enable people to do in cold blood things that they could otherwise do only in the heat of passion. Two-valued propaganda, seriously believed, has precisely this effect.

The Marxist Two-Valued Orientation

The orientation of Russian communist spokesmen is also notoriously two-valued, the world being divided, in their view, into "peace-loving, progressive, scientific, materialist socialists," like themselves, and "warmongering, bourgeois, reactionary, idealist, imperialistic capitalists," like us—or anyone else who disagrees with their views. Because the communists are extremely concerned with ideology, there is no talk of "blood," "instinct," and "soul" as there was in Nazi Germany, and much talk about "historical necessity," "the class struggle," "objective reality," and "the nature of capitalist exploitation and colonialism." Nazi Germany offers classic examples of the two-valued orientation in rabble-rousing and popular oratory. Russian communism offers the best examples of the two-valued orientation among social theorists, philosophers, and intellectuals.

Lenin molded the theories of Karl Marx into a political weapon, and the combative fervor of the revolutionist has remained an important ingredient of communist oratory and orientation ever since. Lenin had, as Anatol Rapoport has explained, "an intense compulsion to view each difference of opinion as irreconcilable":

> If someone whom he considered to be in the enemy camp expressed any view acceptable to him, he took great pains to prove that the opponent was either guilty of inconsistency or was muddle-headed, or else (a favorite explanation) was masking his real nature. If someone in his own camp expressed a view unacceptable to him, he again either accused him of muddle-headedness or argued that eventually this view would drive his erring colleague to the complete acceptance of the enemy position. As Lenin wrote, "Enmesh a single claw and the bird is caught. . . . You cannot eliminate one basic assumption, one substantial part of this philosophy of Marxism (it is as if it were a block of steel) without abandoning objective truth, without falling into the arms of bourgeois-reactionary falsehood."[2]

In short, you either agree *completely* with Lenin (or whoever is running the party at the moment) or you are an outcast.

There is a curious preoccupation with *labeling* in Marxist polemics —a need to characterize the ideological position of an individual or a school of thought with an epithet. In analyzing an author's outlook, a philosophical tendency, or a scientific theory, the Marxist critic first of all has to decide "what it *is*." Is it "idealism" or "materialism"? Is it "agnosticism," "bourgeois charlatanism," "empirio-criticism," "fideism," "formalism," "immanentism," or "revisionism"? Is it "Trotskyism," "Kautskyism," "Machism," "Kantianism," or "Berkeleianism"? Is it "Michurinism" or "Weismannism"? Some of these "-isms" are "good," some "bad."

When Marxist polemicists decide that something deserves one of the "bad" labels, they let go with both barrels. Thus, B. Bykhovsky, writing in 1947 on "Semantic Philosophy," found it to be "nothing but . . . a neo-nominalism" which is trying to bring back to life a discredited "subjective idealism." Then comes the blast:

> The sematic fad in Anglo-American philosophy is one of the manifestations of the decomposition and decay which characterize the idealist philosophy of the imperialist epoch. . . . The grimaces of the semantic obscurantists, that is, the Walpurgis Night, is celebrated in the darkness which pervades the spiritual life of the modern bourgeoisie. . . . Like all the currents of modern idealist philosophy, semantic idealism is a spiritual weapon of imperialism in its struggle against the progressive ideas of our time. Poisoning the consciousness of the intellectuals with the poison of scepticism, nihilism, and agnosticism, scientific, moral, political, the semanticists are the most vicious enemies of progressive ideas.[3]

[2] "Death of Communication with Russia?" *ETC.*, VIII (1950), p. 89.

[3] B. Bykhovsky, "The Morass of Modern Bourgeois Philosophy" (trans. Anatol Rapoport), *ETC.*, VI (1948), pp. 13–15. The article appeared originally in the *Bolshevik: A Theoretical Political Journal* (Moscow), August 30, 1947. With the passage of time and the passing of Stalin, a much more temperate view of semantics has emerged from Marxist circles. See *Introduction to Semantics*, by the Polish philosopher Adam Schaff (1962); also G. Brutyan, *Teoria Poznaniya v Obschchei Semantike* [Theory of Cognition in General Semantics] (Erevan: Academy of Sciences of the Armenian S.S.R., 1959). The books by Schaff and

The two-valued character of Soviet orientations is ironically illustrated by the career of Stalin. Long idolized as a great leader, the epitome of strength and wisdom and communist virtue (a "good guy"), he was after his death accused of numberless crimes, among them that of building up a "cult of personality" for the sake of personal power and self-aggrandizement. Towns and streets which had been named after him were renamed, and his body was removed from enshrinement and hauled away to be buried in obscurity (a "bad guy"). Apparently official ideology could find no middle ground for him at some point between "great hero" and "great villain."

The present generation in Soviet Russia is not engaged, as an earlier generation was, in the task of building a new social order. The revolution having been won, there is no longer any need for the revolutionary spirit, so that one of the problems for Soviet leadership is the apathy of the public toward yesterday's fighting slogans and fiery polemics. Soviet leaders respond to this apathy by creating crises to keep people united in a common purpose against "threats to peace"—a technique not unknown in other parts of the world. There are indications that more and more young people, instead of being aroused to patriotic fervor by such propaganda, simply get bored.

The official ideology, however, remains as two-valued as ever. The following account of an interview with a Soviet professor of philosophy is given by Maurice Hindus, who has studied the development of the Soviet Union over many years:

> "Suppose," I asked, "a student questions the validity of dialectical materialism?"
>
> "You must remember," the professor replied, "that throughout his five years in the university our student takes courses in dialectical materialism and related subjects. Besides, the study of all our courses is permeated with this philosophy. The student cannot possibly question its validity."
>
> "Suppose he disagrees with the professor's position that there is no truth other than what the dialectical materialism he studies reveals to him? In America, students are free to disagree with their professors."
>
> "Then we reason with the student. On the conclusion of a lecture we have from ten to fifteen minutes of questions and the student is free to bring up whatever arguments come to his mind. The professor takes up the arguments one by one and proves them false. . . ."
>
> "Einstein," I said, "was one of the greatest scientists of all time, and so far as I know he never accepted the philosophy of dialectical materialism."
>
> "We have translated the book Einstein wrote with Enfield [Infeld]. We study the book because the authors are great scientists. But we reject their idealistic doctrines."

Brutyan are discussed by Rapoport in "Two Marxist Critiques of General Semantics," *ETC.*, XVIII (1961), pp. 289–314. The chapter on "General Semantics" from Schaff's book appears in translation in *ETC.*, XIX (1962), pp. 401–18.

"Suppose the student sees merit in these doctrines?"

"We argue him out of it."

"But suppose he remains unconvinced?"

"Impossible. We have the question period and we hold seminars and in the end we defeat our ideological enemies."

"But if the student persists in contradicting the professor?"

"It doesn't happen. It cannot happen. Our arguments are incontrovertible."

"And if it were to happen?"

This time the professor replied solemnly: "Then the student would place himself outside our Soviet society."[4]

Two-Valued Logic

The term "two-valued orientation" was originated by Alfred Korzybski, whose main concern was with the orientations that determine health or disorder in people's semantic reactions. Although he described the two-valued orientation as characteristic of a primitive or emotionally disturbed outlook, he was not attacking two-valued *logic*. Ordinary logic, such as we use in arithmetic, is strictly two-valued. Within the framework of ordinary arithmetic, two plus two are four. This is the "right" answer, and all other answers are "wrong." Many demonstrations in geometry are based on what is called "indirect proof": in order to prove a statement, you take its opposite and assume it to be "true" until you find in the course of further calculation that it leads to a flat contradiction; such a contradiction proves it to be "false," whereupon the original statement is regarded as "true." This too is an application of two-valued logic. Korzybsky had no quarrel with arithmetic or geometry, and neither do I.

Logic is a set of rules governing *consistency in the use of a language.* When we are being "logical," our statements are consistent *with each other;* they may be accurate "maps" of real "territories" *or they may not,* but the question whether they are or are not is *outside the province of logic.* Logic is language about language, not language about things or events. The fact that two quarts of marbles plus two quarts of milk do not add up to four quarts of the mixture does not affect the "truth" of the statement, "Two plus two are four," because all that this statement says is that "four" *is the name of* "the sum two and two." Of such a statement as "Two plus two are four," a two-valued question may be asked: "Is it true or false?"—meaning, "Is it or is it not consistent with the rest of our system? If we accept it, shall we be able to talk consistently without eventually contradicting ourselves?" As a set of rules for establishing discourse, a two-valued logic is one of the possible instruments for creating order out of linguistic chaos. It is indispensable, of course, to most of mathematics.

[4]Maurice Hindus, *House Without a Roof* (1961).

In some areas of discourse and within some special groups of people, it is possible, so to speak, to "police" the language so that it comes to have some of the clarity and freedom from ambiguity enjoyed by mathematics. In such cases, people may agree to call certain animals "cats," certain forms of government "democracy," and a certain gas "helium." They would also have clear agreements as to what *not* to call "cats," "democracy," or "helium." The two-valued rule of traditional (Aristotelian) logic, "A thing is either a cat or not a cat," and the Aristotelian "law of identity," "A cat is a cat," make a great deal of sense when we understand them as *devices for creating and maintaining order in one's vocabulary.* They may be translated, "We must, in order to understand one another, make up our minds whether we are going to call Tabby a 'cat' or 'not a cat.' *And once we have entered into an agreement as to what to call him, let's stick to it.*"

Such agreements do not, of course, *completely* solve the problem of what things to call by what names, nor do they guarantee the certainty of statements logically deduced. In other words, definitions, as stated in Chapter 10, say nothing about things, but only describe (and often prescribe) people's linguistic habits. Even with the strictest of agreements, therefore, as to what to call "cats" and what not to call "cats," whatever we may logically deduce about cats *may* turn out, on extensional examination of Tabby, Cinders, or Fluff, not to be true.

> Cats are creatures that meow.
> Tabby, Cinders, and Fluff are cats.
> Therefore Tabby, Cinders, and Fluff meow.

But what if Fluff has a sore throat and cannot meow? The *intensional* cat (the cat by definition, *whatever* our definition may be, "creatures that meow" *or any other*) IS NOT the *extensional* cat (Fluff, April 16, 2 P.M.). Each cat is different from every other cat; each cat also, like Bessie the Cow, is a *process,* undergoing constant change. Therefore, the only way to guarantee the "truth" of logically deduced statements and to arrive at agreements through logic alone is to talk only about cats-by-definition, and not about actual cats at all. The nice thing about cats-by-definition is that, come hell or high water, they *always* meow (although, to be sure, they only meow-by-definition).

This principle is well understood in mathematics. The mathematical "point" (which "has position but occupies no space") and the mathematical "circle" (which is a "closed figure in which all points are equidistant from the center") exist *only as definitions;* actual points occupy *some* space, and actual circles are never *exactly* circular. Hence, in Einstein's words, "As far as the laws of mathematics refer to reality, they are not certain; and as far as they are certain, they do not refer to reality." Therefore, even in an area such as chemistry, in which the vocabulary is quite strictly "policed," statements logically deduced *still have to be checked* against extensional observation. This is another reason why the rule for extensional orientation—cat_1 is not cat_2—is extremely important. No matter how carefully we have defined the word "cat," and no matter how logically we have reasoned, extensional cats still have to be examined.

The belief that logic will substantially reduce misunderstanding is widely and uncritically held, although, as a matter of common experience, we all know that people who pride themselves on their logic are usually, of all the people we know, the hardest to get along with. Logic can lead to agreement only when, as in mathematics or the sciences, there are *pre-existing,* hard-and-fast agreements as to what words stand for. But among our friends, business associates, and casual acquaintances—some of them Catholic and some Protestant, some of them no-nonsense scientists and some mystics, some sports fans and some interested in nothing but money—only the vaguest of linguistic agreements exist. In ordinary conversation, therefore, we have to learn people's vocabularies in the course of talking with them—which is what all sensible and tactful people do, without even being aware of the process.

On the whole, therefore, except in mathematics and other areas where clear-cut linguistic agreements either exist or can be brought into existence, the assiduous study and practice of traditional, two-valued logic is not recommended.[5] The habitual reliance on two-valued logic *in everyday life* quickly leads to a two-valued orientation—and we have already seen what *that* leads to.

Korzybski was rarely concerned with the specific *content of* people's beliefs—whether people were religious or unreligious, liberal or conservative. He was concerned, rather, with how people held their beliefs and convictions: whether with a two-valued orientation ("I am right and everybody else is wrong") or a multi-valued orientation ("I don't know—let's see"). Korzybski saw the two-valued orientation as an *internalization* of the laws of Aristotelian logic, which say that:

> *A* is *A* (law of identity);
> Everything is either *A* or not-*A* (law of the excluded middle);
> Nothing is both *A* and not-*A* (law of non-contradiction).

These "laws of logic" frequently mislead us. Aristotelian logic suggests that if something is "good," it must be "all good" (identity); that that which is "not good" must be "bad" (exclusion); and that nothing can be "good" and "bad" at the same time (contradiction). In real life, however, good and bad are usually mixed and it is seldom possible to impose such simplistic categories upon experience. The difficulty with Aristotle's "laws of logic" is that while they *seem* to be sensible, in fact they are

[5]It is interesting to note that even in mathematics, stress is laid today on the fact that two-valued logic is only one of many possible systems of logic. The logic of probability, on the basis of which insurance companies quote premiums, bookmakers quote odds, and physicists predict the behavior of neutrons, may be regarded as an infinite-valued logic.

inadequate to deal with reality, forcing us to press it into narrow confines.

For example, a football game may be "good" (exciting) and "bad" (your team loses). A book may be "good" (full of useful information) and "bad" (difficult). Aristotle forces one to make oversimplified all-inclusive generalizations, a problem Korzybski was concerned with. He regarded his own system as an internalization of modern, multi-valued and infinite-valued logics. He therefore called general semantics a *"non-Aristotelian* system." This has led some people to believe that Korzybski was fighting Aristotle. He was not. He was simply fighting unsanity, whether individual or national. As for Aristotle, he must have been one of the sanest men of his time; but anyone whose knowledge and thinking are limited to Aristotle's can hardly behave sanely in *our* time.

Defeating One's Own Ends

Action resulting from two-valued orientations notoriously fails to achieve its objectives. The mobs that tried to force dissenting pacifist or religious groups to kiss the flag during World War I did not advance the cause of national defense; they weakened it by creating burning resentments among those minorities. Southern lynch mobs did not solve the Negro problem; they simply made matters worse. What hardens "hardened criminals" is usually the way they are treated by a two-valued society and two-valued policemen. In short, the two-valued orientation increases combativeness but sharply diminishes the ability to evaluate the world accurately. When guided by it for any purpose other than fighting, we practically always achieve results *opposite from* those intended.

Nevertheless, some orators and editorial writers employ the crude, unqualified two-valued orientation with extraordinary frequency, although allegedly in the interests of peace, prosperity, good government, and other laudable aims. Do such writers and speakers use this primitive approach because they know no better? Or are they so contemptuous of their audiences that they feel that "it don't pay to be subtle"? Another possibility is that they are sincere; like some physicians at the mention of "socialized medicine," they cannot help having two-valued reactions when certain hated subjects come into their minds. And still another explanation, less pleasant to think about but in many instances highly probable, is that the two-valued furor is a means of diverting public attention from urgent and practical issues. By making enough of an uproar about "atheism in the state university," "communists on the government payroll," or "who's to blame for the mess in South-East Asia," one can keep people from noticing what is going on in legislative lobbies "crowded," as Winston Churchill once said, "with the touts of protected industries."

APPLICATIONS

I. Fervid belief in a cause is one of the strongest and most uncompromising promoters of the two-valued orientation. The Ku Klux Klan, SDS, the WCTU, ardent pacifists, smitten lovers, etc. may find it difficult to avoid the two-valued orientation. Write an essay discussing the pros and cons of the two-valued orientation in a particular situation involving strong convictions of your own.

II. The two-valued orientation appears in each of the following passages at higher levels of feeling as well as in crude form, qualified as well as unqualified. Analyze each statement carefully, especially in the light of the questions: "How much confidence can I safely repose in the judgment of the author of this passage? A great deal? None at all? Or is there not enough evidence to be able to say?"

1. It's time we hit the sawdust trail. It's time we revived the idea that there is such a thing as sin. . . . It's time we brought self-discipline back into style. . . . So I suggest:

Let's look at our educational institutions at the local level, and if Johnny can't read by the time he's ready to get married let's find out why.

Let's look at the distribution of public largesse, and if, far from alleviating human misery, it is producing the sloth and irresponsibility that intensifies it, let's get it fixed.

Let's quit being bulldozed and bedazzled by self-appointed longhairs. Let's have the guts to say that a book is dirt if that's what we think of it. . . . And if some beatnik welds together a collection of rusty cogwheels and old corset stays and claims it's a greater sculpture than Michelangelo's "David" let's have the courage to say that it looks like junk and may well be. . . .

I am fed up to here with the medicine men who try to pass off pretense for art and prurience for literature. . . .

In this hour of misbehavior, self-indulgence and self-doubt . . . let there be a fresh breeze of new pride, new idealism, new integrity.

JENKIN LLOYD JONES, address to the American Society of Newspaper Editors

2. If you're not part of the solution, you're part of the problem.

Black Panther slogan

3. *Coffee and Tea*

Molly, my sister, and I fell out,
And what do you think it was all about?
She loved coffee and I loved tea,
And that was the reason we couldn't agree.

MOTHER GOOSE

4. The right of citizens of the United States to vote shall not be denied or abridged by the United States or by any State on account of race, color, or previous condition of servitude.

Section One, Amendment XV to the Constitution of the United States

5. War is the product of imperialism and the system of exploitation of man by man. Lenin said that "war is always and everywhere begun by the exploiters themselves, by the ruling and oppressing classes." So long as imperialism and the system of exploitation of man by man exist, the imperialists and reactionaries will invariably rely on armed force to maintain their reactionary rule and impose war on the oppressed nations and peoples. This is an objective law independent of man's will. . . .

   In the last analysis, whether one dares to wage a tit-for-tat struggle against armed aggression and suppression by the imperialists and their lackeys, whether one dares to fight a people's war against them means whether one dares to embark on revolution. This is the most effective touchstone for distinguishing genuine from fake revolutionaries and Marxist-Leninists.

   LIN PIAO, "Long Live the Victory of the People's War"

6. We meet in the midst of a nation brought to the verge of moral, political, and material ruin. Corruption dominates the ballot-box, the Legislatures, the Congress, and touches even the ermine on the bench. The people are demoralized; most of the states have been compelled to isolate the voters at the polling place to prevent universal intimidation or bribery. The newspapers are largely subsidized or muzzled, public opinion silenced, business prostrated, our homes covered with mortgages, labor impoverished, and the land concentrating in the hands of capitalists. . . . The fruits of the toil of millions are boldly stolen to build up colossal fortunes for a few, unprecedented in the history of mankind, and the possessors of these in turn despise the Republic and endanger liberty. From the same prolific womb of governmental injustice we breed the two greatest classes—tramps and millionaires.

   IGNATIUS DONNELLY, Preamble to the platform of the first national convention of the People's Party, Omaha, Nebraska, July 4, 1892

7. The history of all hitherto existing society is the history of class struggles. Free man and slave, patrician and plebian, lord and serf, guild master and journeyman, in a word, oppressor and oppressed, stood in constant opposition to one another, carried on an uninterrupted, now hidden, now open fight, a fight that each time ended either in a revolutionary reconstitution of society at large or in the common ruin of the contending classes.

   MARX and ENGELS, *The Communist Manifesto*

8. Those who uphold the necessity of dependence upon violence usually much oversimplify the case by setting up a disjunction they regard as self-evident. They say that the sole alternative is putting our trust in parliamentary procedures as they now exist. This isolation of law-making from other social forces and agencies that are constantly operative is wholly unrealistic. Legislatures and congresses do not exist in a vacuum—not even the judges on the bench live in completely secluded sound-proof chambers. The assumption that it is possible for the constitution and activities of law-making bodies to persist unchanged while society itself is undergoing great change is an exercise in verbal formal logic.

   JOHN DEWEY, *Liberalism and Social Action*

III. For those interested in exploring the subject of logic in greater detail, there are a number of excellent books on the subjects of logic and logical thinking.

Morris Cohen and Ernest Nagel, *An Introduction to Logic and Scientific Method* (1934), which contains a fine discussion of Aristotle's laws of thought in Chapter 9, "Some Problems in Logic."

John Passmore, *A Hundred Years of Philosophy* (1957), Chapter 17 being particularly relevant to the matters discussed in this chapter. The discussion of John Stuart Mill and British Empiricism is also useful.

Stuart Chase, *Guides to Straight Thinking* (1956), which has many amusing examples of errors in the thinking process.

Robert H. Thouless, *How to Think Straight* (1950), which is especially good on the subject of *enthymeme*, or syllogism with one of its propositions missing.

Faith in reason is not only a faith in our own reason but also —and even more—in that of others. Thus a rationalist, even if he believes himself to be intellectually superior to others, will reject all claims to authority since he is aware that, if his intelligence is superior to that of others (which is hard for him to judge), it is so only in so far as he is capable of learning from criticism as well as from his own and other people's mistakes, and that one can learn in this sense only if one takes others and their arguments seriously. Rationalism is therefore bound up with the idea that the other fellow has a right to be heard, and to defend his arguments.

Karl R. Popper

the multi-valued orientation

A Matter of Degree

Except in quarrels and violent controversies when our emotions tend to lead us astray, the language of everyday life shows what may be termed a multi-valued orientation. We have *scales* of judgment. Instead of "good" and "bad," we have "very bad," "bad," "not bad," "fair," "good," "very good"; we also have mixed judgments: in some respects "good" and in others "bad." Instead of "sane" and "insane," we have "quite sane," "sane enough," "mildly neurotic," "sane on most subjects," "neurotic," "extremely neurotic," and "psychotic." The greater the number of distinctions, the greater becomes the number of courses of action suggested to us. This means that we become increasingly capable of reacting *appropriately* to the many complex situations life presents. The physician does not lump all people together into the two classes of the "healthy" and the "ill." He distinguishes an indefinite number of conditions that may be described as "illness" and has an indefinite number of treatments or combinations of treatments.

The two-valued orientation is an orientation based ultimately, as we have seen, on a single interest. But human beings have many interests: they want to eat, to sleep, to have friends, to publish books, to sell real estate, to build bridges, to listen to music, to maintain peace, to conquer disease. Some of these desires are stronger than others, and life presents a perpetual problem of weighing one set of desires against others and making choices: "I like having the money, but I think I would like having that car even better." "I don't like to stand in line for tickets, but I do want to see that show." "I'd like to fire the strikers, but I think it's more important to obey the labor board." "I'd like to uphold the Constitution, but I don't want to admit Negroes to the University." For weighing the various and complicated desires that civilization gives rise to, an increasingly finely graduated scale of values is necessary, as well as foresight, lest in satisfying one desire we frustrate even more important ones. The ability to see things in terms of more than two values may be referred to as a *multi-valued orientation.*

The Multi-Valued Orientation and Democracy

The multi-valued orientation shows itself, of course, in almost all intelligent or even moderately intelligent public discussion. The editors of responsible papers, such as *The New York Times*, Chicago *Sun-Times*, Milwaukee *Journal*, St. Louis *Post-Dispatch*, Louisville *Courier-Journal*—to name only a few—and the writers for reputable magazines, such as *New Republic*, *Harper's*, *Atlantic Monthly*, *Encounter*, or *Commonweal*, almost invariably avoid the unqualified two-valued orientation. They may condemn communism, but they try to see what makes communists act as they do. They may denounce the actions of a foreign power, but they do not forget the extent to which American actions may have provoked the foreign power into behaving as it did. They may attack a political administration, but they do not forget its positive achievements. It does not matter whether it is from fair-mindedness or timidity that some writers avoid speaking in terms of angels and devils, pure "good" and pure "evil." The important thing is that they do avoid it, and by so doing they keep open the possibility of adjusting differences, reconciling conflicting interests, and arriving at just estimates. There are people who object to this "shilly-shallying" and insist upon an "outright yes or no." They are the Gordian-knot cutters; they may undo the knot, but they ruin the rope.

Indeed, many features of the democratic process presuppose the multi-valued orientation. Even that most ancient of judicial procedures, the trial by jury, restricted to the conclusions "guilty" and "not quilty," is not as two-valued as it looks, since in the very selection of the charge to be brought against the defendant a choice is made among many possibilities, and also, in the jury's verdict as well as in the judge's sentence, guilt is often modified by recognition of "extenuating circumstances." Modern administrative tribunals and boards of mediation, not tied down by the necessity of arriving at clear verdicts of "guilty" and "not quilty," and empowered to issue "consent decrees" and to close agreements between litigants, are even more multi-valued than the trial by jury and therefore, for some purposes, considerably more efficient.

To take another example, very few bills ever pass a democratic parliamentary body in exactly the form in which they were proposed. Opposing parties argue back and forth, make bargains and compromises with each other, and by this process tend to arrive at decisions that are more nearly adjusted to the needs of everyone in the community than the original proposals. The more fully developed a democracy, the more flexible become its orientations, and the more fully does it reconcile the conflicting desires of the people.

Even more multi-valued is the language of science. Instead of saying "hot" and "cold," we give the temperature in *degrees on a fixed and agreed-upon scale:*—20° F., 37° C., and so on. Instead of saying "strong" and "weak," we give strength in *horsepower* or *voltage;* instead of "fast" and "slow," we give speed in miles per hour or feet per second. Instead of being limited to two answers or even to several, we have an infinite number when we use these numerical methods. The language of science, therefore, can be said to offer an *infinite-valued orientation.* Having at its command the means to adjust action in an infinite number of ways according to the exact situation at hand, science travels rapidly and gets things done.

The Pitfalls of Debate

In spite of all that has been said to recommend multi-valued and infinite-valued orientation, it must not be overlooked that in the *expression of feelings,* the two-valued orientation is almost unavoidable. There is a profound "emotional" truth in the two-valued orientation that accounts for its adoption in strong expressions of feeling, especially those that call for sympathy, pity, or help in a struggle. "Fight polio!" "Down with slums and up with better housing!" "Throw out the crooks! Vote the Reform ticket!" The more spirited the expression, the more sharply will things be dichotomized into the "good" and the "bad."

Where there are expressions of feeling and therefore affective elements in speaking and writing, the two-valued orientation almost always appears. It is hardly possible to express strong feelings or to arouse the interest of an apathetic listener without conveying to some extent this sense of conflict. Everyone who is trying to promote a cause, therefore, shows the two-valued orientation somewhere in the course of his writing. It will be found, however, that the two-valued orientation is *qualified* in all conscientious attempts at presenting what is believed to be truth—qualified sometimes, in the ways explained above, by pointing out what can be said against the "good" and what can be said for the "bad"—qualified at other times by the introduction, elsewhere in the text, of a multi-valued approach to the problems.

The two-valued orientation, in short, can be compared to a paddle, which performs the functions, in primitive methods of navigation, both of starter and steering apparatus. In civilized life the two-valued orientation may be the starter, since it arouses interest with its affective power, but the multi-valued or infinite-valued orientation is the steering apparatus that directs us to our destination.

Although we like to think of ourselves as rational beings, there are few among us who do not exhibit the two-valued orientation when we are stirred up by controversy. In the course of a debate, if *one* of the debaters has a two-valued orientation which leads him to feel that the Democrats, for example, are "entirely good" and the Republicans "entirely bad," he unconsciously forces his opponent into the position of maintaining that the Democrats are "entirely bad" and the Republicans "entirely good." If we argue with such a person at all, there is hardly any way to escape being put into a position that is as extreme on one side as his is on the other. This fact was well stated by Oliver Wendell Holmes in his *Autocrat of the Breakfast-Table,* where he speaks of the "hydrostatic paradox of controversy":

> Don't you know what that means?—Well, I will tell you. You know that, if you had a bent tube, one arm of which was of the size of a pipestem, and the other big enough to hold the ocean, water would stand at the same height in one as in the other. Controversy equalizes fools and wise men in the same way—*and the fools know it.*

Disputes in which this "equalization" is likely to occur are, of course, a waste of time. The *reductio ad absurdum* of this kind of discussion is often to be found in the high school and college debate as still practiced in some localities. Since both the "affirmative" and "negative" can do little other than exaggerate their own claims and belittle the claims of the opposition, the net intellectual result of such encounters is usually negligible—unless teachers consciously guide the discussions in the direction of multi-valuedness, and draw attention to the processes of abstraction underlying the question under debate. Parliaments and congresses, it will be observed, do not try to conduct much of their serious discussion on the floor. Speeches are made principally for the constituents back home and not for the other legislators. The main work of government is done in the committee room, where the traditional atmosphere of debate is absent. Freed from the necessity of standing resolutely on "affirmative" and "negative" positions, legislators in committee are able to thresh out problems, investigate facts, and arrive at workable conclusions that represent positions between the possible extremes. It would seem that, in training students to become citizens in a democracy, practice in being members of and testifying before committees of inquiry would be more suitable than debating, after the fashion of medieval schoolmen, for "victory."

In the course of everyday conversation, most of us need to watch for the two-valued orientation in ourselves. In a competitive society, conversation is often a battleground in disguise on which we are constantly (and unconsciously) trying to win victories—showing up the other fellow's errors, exposing his lack of information, confronting him (and all others present) with the superiority of our own erudition and logic. This habit of jousting for status is so deeply ingrained in most of us (especially in professional and university circles) that every meeting of intellectuals and every literary cocktail party is likely to include, as part of the entertainment, some sort of verbal dogfight among those present.[1] Most people in such circles are so accustomed to this jousting that they rarely take offense at the remarks of their opponents. Nevertheless, they waste in argument a good deal of time that might more profitably be spent exchanging information and views. An unconscious assumption, convenient for the purposes of those who are looking for occasions to argue and therefore underlying most of this kind of conversation, is that statements are either "true" or "false."

An important way to get the most out of conversation (and out of other forms of communication) is the following *systematic* application of the multi-valued orientation. Instead of assuming a statement to be "true" or "false," one should assume that it has a *truth-value* that stands somewhere *between* 0 and 100 percent. For example, let us say that we are sympathetic to organized labor, and someone says to us, "Labor unions are rackets." Our immediate temptation is to say, "They are not" —and the battle would be on. But what is the truth-value of the man's statement? It is clearly neither 0 percent ("No unions are rackets") nor 100 percent ("All unions are rackets"). Let us then silently grant a *tentative* truth-value of 1 percent ("One union out of 100 is a racket") and say to him, "Tell me more." If he has no more basis for his remark than the vague memory of something somebody once wrote in a newspaper column, he will fizzle out shortly, so that we need not be bothered with him any more. But if he does have experience with even *one* instance of union racketeering, he is talking about something quite real to him, although he may be vastly overgeneralizing his experience. If we listen sympathetically to his experience, the following are some of the things that may happen:

[1]The fame and popularity of Stephen Potter's concept of "one-upmanship" is an amusing commentary on the not-too-well-concealed struggle for status that characterizes our social life. See his *Gamesmanship* (1948) and *Lifemanship* (1951).

1. We may learn something we never knew before. We may, without giving up our pro-union sympathies, at least modify them so that they rest upon a clearer recognition of the shortcomings of unions as well as of their advantages.

2. He may moderate his statement with such an admission as, "Of course, I haven't had experience with many unions." Again, if he tries to describe as extensionally as possible his experience with a labor union, he may find that some term other than "racketeering" more accurately fits the facts. In these and other ways, then, he may modify his remarks and make them increasingly acceptable as he proceeds.

3. By inviting him to communicate to us, we establish lines of communication with him. This enables us later to say things to him which he may then be disposed to listen to.

4. Both may profit from the conversation.

To attempt to converse in this way is to make all our social contacts occasions for what we have earlier called "the pooling of knowledge." We can, if we are able to listen as well as to speak, become better informed and wiser as we grow older instead of being stuck, like some people, with the same little bundle of prejudices at sixty-five that we had at twenty-five.

Statements made in everyday conversation, even if based on slipshod inferences and hasty overgeneralizations, can usually be found to have *some* modest degree of truth-value. To find the needle of meaning in the haystacks of nonsense that the other fellow is talking is to learn something, even from the apparently prejudiced and uninformed. And if the other fellow is equally patient about looking for the needle of meaning in *our* haystacks of nonsense, he may learn something from us. Ultimately, all civilized life depends upon the willingness on the part of all of us to learn as well as to teach. To delay one's reactions and to be able to say "Tell me more," and then *to listen before reacting*—these are practical applications of some of the theoretical principles with which this book has been concerned: no statements, not even our own, say all about anything; inferences—for example, that the man who made the nasty remarks about unions is a "labor-hating reactionary"—need to be checked before we react to them; a multi-valued orientation is necessary to democratic discussion and to human cooperation.

The Open and Closed Mind

Important insights into the two-valued orientation are to be found in *The Open and Closed Mind* (1960), by Milton Rokeach of Michigan State

University. First, Rokeach says, let us divide a communicative event into two elements, the *speaker* and the *statement*. To put matters as simply as possible, the listener may either accept or reject (like or dislike) the speaker; he may likewise accept or reject (agree or disagree with) the statement. Then the following are the possible ways for the listener to react to the communication:

1. he may accept the speaker and accept his statement;
2. he may accept the speaker but reject his statement;
3. he may reject the speaker but accept his statement;
4. he may reject the speaker and reject his statement.

A person with what Rokeach calls a "closed mind" is able to have only reactions (1) and (4): he either accepts the speaker *and* his statement, or rejects the speaker *and* his statement. The person with the "open mind," however, is able to have, in addition to reactions (1) and (4), the more complex reactions (2) and (3): of accepting the speaker but rejecting his statement, or rejecting the speaker but accepting his statement.

The person with the closed mind is apparently one who finds life threatening. If *either* the speaker *or* the statement is unacceptable to him, he rejects *both*. As the reader will recall, according to Anatol Rapoport's account of Lenin's evaluations, this is exactly the orientation Lenin habitually exhibited: an individual on his side who said anything unacceptable to him was shown to be either muddle-headed or "unconsciously" on the enemy side; anyone on the "enemy" side who said anything acceptable to him was also declared to be either muddle-headed or "masking his true nature." In short, the closed mind is definitely two-valued in its orientation: you have to like *everything* about the speaker or *nothing*.

Psychologically, Rokeach says, all human beings are engaged simultaneously in two tasks: (1) they seek to know more about the world, and

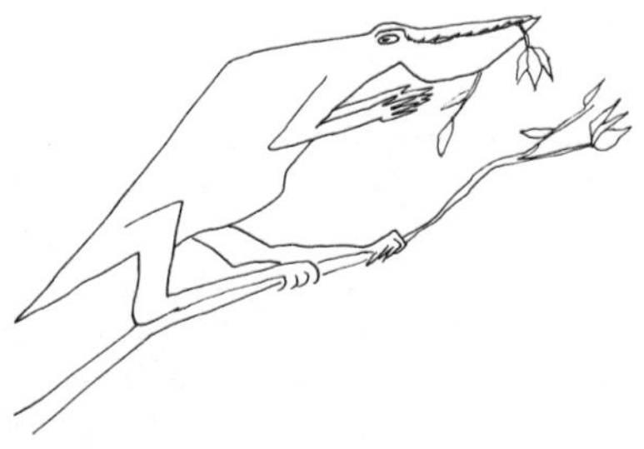

Snap judgment killing a budding thought

(2) they wish to protect themselves from the world—especially from information that might prove upsetting. As the need for defense against disturbing information gets stronger, curiosity about the world gets weaker. ("A person will be open to information *insofar as possible*, and will reject it, screen it out, or alter it *insofar as necessary*.")

Rokeach refers to the things you believe in as your "belief system," and to the things you don't believe in as your "disbelief system." (For example, if you are a Catholic, Catholicism is your "belief system," and your "disbelief system" would be Protestantism, Judaism, Buddhism, and so on.) If you are a reasonably secure and well-organized individual, you enjoy your own belief system, but you are also open to information about your disbelief system. (You are able, although Catholic, to take in information about Protestantism, Judaism, Buddhism, and so on, and *to see the differences* among the various bodies of ideas that you *do not* believe in.) *To be open to information about the disbelief system,* says Rokeach, *is to have an open mind.*

However, if you are chronically insecure or anxious or frightened, you cling desperately to your belief system, and you are too busy defending yourself against real or imagined threats to take in information about the disbelief system. That is, if "communism" and "socialism" are both part of your disbelief system, *the more frightened you are, the less you are able to distinguish between them.*

The term "socialism" is used in a variety of ways in a number of contexts. There is the Russian kind of state capitalism organized under the banner of the Union of Soviet *Socialist* Republics. There is "democratic socialism" (Sweden, Britain), with "socialistic" measures (health, welfare, unemployment benefits, and such) instituted through democratic, parliamentary procedures. There are also "socialistic" measures imposed by armed dictatorships with the help of informers and secret police (for example, the collectivization of farms in Russia and China). Then there are all the measures *called* socialistic by their opponents: prepaid medical care, the income tax, social security, aid to dependent children, or whatever. The frightened individual's reaction to all of these *different* measures is *to see them as alike:* "One is just as bad as the other—they are all 'socialism,' which means that they are all 'communism.'" Other disturbing areas are also seen as "communism"; the fluoridation of the public water supply, abstract art, or the Negro demand for equal rights. According to Rokeach, *this inability to see the differences among the various things you do not believe in characterizes the closed mind.*

With such a view, the individual with the closed mind looks around at the world through frightened eyes, and he sees what he calls "communism" making progress everywhere. (He does not observe communist setbacks.) From here it takes only a short inferential step to conclude that all these "communists" are secretly united in a vast conspiracy.

Further inferences are made to explain why this "conspiracy" is so "successful." Furthermore, it is believed, our own government has been penetrated by "communists," their "dupes," and "sympathizers." Therefore, it is argued, the most urgent task is to expose and drive from office all the "communists" now occupying high places in our society—especially in government and education. "The greatest dangers to America are internal!"

Robert Welch, who said that "Dwight Eisenhower is a dedicated and conscious agent of the Communist conspiracy" and who in his major opus, *The Blue Book of the John Birch Society,* said that President Roosevelt and General George C. Marshall were guilty of "plain unadulterated treason" (p. 99),[2] gives frequent and eloquent expression to this two-valued orientation and its logical consequences. He says that communists control, or are about to control, all the Moslem nations of the Mediterranean in addition to controlling Eastern Europe. Most of Western Europe is also in communist hands: "Any idea that Norway is not, for all practical purposes, now in Communist hands, or that Iceland and Finland are not completely so, is in my opinion . . . unrealistic" (pp. 18–19). Communists have taken over most of Asia "with the full help of our government, completely misled by Communist influence" (p. 14). Nehru is a communist; so is Nasser. Communists control most of Latin America. They have a "stranglehold on the economic life of Hawaii . . . so great that it constitutes virtual political control" (pp. 20–21). Communists are well entrenched in the State Department; they exercise enormous influence on the press, radio, and television (p. 21). There are "at least thirty huge Communist espionage rings operating in this country today." "Scores of known Communist sympathizers have been restored, by Supreme Court rulings, to their former jobs within our Federal Government" (p. 24).

> The [communist] conspiracy is incredibly well organized. It is so well financed that it has billions of dollars annually just to spend on propaganda. It has the benefit of decades of successful experience. . . . And it is guided by men who had to have supreme cunning and ruthlessness to have achieved their present positions within the conspiracy itself.
>
> This octopus is so large that its tentacles now reach into all of the legislative halls, all of the union labor meetings, a majority of the religious gatherings, and most of the schools *of the whole world.* It has a central nervous system which can make its tentacles in the labor unions of Bolivia, in the farmers' co-operatives of Saskatchewan, in the caucuses of the Social Democrats in West Germany, in the classrooms of the Yale Law School, all retract or reach forward simultaneously. It can make all of these creeping tentacles turn right or left, or a given percent-

[2] *The Blue Book* is based, according to its author, on a series of lectures given before eleven men in an Indianapolis hotel on December 8 and 9, 1958. The John Birch Society was founded at that time by Robert Welch and these eleven. The book is privately printed; page references are to the fourth printing, 1961. Welch's comment on President Eisenhower is from his earlier, privately circulated book, *The Politician.*

age turn right while the others turn left, at the same time, in accordance with the intentions of a central brain in Moscow or Ust'-Kamenogorsk. The human race has never before faced any such monster of power which is determined to enslave it (pp. 72–73).

A generation ago, when liberals and conservatives alike were deeply (and rightly) concerned with the rising fascism of Germany and Italy, the more doctrinaire liberals (and the communists) saw fascists in almost as many places as Mr. Welch and his friends see communists today. Two-valued orientation, whether of the right or the left, makes raving fools of all who succumb to it.

APPLICATIONS

I. Classify the following questions as two-valued or multi-valued, giving your reasons in each instance:

1. Did our team win the baseball game yesterday?
2. What grade did you receive in English?
3. Did you pass your English course?
4. Is the paint blue or turquoise?
5. Who is the right man to represent us in Congress?
6. Is Mary at home, or did she go out?
7. Am I going to be all right, doctor?
8. What kind of girl is right for me?
9. Are you sad?
10. Do you like modern jazz or not?

II. The essential feature of the multi-valued orientation is its inherent capacity to enable us to see more deeply into reality, or to appreciate its finer shadings and subtle nuances of possibilities. However, as with the levels of abstraction discussed in Chapters 10 and 11, the multi-valued orientation contains certain dangers as well as advantages. Discuss the following passage in the light of this and the preceding chapter. Does this passage imply we would be better off with a simpler method of evaluation? Is it easier to act with a two-valued orientation?

He who sees different ways to the same end will, unless he watches carefully over his own conduct, lay out too much of his attention upon the comparison of probabilities, and the adjustment of expedients, and pause in the comparison of probabilities, and the adjustment of expedients, and pause in the choice of his road, till some accident intercepts his journey. He whose penetration extends to remote consequences, and who, whenever he applies his attention to any design, discovers new prospects of advantage, and possibilities of improvement, will not easily be persuaded that his project is ripe for execution; but will superadd one contrivance to another, endeavor to unite various purposes in one operation, multiply complications, and refine niceties, till he is entangled in his own scheme, and bewildered in the perplexity of various intentions.

SAMUEL JOHNSON, *The Rambler*

III. Observe the frequency of two-valued situations in television programs, for instance in mysteries, quiz shows, and soap operas. Why do you think television is saturated with these situations? Does real life contain many such situations?

IV. One of the most effective ways of understanding and applying some of the central ideas in this chapter is to experiment, along with other people who have read it, in seeing how these ideas work.

For example, in a group of people who are familiar with the distinctions made here, choose some controversial subject of genuine interest to the group, such as the censorship of movies or of television, the abolition of college fraternities and sororities, world government, national health insurance by the federal government, pacifism, or the closed shop. Ask two members of the group to present a discussion of the chosen subject with one person persistently maintaining a two-valued orientation on the subject ("All censorship is bad," "The closed shop is undemocratic") and with the other person taking an opposing two-valued orientation.

Then ask two other members of the group to discuss the same subject, again with one of them maintaining a two-valued orientation but this time with the second person using the approach suggested in this chapter ("Tell me more," "Let's see").

The role-playing suggested here need not be lengthy—a three- to five-minute demonstration will usually suffice. A discussion of the demonstration, followed perhaps by another demonstration, will help to get the "feel" of "verbal jousting" as compared with the "systematic application of multi-valued orientation." In general discussion following such a demonstration, let the role-taker who has been most "on the spot" have the first chance to criticize what has been done, then his collaborator, and then those who were present as spectators.

I've snuff and tobaccy and excellent jacky;
I've scissors and watches and knives;
I've ribbons and laces to set off the faces
Of pretty young sweethearts and wives.

W. S. Gilbert

The advertisement is one of the most interesting and difficult of modern literary forms.

Aldous Huxley

poetry and advertising

The Poet's Function

One does not often mention poetry and advertising in the same breath. Poetry is universally conceded to be the loftiest of the verbal arts. Advertising, on the other hand, is not even an autonomous art; it is but the handmaiden of commerce. Its name carries connotations, often well deserved, of half-truth, deception, and outright fraud; of appeals to vanity, fear, snobbery, and false pride; of radio and television programs hideous with wheedling voices.

There are many more contrasts. The best poetry seems to be fully appreciated only by the few and to be beyond the comprehension of the many. The best advertising, however, is thought about, laughed over, and acted upon by multitudes. Poetry is, in the general apprehension, something special, to be studied in schools, to be enjoyed by cultivated people who have time for that sort of thing, to be read on solemn or momentous occasions. Advertising is part of everyday life.

Nevertheless, poetry and advertising have much in common. To begin with, they both make extensive use of rhyme and rhythm ("What's the word? Thunderbird!"). They both use words chosen for their affective and connotative values rather than for their denotative content ("Take a puff . . . it's springtime! Gray rocks and the fresh green leaves of springtime reflected in a mountain pool. . . . Where else can you find air so refreshing? And where can you find a smoke as refreshing as Salem's?"). William Empson, the English critic, said in his *Seven Types of Ambiguity* that the best poems are ambiguous; they are richest when they have two or three or more levels of meaning at once. Advertising, too, although on a much more primitive level, deliberately exploits ambiguities and plays on words: a vodka is advertised with the slogan, "Leaves you breathless"; an automobile is described as "Hot, Handsome, a Honey to Handle."

But the most important respect in which poetry and advertising resemble each other is that they both strive to give meaning to the data of everyday experience; they both strive to make the objects of experience symbolic of something beyond themselves. Speaking of the untutored, "wild and rude" Peter Bell in the poem of that name, William Wordsworth said:

> A primrose by the river's brim,
> A yellow primrose was to him,
> And it was nothing more.

A poet, however, cannot let a yellow primrose remain merely a yellow primrose; his function is to invest it with meanings. In the poet's eye the primrose comes to symbolize many things: the joy of early spring, his love of his darling Lucy, the benevolence of God, the transitoriness of life, or other things.

Similarly, an advertising writer cannot permit a cake of soap to remain a cake of soap and "nothing more." Whatever the object for sale is, the copywriter, like the poet, must invest it with significance so that it becomes symbolic of something beyond itself—symbolic of domestic happiness (like Van Camp's pork and beans), of aristocratic elegance (like Chanel No. 5), of rugged masculinity (like Marlboros), or of solid, traditional American virtues (like Log Cabin syrup). Whether he writes about toothpaste or tires, convertibles or colas, the task of the copywriter is *the poeticizing of consumer goods.*

Art and Life

All literary and dramatic enjoyment involves to some degree, as stated in Chapter 8, the reader's imaginative identification of himself with the roles portrayed in the story or play, and his projection of himself into the situations described. The same principles hold for poetry and advertising, of course. In reading poetry, we identify ourselves with the characters the poet creates, or with the poet himself. Advertisers also invite us to identify ourselves with the roles they portray. "Put yourself in this picture!" says the advertiser, showing radiant groups of young people drinking

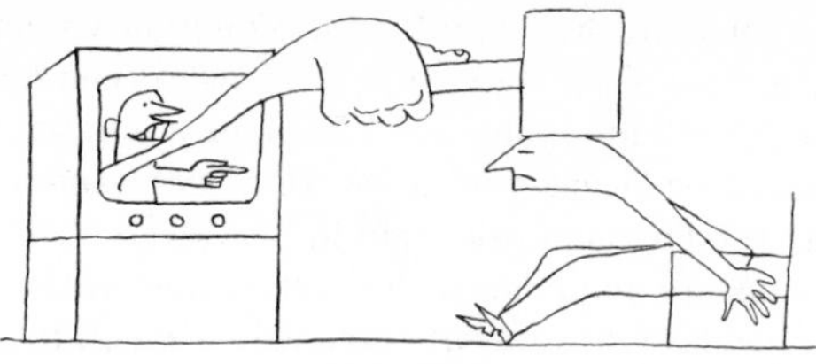

Hard sell

Seven-Up; families wide-eyed with joy as they try out their new Dodge Dart or sit down to their dinner of fried chicken made with new, improved Mazola; aristocratic gentlemen and sportsmen wearing Hathaway shirts; and the lovely young woman who, having found a toothpaste that cleans her breath while it cleans her teeth, is now a happy bride.

The identification which great poets invite us to make requires of the reader both close attention and imaginative strenuousness; it is not everyone who can empathize with Lucifer in Milton's *Paradise Lost* or with "The Ancient Mariner" of Coleridge. The identifications which advertisers invite us to make are easy and pleasant: most of us would *like* to be as handsome and well-dressed and joyous and radiant as the people in the advertisements. Looking at the four-color picture of the serene mother standing by her Norge washer with spotless children and piles of fluffy towels, the harassed housewife readily dreams herself into the picture and says, "*That's* for me!" According to the advertisements, happiness is always within reach.

In spite of this marked contrast in the demands which poetry and advertising make upon their audiences, both have the common function of entering into our imaginations and shaping those idealizations of ourselves that determine, in large measure, our conduct. "Life," said Oscar Wilde, "is an imitation of art." Insofar as both poetry and advertising exact this tribute of imitation, they are both, in a real sense, "creative." Outsiders to the advertising business are often surprised and sometimes amused to learn that the art and copy departments of advertising agencies are known as "creative departments" and their head is known as "creative director." The more you think about it, the more appropriate the term becomes—whether or not you approve of what is created.

Let us call this use of verbal magic (or verbal skulduggery) for the purpose of giving an imaginative, symbolic, or ideal dimension to life and all that is in it, *poetry*. If we speak separately of what we ordinarily call poetry and advertising, let us speak of the latter as *sponsored poetry*, and of the former as *unsponsored poetry*.

Using our terms in this way, we see that our age is by no means deficient in poetry, if we include under that term the poetry of consumer goods. We have more access to poetry (or perhaps we should say that poetry has more access to us) than people have had at any other time in history. It is not possible to listen to most radio stations for five minutes, or to television stations for ten, without running into a panegyric for a beer, a spray deodorant, or a chewing gum. Most American large-circulation magazines are so full of sponsored poetry about breakfast foods, hams, electric appliances, clothing, liquor, and automobiles, and this poetry is so lavishly illustrated by the most expensive processes of color-reproduction and printing in order to attract attention, that reading the articles and stories is like trying to do your algebra homework in Times Square on New Year's Eve.

The Laureate's Task

To say that poetry is sponsored, however, is not to say that it is necessarily bad. Poets have been sponsored in times past, although the conditions of their sponsorship were different. The court poet, or poet laureate, is a typical example of the sponsored poet of a previous age. Such a poet, a paid retainer in the court of an emperor, king, or nobleman, had the task of saying, in odes and epics on suitable occasions, how great and powerful was the ruler who employed him, and how happy the people were under that ruler's benign and just government. Good poet laureates rose above the level of personal flattery of the kings they worked for, and sometimes gave expression to the highest ideals of their times and of their nation. Virgil was poet laureate to the Emperor Augustus. When Virgil wrote *The Aeneid,* according to the *Encylopaedia Britannica* (11th edition), "The problem before him was to compose a work of art on a large scale, which should represent a great action of the heroic age, and should at the same time embody the most vital ideas and sentiments of the hour —which in substance should glorify Rome and the present ruler of Rome." In brief, Virgil had a sponsor and was working under assignment. Nevertheless, because of the character of Virgil as a poet and as a man, and because of his genuine dedication to his task, the fulfillment of his assignment turned out to be a very great poem indeed—many would say the greatest poem of his age.

Another example of a poet laureate is Alfred, Lord Tennyson, who held that post under Queen Victoria. In 1852 Tennyson was called upon to write a poem on the occasion of the burial of the Duke of Wellington in Westminster Abbey. His task was to express the sentiments of his queen and his nation at the death of a national hero. These opening lines from his "Ode on the Death of the Duke of Wellington" (a poem of over 500 lines) show unmistakably that sponsored art can also be art of a very impressive kind, certainly worthy of attentive study in a course in English literature:

Bury the Great Duke
    With an empire's lamentation,
Let us bury the Great Duke
    To the noise of the mourning of a mighty nation,
Mourning when their leaders fall,
Warriors carry the warrior's pall,
And sorrow darkens hamlet and hall.

Where shall we lay the man whom we deplore?
Here, in streaming London's central roar.
Let the sound of those he wrought for,
And the feet of those he fought for,
Echo round his bones for evermore.

Lead out the pageant: sad and slow,
As fits an universal woe,
Let the long long procession go,
And let the sorrowing crowd about it grow,
And let the mournful martial music blow;
The last great Englishman is low.

It is a curious fact that American advertising has also shown itself capable of performing a poet laureate's function—that of giving expression to a nation's ideals and sentiments on an important public occasion. In 1950 the tomb of the Unknown Soldier of World War II was dedicated in Washington, and at that time the following advertisement appeared in the newspapers of Boston and in national magazines:

He Is the Stranger Who Is My Brother

This is the story of a man I never knew, and yet I know all about him.

He is dead now, and he lies in a tomb of polished marble whose splendor would surprise him. And people come from everywhere to stand here with their heads bowed, their eyes serious, their hearts filled with mourning for this man they never knew.

Because he wore a uniform when he died, they call him the Unknown Soldier. I think he was a good soldier, though fighting was never his business. He was a man of peace, I'm sure, though he never told me.

He was born on a farm in the Dakotas . . . or was it a miner's cottage in Pennsylvania, a tenement in the Bronx, a ranch house in Texas, a duplex apartment on Park Avenue? I can't be sure, as I stand here with my hat in my hand, reverent at the grave of this man I never knew.

Was he a poet, bookkeeper, truck driver, surgeon, lumberjack, errand boy, student? Was he telling a joke, or cursing his sergeant, or writing to his family, when the missile came?

I don't know. For when they picked this man, from among all our nameless dead, he was lying quiet in a closed coffin, and known only to God.

But I do know that he is deserving of honor and respect. For, whoever he may be, I feel sure he must have believed, as I do, in the equality of men, the promise of men, the duty of men to live justly with each other and with themselves.

And that is why I stand here with my hat in my hand, reverent at the grave of the stranger who is my brother, my father, my son, my countryman, my friend.

John Hancock Mutual Life Insurance
Company, Boston, Massachusetts

A comparison of this advertisement with Tennyson's "Ode" is instructive. Both express a nation's mourning. Both express, too, something of the spirit of the nations that produced them: Tennyson's poem, the pomp and military pride of the British Empire of the mid-nineteenth century; the insurance company advertisement, the simple, colloquial accents of the democratic America of the mid-twentieth century. The advertisement, necessarily addressed to a wider public than the poem, makes freer use of clichés; the reader trained in literary appreciation would find its language commonplace. Nevertheless, the writer of this advertisement performed on this occasion a laureate's task for a nation that has no poet laureate.

The Problems of the Unsponsored Poet

Let us turn from sponsored poetry to unsponsored poetry—the kind poets write not to satisfy any external demand, but to satisfy themselves. For decades there has been much wringing of the hands at the sad state of modern poetry. Robert Hillyer, a poet himself, in an article on "Modern Poetry vs. the Common Reader" in the *Saturday Review*, speaks of the poets of today as being in a "welter of confusion and frustration." He is distressed by their obscurity of language—"the flight from clarity," as he calls it. He is certain that both the unintelligibility and the tone of despair characteristic of much modern verse are due to the moral defects of the poets themselves. "Their confusion," he writes, "is a sign of artistic effeminacy and egotism."

It is true that many modern poets, from T. S. Eliot to Ezra Pound to Wallace Stevens to Delmore Schwartz to Robert Lowell, are not easy to understand on first reading, or even on second or third reading. But Mr. Hillyer is mistaken, it seems to me, in blaming the difficulties of modern poetry on the moral shortcomings of poets. He fails to take into account the *context* in which the unsponsored poet has to write today.

The unsponsored poet of today works in a semantic environment in which almost all the poetry that ordinary poeple hear and read is the sponsored poetry of consumer goods. Poetic language is used so constantly and relentlessly for the purposes of salesmanship that it has become almost impossible to say anything with enthusiasm or joy or conviction without running into the danger of sounding as if you were selling something. John Keats could write:

To one who has been long in city pent
'Tis very sweet to look into the fair

And open face of heaven,—to breathe in prayer
Full in the smile of the blue firmament. . . .

Today, anyone writing like this would immediately be suspected of working for the Hawaii Visitors Bureau or for the American Export Line promoting Mediterranean cruises.

Robert Herrick could write without self-consciousness about the beauty of women:

Whenas in silks my Julia goes,
Then, then, methinks, how sweetly flows
The liquefaction of her clothes

And so could William Wordsworth:

She was a phantom of delight
When first she gleamed upon my sight;
A lovely apparition sent
To be a moment's ornament;
Her eyes as stars of twilight fair

Today, such lines remind us inevitably of the promises of advertising copy. Herrick's Julia is a testimonial to the effects of wearing Van Raalte lingerie and Hanes' hosiery, while Wordsworth's unnamed beauty obviously exemplifies the results of using Clairol and the new Max Factor eye shadow. Indeed, anyone who is moved to express his thankfulness for the freedoms we enjoy in America will soon begin to sound like an advertisement of the Investor-Owned Electric Light and Power Companies on the necessity of keeping the government out of the utilities business.

The Symbols We Live By

To repeat, advertising is a symbol-manipulating occupation. The symbols of fashion and elegance are used to glamorize clothing and cosmetics. The symbols of youthful gaiety sell soft drinks and candy bars. The symbols of adventure and sportsmanship are used to promote cigarettes and liquor. The symbols of love and delight in one's new baby have been completely appropriated by the sellers of prepared baby foods, canned milk, and diaper services. Advertising is a tremendous creator and devourer of symbols. Even the symbols of patriotism are used for the purposes of salesmanship. There are advertisers who assure us that "It's *American* to want something better," while a beer called "Lucky Lager" advertises with the slogan, "It's *Lucky* if you live in America." Not even the symbols of religion are off limits—Christmas and Easter are so strenuously exploited commercially that they almost lose their religious significance. And there are other examples of the commercial use of religious symbols: a Midwestern flour company, for example, once organized the women's auxiliaries of churches into listener clubs for a quasi-religious program it was sponsoring. The women were urged to save box-tops from the company's cake flour in order to earn furniture and equipment for their churches—with the result that these churches were converted in effect into promotional outlets for that company's cake flour.

The problems of the unsponsored poet in an environment dominated by advertising are therefore difficult. Poets, too, must work with the symbols that exist in the culture, and they must create new ones as well. Almost all the symbols of daily living—especially those symbols that have any connotations of happiness and joy—have been appropriated by the advertisers. If unsponsored poets seem to concern themselves too much with negative moods, such as disillusionment, despair, or cynicism, part of the reason may well be that the positive moods have come to smell too much of salesmanship. Also, the verse of unsponsored poets is often difficult to understand and full of obscure symbolism. For at least a generation there have been no poets—not even Robert Frost or Carl Sandburg—who could communicate with as large a portion of the literate public as Tennyson and Longfellow did in their time. One reason for the obscurity of modern poets may again be that the familiar symbols of courtship, home, mother, nature, and love of country have been so completely appropriated for commercial purposes as to appear unusable to the unsponsored poet. He is practically driven to use obscure symbols out of the Upanishads or Zen Buddhism in his search for something the advertisers have not already used.

Some poets, more aware of the world around them than other poets, have known very clearly who their chief rivals are in the business of manufacturing dreams—and, therefore, patterns of living. E. E. Cummings, in his famous "Poem, or Beauty Hurts Mr. Vinal" which remains quite timely, equates advertising with bad poetry. More recently, the so-called "beat" poets have made something of a cult of rejecting the consumer-advertising culture. The definition of a "square" in beat circles is a person who believes the advertisements, and who is therefore caught in the rat-race of late-model cars, wall-to-wall carpeting, installment payments, conformity, and constant financial anxiety. To be "hip" is, among other things, to have ceased believing the ads. "I can do *without* things," cries a newly liberated young lady of Venice, California, quoted by Lawrence Lipton in *The Holy Barbarians.* "God!—do you know what a relief that is?"

Symbols for Our Times

"Poets," said Shelley, "are the unacknowledged legislators of the world." Poets, by creating new ways of feeling and perceiving, help to create the new ways of thinking that bring us to terms with a changing world. Every age finds its appropriate symbols. In medieval times, religious images symbolized what people believed in and lived by: God, the angels, and the saints. In Renaissance times, the prevailing image was that of the human body, which was used in endless ways to symbolize the ideas of an age of humanism.

With what symbols shall the poet bring us to terms with the realities of our own times? In the past few decades whole new areas of thought and exploration have been opened up by the sciences—by electronics, by astrophysics, by microbiology, by photo-elasticity studies, by the study of nucleo-proteins and their role in genetics, by radioactive tracer studies, and by nuclear physics. Every few months a newly born nation seeks membership in the United Nations, and parts of the world that we had never thought about before suddenly become objects of concern. Astronauts shoot through space, so that the limits of the planet we live on are no longer the limits of our exploration. We can, and do, describe these new developments in the language of science, but how are we to take these new and urgent realities into our hearts as well as our minds, unless poets give us new images with which to experience them?

APPLICATIONS

I. Examine the following advertisements, keeping in mind the assertion that "whatever the object for sale is, the copywriter, like the poet, must invest it with significance so that it becomes symbolic of something beyond itself" (p. 219). The great reliance of advertising upon affective connotations, coupled with a relative absence of information, is well known. But it is useful to examine specific advertisements, separating verifiable information about the product from affective and symbolic meanings, to see exactly how each advertisement "works." What do the products symbolize? Place the two kinds of assertions, the informational and the affective and symbolic, side-by-side and see what you come up with.

1. You'll enjoy *different* tomato juice made from *aristocrat* tomatoes.

Advertisement

SAMPLE ANALYSIS:

Information About Product	*Affective and Symbolic Meanings*
Tomato juice is made from tomatoes.	Because you have cultivated and discriminating tastes, you will prefer tomato juice made from superior, exclusive tomatoes to that made from common ordinary tomatoes. An average person may not notice the difference, but you will. To drink our tomato juice is to symbolize your own aristocratic taste and aristocratic way of life.

2. For men of Distinction . . . LORD CALVERT. It is only natural that Lord Calvert is the whiskey preferred by so many of America's most distinguished men. For this "custom" blended whiskey . . . so *rare* . . . so *smooth* . . . so *mellow* . . . is produced expressly for those who appreciate the finest. (For an interesting analysis of this advertisement, see Marshall McLuhan's *The Mechanical Bride*. His more recent work, *Culture Is Our Business*, also deals with advertising.)

3. Lead women around by the nose. Flying Dutchman. Mysteriously aromatic. Blended from 18 of the world's most savory tobaccos. You'll like it. Women love it.

4. Maybe you'll never tell her
   how you got the shakes just before the wedding
   Back when you thought you were
   giving up your freedom forever.
   But look what you got.
   A life fuller than you ever realized was possible.
   And you can tell her that.

   Diamonds make a gift of love.

5. Smirnoff leaves you breathless.

6. Alka-Seltzer. For people in Love. You've all been there before. You know the feeling. You can't eat. You can't sleep. You can't think. With Alka-Seltzer, though, you can weather the storm. With Alka-Seltzer by your side, you can relieve a love-sick stomach, a tension headache, a foolish heartburn, and spring fever. When it isn't even spring.

7. New Virginia Slims. What is this new extra-long cigarette for women? Is it just a normal ordinary cigarette we call "a woman's cigarette"? No. We tailor it for women. We tailor it for the feminine hand. Virginia Slims are slimmer than the fat cigarettes men smoke. They have the kind of flavor women like—rich, mild, Virginia flavor. YOU'VE COME A LONG WAY.

II. Read and discuss the following passage:

Consider the advertisement for *Pango Peach*, a new color introduced by Revlon in 1960. A young woman leans against the upper rungs of a ladder leading to a palm-thatched bamboo tree-house. *Pango Peach* are her *sari*, her blouse, her toe and finger nails, and the cape she holds. A sky of South Pacific blue is behind her, and the cape, as it flutters in the wind, stains the heavens *Pango Peach*. "From east of the sun—west of the moon where each tomorrow dawns . . ." beckons the ad, in corny pecuniary lingo. But when you are trying to sell nail polish to a filing clerk with two years of high school you don't quote Dylan Thomas! The idea of the ad is to make a woman think she is reading real poetry when she is not, and at the same time to evoke in her the specific fantasy that will sell the product. Millions will respond to poetry as a value and feel good when they think they are responding to it, and this process of getting people to respond to pseudo-values as if they were responding to real ones is called here *pecuniary distortion of values*.

In the ad Pango Peach is called "A many splendoured coral . . . pink with pleasure . . . a volcano of color! It goes on to say that "It's a full ripe peach with a world of difference . . . born to be worn in big juicy slices. Succulent on your lips. Sizzling on your fingertips . . . Go Pango Peach . . .

your adventure in paradise." Each word in the advertisement is carefully chosen to tap a particular yearning and hunger in the American woman. "Many splendoured," for example, is a reference to the novel and movie *Love Is a Many Splendoured Thing,* a tale of passion in an Oriental setting. "Volcano" is meant to arouse the latent wish to be a volcanic lover and be loved by one. The mouthful of oral stimuli—"ripe," "succulent," "juicy," —puts sales resistance in double jeopardy because mouths are even more for kissing than for eating. "Sizzling" can refer only to *l'amour à la folie. . . .*

JULES HENRY, *Culture Against Man*

Notice that Henry, while he does not use the terms used in this book, is concerned with many of the same problems. If advertisements do tap yearnings and hungers of the American woman, what picture of women do we get from advertising? Select some interesting advertisements from magazines and write a 1,000-word essay on "the image of women in advertising."

III. The following unsponsored poem was written by a distinguished American poet about a well-known American automobile. Compare this poem with magazine or television advertisements for the same product. Would General Motors do well to use this poem to advertise its automobile? What kind of people, if any, would be persuaded to purchase a Buick after having read this peom?

Buick

As a sloop with a sweep of immaculate wing on her delicate spine
And a keel as steel as a root that holds in the sea as she leans,
Leaning and laughing, my warm-hearted beauty, you ride, you ride,
You tack on the curves with parabola speed and a kiss of goodbye,
Like a thoroughbred sloop, my new high-spirited spirit, my kiss.

As my foot suggests that you leap in the air with your hips of a girl,
My finger that praises your wheel and announces your voices of song,
Flouncing your skirts, you blueness of joy, you flirt of politeness,
You leap, you intelligence, essence of wheelness with silvery nose,
And your platinum clocks of excitement stir like the hairs of a fern.

But how alien you are from the booming belts of your birth and the smoke
Where you turned on the stinging lathes of Detroit and Lansing at night
And shrieked at the torch in your secret parts and the amorous tests,
But now with your eyes that enter the future of roads you forget;
You are all instinct with your phosphorous glow and your streaking hair.

And now when we stop it is not as the bird from the shell that I leave
Or the leathery pilot who steps from his bird with a sneer of delight,
And not as the ignorant beast do you squat and watch me depart,
But with exquisite breathing you smile, with satisfaction of love,
And I touch you again as you tick in the silence and settle in sleep.

KARL SHAPIRO

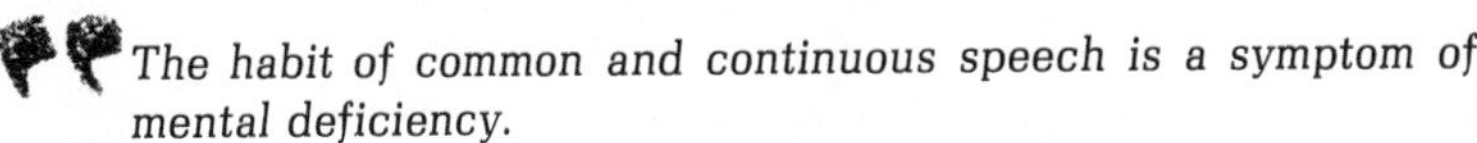

The habit of common and continuous speech is a symptom of mental deficiency.

Walter Bagehot

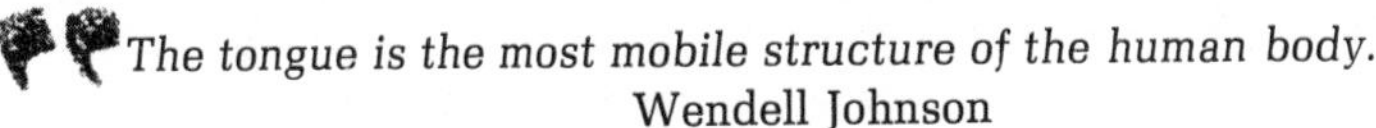

The tongue is the most mobile structure of the human body.

Wendell Johnson

the dime in the juke-box

Many a practical-minded lecturer and clergyman has no doubt discovered for himself the principle that when someone in the audience asks a question you cannot answer, the thing to do is to make an *appropriate-sounding* set of noises, and few people will notice that the question has not been answered. Words are used sometimes intentionally, often unintentionally, as smoke screens for ignorance and the absence of ideas.

At one time when the then governor of Wisconsin forced the resignation of the then president of the state university, the merits and demerits of the case were heatedly debated in newspapers throughout the state. I was an extension lecturer for the University of Wisconsin at the time and often encountered acquaintances and strangers who asked, "Say, doc, what's going on down there in Madison? It's all politics, isn't it?" I never found out what anybody meant by "It's all politics," but in order to save trouble I usually answered, "Yes, I suppose it is." Thereupon the questioner would look pleased with himself and say, "That's what I thought!" In short, "politics" was the appropriate-sounding word in this context. The question at the heart of the controversy—namely, whether the governor had *abused his political powers* or had *carried out his political duty*—was never asked and never answered.

Intensional Orientation

In previous chapters, we have analyzed particular kinds of misevaluation. All of these can now be summed up under one term: *intensional orientation*—the habit of guiding ourselves by *words alone*, rather than by the facts to which words should guide us. We all tend to assume, when professors, writers, politicians, or other apparently responsible individuals open their mouths, that they are saying something meaningful. When we open our own mouths, we are even more likely to make that assumption. As Wendell Johnson says, "Every man is his most interested and affected listener." The result of such indiscriminate lumping together of sense and nonsense is that "maps" pile up independently of "territory." And, in the course of a lifetime, we may pile up entire systems of meaningless noises, placidly unaware that they bear no relationship to reality whatever.

Intensional orientation may be regarded as a general term covering the multitude of more specific errors already pointed out: (1) the unawareness of contexts; (2) the tendency toward automatic reactions; (3) the confusion of levels of abstraction (confusing what is inside one's head with what is outside); (4) the consciousness of similarities, but not of differences; (5) the habit of being content to explain words by means of definitions, that is, more words. When we are intensionally oriented, "capitalists," "bureaucrats," and "labor bosses" *are* what we *say* they are. People in communist countries *must* be unhappy because they are ruled by communists. (The intensional communist meanwhile believes that people in capitalist countries *must* be unhappy because they are ruled by "imperialist warmongers.") Atheists *must* be immoral because if people do not fear God they have "no reason to behave themselves." Politicians *must* be untrustworthy because all they do is "play politics."

Oververbalization

Let us take a term, such as "churchgoer," which *denotes* Smith_1, Smith_2, Smith_3 . . . , who attend divine services with moderate regularity. Note that the *denotation* says nothing about the "churchgoer's" character. It simply says that he goes to church. The *intensional* meanings or *connotations* of the term, however, are quite a different matter. "Churchgoer" *suggests* "good Christian"; "good Christian" *suggests* fidelity to wife and home, kindness to children, honesty in business, sobriety of living habits, and a whole range of admirable qualities. These suggestions further *suggest*, by two-valued orientation, that non-churchgoers are likely not to have these qualities.

If our intensional orientations are serious, therefore, we can manufacture verbally a whole system of values—a whole system for the classi-

Hypnotic effect of one's own words

fication of mankind into sheep and goats—out of the connotations, informative and affective, of the term "churchgoer." That is to say, once the term is given, we can, by proceeding from connotation to connotation, keep going indefinitely. A map is independent of territory, so that we can keep on adding mountains and rivers after we have drawn in all the mountains and rivers that actually exist in the territory. Once we get started, we can spin out whole essays, sermons, books, and even philosophical systems on the basis of the word "churchgoer"—without paying a particle of further attention to churchgoer_1, churchgoer_2, churchgoer_3. . . .

There is no way of stopping this process by which free associations, one word "implying" another, can be made to go on and on. That is why, of course, there are so many people in the world whom one calls windbags. That is why many orators, newspaper columnists, commencement-day speakers, politicians, and high-school elocutionists can speak at a moment's notice on any subject whatever. Indeed, a great many of the "personality development" and "dynamic salesmanship" courses offered commercially, and some English and speech courses in our schools, are merely training in this very technique—how to keep on talking importantly when one hasn't a thing to say.

The kind of associative "thinking" we have been discussing, which is the product of intensional orientation, is called *circular* because, since all the possible conclusions are contained in the connotations of the word to start with, we are bound, no matter how hard or how long we "think," to come back to our starting point. Indeed, we can hardly be said ever to leave our starting point. Of course, as soon as we are face to face with a fact, we are compelled to shut up, or start over again somewhere else. That is why it is so rude in certain kinds of meetings and conversations to bring up any facts. They spoil everybody's good time.[1]

Now let us say that while $\text{churchgoers}_{1,2,3,\text{etc.}}$ prove to be the fine people that we (intensionally) expect them to be, churchgoer_{17} is dis-

[1] "When Harold Stassen in a 'Forum of the Air' radio debate charged that no great advance like penicillin had ever come from a country with a medical-insuranoe plan. Oscar Ewing quietly pointed out that penicillin came from England." *New Republic.*

covered to be unfaithful to his wife and dishonest in his trusteeship of other people's funds. Some people find such a case completely bewildering: how *can* a man be a churchgoer and such a rascal at the same time? Unable to separate the intensional from the extensional "churchgoer," such people are forced to one of three conclusions, all absurd:

1. "This is an exceptional case"—meaning, "I'm not changing my mind about churchgoers, who are *always* good people no matter how many exceptions you can find."
2. "He isn't *really* that bad. He *can't* be!"—that is, denying the facts in order to escape the necessity of accounting for them.
3. "A man can't believe *anything* any more. I'll never trust another churchgoer as long as I live."

An unfounded complacency, which can so easily be followed by "disillusionment," is perhaps the most serious consequence of intensional orientation. And, as we have seen, we all have intensional orientation regarding some subjects. In the 1930's the federal government, confronted by mass unemployment, created the Works Progress Administration, an agency which hired men and women and thought up public projects for them to work on. These WPA jobs were described scornfully by opponents of the administration as "made work," to be distinguished from "real work" such as private industry was at that time failing to provide. It became a matter of pious faith on the part of these critics of the administration to believe that "WPA workers don't ever *really* work." The capacity for verbal autointoxication being as great as it is in some people, many of the believers in this faith were able to drive daily past gangs of WPA workers sweating over the construction of roads and bridges and still to declare quite honestly, "I've never yet seen a WPA worker do any work!" Another instance of this same self-induced blindness is to be found in widespread attitudes toward "women drivers." Many men encounter hundreds of cars daily that are expertly driven by women; yet they declare, again quite honestly, "I never saw a woman yet who could *really* drive a car." By *definition*, driving is a "man's job"; women are "timid," "nervous," "easily frightened," and therefore they "can't drive." If the critics happen to know women who have driven successfully for years, they maintain that those women "have just been lucky," or that "they don't drive like women."[2]

The important fact to be noticed about such attitudes toward "churchgoers," "WPA workers," and "women drivers" is that we should never have made such mistakes nor so blinded ourselves if we had never heard anything about them beforehand. Such attitudes are not the prod-

[2] As is well known now, the statistics of insurance companies indicate clearly that women have much better safety records than men do. Nor do insurance companies raise their rates for families with daughters of driving age, as they do for families with sons of driving age.

uct of ignorance; genuine ignorance doesn't have attitudes. They are the result of false knowledge—false knowledge that robs us of whatever good sense we were born with. As we have already seen, part of this false knowledge we make up for ourselves with our confusions of levels of abstraction and other evaluative errors described in earlier chapters. However, a great deal of it is *manufactured* simply through our universal habit of *talking too much*.

Many people, indeed, move in a perpetual vicious circle. Because of intensional orientation, they are oververbalized; by oververbalization, they strengthen their intensional orientation. Such people burst into speech as automatically as juke boxes; a dime in the slot, and they're off. With habits of this kind, it is possible for us to *talk ourselves into un-sane attitudes,* not only toward "women drivers," "Jews," "capitalists," "bankers," and "labor unions," but also toward our personal problems: "mother," "relatives," "money," "popularity," "success," "failure"—and, most of all, toward "love" and "sex."

Advertising and Intensional Orientation

Among the forces in our present culture contributing to intensional orientation, advertising must be counted as one of the most important. The fundamental purpose of advertising—the announcing of products, prices, new inventions, or special sales—is not to be quarreled with; such announcements deliver needed information, which we are glad to get. But in national advertising directed to the consumer, the techniques of persuasion are rarely informative. As stated in the previous chapter on "Poetry and Advertising," the main endeavor is to "poeticize" or glamorize the objects you wish to sell by giving them brand names and investing those names with all sorts of desirable affective connotations suggestive of health, wealth, popularity with the other sex, social prominence, domestic bliss, fashion, and elegance. The process is one of creating intensional orientations toward brand names:

> If you want love interest to thrive, then try this dainty way. . . . For this way is glamorous! It's feminine! It's alluring! . . . Instinctively, you prefer this costly perfume of Verona Soap. . . . It's a fragrance men love. Massage each tiny ripple of your body daily with this delicate, cleansing lather. . . . Thrill as your senses are kissed by Verona's exquisite perfume. Be radiant.

Advertisers further promote intensional habits of mind by playing on words: the "extras" of skill and strength that enable champions to win games are equated with the "extras" of quality that certain products are claimed to have; the "protective blending" that harmonizes wild animals with their environment and makes them invisible to their enemies is equated with the "protective blending" of whiskies.

There is another subtle way in which advertising promotes intensional habits: through the practice of making slogans out of commonplace facts, advertisers make the facts appear to be unique to particular products. Rosser Reeves, head of Ted Bates and Company advertising agency, cites with admiration a number of phenomenally successful campaigns using this technique—the parenthetical comments are his own: "OUR BOTTLES ARE WASHED WITH LIVE STEAM" ("His client protested that every other brewery did the same"); "IT'S TOASTED" ("So, indeed, is every other cigarette"); "GETS RID OF FILM ON TEETH" ("So, indeed, does every other toothpaste"); "STOPS HALITOSIS" ("Dozens of mouth-washes stop halitosis"); "STOPS B.O." ("All soaps stop body odor").[3] The skill that advertisers and propagandists often display in this kind of slanting reminds us of William Blake's famous warning:

> A truth that's told with bad intent
> Beats all the lies you can invent.

When advertising by verbal hypnotism succeeds in producing these intensional orientations, the act of washing with Verona Soap becomes, in our minds, a thrilling experience indeed. Brushing our teeth with Colgate toothpaste becomes a dramatic and timely warding off of terrible personal calamities, like getting fired or losing one's girl friend. The smoking of Marlboros becomes an assertion of masculinity (instead of a possible invitation to lung cancer)—making one a rugged, outdoor, he-man type, like a telephone lineman or a paratrooper—even though in actuality one may be simply a clerk at a necktie counter. The taking of unnecessary (and even dangerous) laxatives becomes "following the advice of a world-renowned Viennese specialist." We are sold daydreams with every bottle of mouthwash and delusions of grandeur with every package of breakfast food.

Advertising, then, has become in large part the art of overcoming us with pleasurable affective connotations. When the consumer demands that, as a step toward guiding himself by facts rather than by affective connotations of brand names, certain products be required by law to have informative labels and verifiable government grading, the advertising industry raises a hue-and-cry about "government interference with business."[4] This is the sort of argument presented against grade-labeling *in spite of the fact that businessmen, both retailers and wholesalers,*

[3]Rosser Reeves, *Reality in Advertising* (1961), pp. 55–57.

[4]For example, a pamphlet called "Your Bread and Butter: A Salesman's Handbook on the Subject of Brand Names," prepared by "Brand Names Research Foundation" (no address given), undertakes to explain "What's Behind All the Smoke" of the consumer movement which, for many years, has demanded grade-labeling of consumer goods. Most of the members of women's organizations in the consumer movement, the pamphlet says, are "honestly concerned with solving the perennial problems of common sense buying," but a "vocal minority" of "self-appointed champions of the consumer" are the "spokesmen." This minority, it is explained, "want to standardize most consumer goods, to eliminate advertising and competing brands, to see government controls extended over production, distribution and profits. They believe in a planned economy, with a government brain trust doing all the planning."

The slogan

rely extensively on grading according to federally established standards when they do their own purchasing.

In other words, many advertisers *prefer* that we be governed by automatic reactions to brand names rather than by thoughtful consideration of the facts about their products. An important reason for this preference lies in the mechanics of present-day retail distribution. Most of the buying of groceries, for example, is done at supermarkets, where the housewife must make choices among huge and dazzling displays of packaged merchandise, with no clerk to explain to her the advantages of one choice over another. Therefore, to use the terminology of the trade, she must be "pre-sold" *before* she gets to the market—and this is done by getting her to remember, through tireless reiteration on radio and television commercials, a brand name, and by investing that name with nothing but pleasant connotations.

Thoughtful purchasing is the last thing many merchandisers want. Once the customer is hooked on a brand name, all sorts of tricks can be played on him (or her). A currently widespread practice is to reduce the contents of a package without reducing its size or price; many items traditionally bought in one-pound and half-pound packages now come in such sizes as 15 oz., 14½ oz., 7 oz., and 6¾ oz. These figures are usually printed in tiny letters on the package in places where they are least likely to be seen. For the unwary housewife, the costs of "brand loyalty" can be high.[5]

[5]Not all proprietors of brand names do this sort of thing, of course. The following comments from readers published in *Consumer Reports* give the other side of the picture: "It has always impressed me how the *Wheatena* cooked-cereal boxes are filled so close to the top that they can hardly be opened without running over. What a happy experience to encounter in today's world of commerce." "I am happy to call attention to the *Hi Ho* crackers package. A one-pound size, so designated in large type on the front and back, was a welcome relief."

Within recent years, the advertising of brand names has climbed to a higher level of abstraction. In addition to the advertising of specific products by their brand name, there is now *advertising of advertising.* As the pamphlet of the Brand Names Research Foundation urges, "So it's up to you as a salesman for a brand name to keep pushing not only YOUR BRAND, but brands in general. *Get on the Brand Wagon!*" A whisky advertisement says: "AMERICA IS NAMES . . . Seattle, Chicago, Kansas City . . . Elm Street, North Main, Times Square . . . Wrigley, Kellogg, Squibb, Ipana . . . Heinz, Calvert . . . Goodrich . . . Chevrolet. Names [the American has] always known . . . names of things he's bought and used . . . believed in. . . . Yes, America is names. *Good* names. Familiar names that inspire confidence. . . . For America *is* names . . . *good* names for good things to have. . . ." This sort of advertising of advertising has become increasingly common. The assumption is dinned into us that if a brand name even *sounds* familiar, the product it stands for must be good. ("The best in the land if you buy by brand.") *A graver example of systematic public miseducation can hardly be imagined. Intensional orientation is elevated to a guiding principle in the life of the consumer.*

Sometimes it seems as if the conflict between the aims of the advertiser and those of the educator is irreconcilable. When the teacher of home economics says, "Buy wisely," she means careful and reflective purchasing in the light of one's real needs and of accurate information about the product. When the advertiser says, "Buy wisely," he often means, "Buy our brand, regardless of your special situation or special needs, because DUZ DOES EVERYTHING!" The teacher's job is to encourage intellectual and moral self-discipline. The job of the advertiser often seems to be to encourage thoughtlessness ("impluse buying") and self-indulgence, even at the cost of life-long bondage to finance companies.

However, I am far from certain that the conflict between the aims of the advertiser and the educator is inevitable. It is inevitable *if* advertising cannot perform its functions *except* through the promotion of mistaken reactions to words and other symbols. Because advertising is both so powerful and so widespread, it influences more than our choice of products; it also influences our patterns of evaluation. It can either increase or decrease the degree of sanity with which people respond to words. Thus, if advertising is informative, witty, educational, and imaginative, it can perform its necessary commercial function and contribute to our pleasure in life without making us slaves to the tyranny of affective words. If, however, products are sold largely by manipulating affective connotations—"*pin-point* carbonation," "*activated* chlorophyll," "*dual-filter* Tareytons," "contains *RD-119*," "*tired blood*"—the influence of advertising is to deepen the already grave intensional orientations widely prevalent in the public. The schizophrenic is one who attributes a greater reality to words, fantasies, daydreams, and "private worlds" than to the actualities around him. Surely it is possible for advertising to perform its functions without aggravating our all-too-prevalent verbomania! Or is it?

Higher Education, Learned Jargon, and Babuism

Education of the wrong kind also contributes tremendously to our intensional orientations. Some people look upon education largely as a matter of acquiring a learned vocabulary (including terms like "intensional orientation") *without* a corresponding concern (and sometimes with no concern at all) for *what the vocabulary stands for.*

In the course of getting an education, students have to read many difficult books. Some of these books, the student feels, are much more difficult to read than they need to be, because of the addiction of many scholars to extremely difficult terminology. Students, like other people, often ask why all books cannot be written more simply.

There are of course two answers to this question. The first is that some books are difficult because the ideas they deal with are difficult. An advanced work in chemistry or economics is difficult to one who knows no chemistry or economics for the simple reason that such a work presupposes on the part of the reader a background of previous study.

But there is another reason why books may be difficult. A learned vocabulary has two functions: first, it has the *communicative function* of giving expression to ideas—including important, difficult, or recondite ideas; secondly, it has a *social function* of conferring prestige upon its users and arousing respect and awe among those who do not understand it. ("Gosh, he must be smart. I can't understand a word he says!") It can be stated as a general rule that *whenever the social function of a learned vocabulary becomes more important to its users than its communicative function, communication suffers and jargon proliferates.*[6] This rule may be illustrated by a passage from an issue of the *American Journal of Sociology:*

> In any formal organization, the goals as reflected in the system of functional differentiation result in a distinctive pattern of role differentiation. In turn, role differentiation, whether viewed hierarchically or horizontally, leads to what Mannheim called "perspectivistic thinking," namely, incumbency in a particular status induces a corresponding set of perceptions, attitudes and values. In an organization, as in society as a whole, status occupants tend to develop a commitment to subunit goals and tasks—a commitment that may be dysfunctional from the viewpoint of the total organizational goals. In other words, "perspectivistic think-

[6]The word "jargon" is used here, as it is defined in *Webster's Third New International Dictionary,* to mean "pretentious or unnecessarily obscure and esoteric terminology."

Brief, as in legal brief

ing" may interfere with the coordination of effort toward the accomplishment of total organizational goals, thus generating organizational pressures to insure adequate levels of performance.

In this passage the author is merely saying (1) that in any formal organization, different people have different tasks; (2) that people sometimes get engrossed in their own special tasks to a degree that interferes with the goals of the organization as a whole; and therefore (3) that the organization has to put pressure on them to get the over-all job done. What is clear from this passage (the *only* thing that is clear) is that the author's concern with his professional standing as a sociologist has almost completely submerged his concern with communicating his ideas. Thus, students are compelled in their studies to read, in addition to material that is intrinsically difficult, material that is made unnecessarily difficult by jargon.

This sociological passage, however, has at least the merit of possessing a discoverable meaning. There are some readings a college student encounters for which even this much cannot be said with certainty. For example:

> The being that exists is man. Man alone exists. Rocks are, but they do not exist. Trees are, but they do not exist. Horses are, but they do not exist. Angels are, but they do not exist. God is, but he does not exist. The proposition "man alone exists" does not mean by any means that man alone is a real being while all other beings are unreal and mere appearances or human ideas. The proposition "man exists" means: man is that being whose Being is distinguished by the open-standing standing-in in the unconcealedness of Being, from Being, in Being. The existential nature of man is the reason why man can represent beings as such, and why he can be conscious of them. All consciousness presupposes ecstatically understood existence as the *essentia* of man—*essentia* meaning that as which man is present insofar as he is man. But consciousness does not itself create the openness of beings, nor is it consciousness that makes it possible for man to stand open for beings. Whither and whence and in what free dimension could the intentionality of consciousness move, if instancy were not the essence of man in the first instance?[7]

The foregoing are only samples of the many kinds of abstract prose that the student—especially the college and university student—encounters daily in his studies. Sometimes his professor, who presumably understands the readings he assigns, lectures at equally high levels of abstraction, so that the student is never quite sure, from the beginning of the course to the end, what it is all about. What is the effect upon students of readings and lectures of this kind? Obviously, the student is left with the impression that simplicity and clarity of style will get him nowhere in intellectual life, and that even a simple idea (or no idea

[7]Martin Heidegger, "The Way Back into the Ground of Metaphysics," in *Existentialism from Dostoevsky to Sartre*, translated and edited by Walter Kaufmann (1957), pp. 214–15.

at all) will gain academic respectability if it is phrased in a sufficiently abstract and incomprehensible vocabulary.

The British in India used to have a derogatory term for the pretentious and often comically inappropriate English used by poorly trained Indian clerks and civil servants: they called it "babu English."[8] The term is admittedly offensive, and the writer uses it only because it contains an idea for which there is no other term. Abandoning its original application, then, let us use "babu English," or "babuism," as a general term to mean *discourse in which the speaker (or writer) throws around learned words he does not understand in order to create a favorable impression.* Babuism probably has existed and will continue to exist in every culture in which there is a learned class of magicians, shamans, priests, teachers, and other professional verbalizers with big vocabularies. Babuism results whenever people who are not learned try to confer upon themselves by purely verbal means the *social* advantages of being considered learned.

Elsewhere in this volume, much has been said of the common tendency to confuse symbols with the things they stand for. The student may do the same: he may confuse symbols of learning (such as an abstract and difficult vocabulary) with learning itself. Not being able to understand the books he is reading, and blaming himself for his failure to understand, he conscientiously applies himself again and again to his assignments until he is familiar with the *vocabulary* of the course—a vocabulary that cannot help becoming a "babu English," since he still does not know what it is all about. If he is verbally clever, he will be able to parrot enough of this vocabulary in his final term paper to make it sound extremely plausible. The teacher reading the paper will also not be too sure what it is all about, but he will recognize the vocabulary as his own and so will give it a passing grade.

Thus the student, by learning to speak and write several kinds of babu—literary babu, psychological babu, educational babu, philosophical babu, the babu of art criticism, etc.—will eventually get his bachelor's degree. Perhaps he will go on to graduate school and get his Ph.D. Then he will teach it to others.

Thus does intensional orientation, like Ol' Man River, keep a-rollin' along.

APPLICATIONS

I. Try to find at least three examples of intensional orientation from pulp fiction magazines, advertising, political statements, or articles

[8]"Babu" (or "baboo") is defined in the Funk and Wagnalls *New Standard Dictionary* as "1. A Hindu gentleman: a polite term of address, equivalent to *sir* or *Mr.* 2. In India, a native merchant or clerk who can write English. 3. A native of India with a smattering of English education: a derogatory term. . . . babuism."

about education. Which of the five semantic errors listed on page 230 can be found in your examples? Is there any way that you could "re-orient" your examples by rewriting them? Do you suspect that the writer is using intensionally oriented words accidentally or on purpose? Why?

II. Occasionally advertising oversteps the legitimate bounds of persuasion, as can be seen in the following "correction" advertisement originally printed in a Chicago newspaper.

> Recently we advertised lots for sale in California City, California. We indicated this property is "In Greater Los Angeles"; "Commuting Distance Los Angeles"; "Already a Large Community"; Parks, Schools, Churches Provided For"; "Running Water, Paved Streets Already In." An illustrated lake was captioned, "Isabella Lake near California City."
>
> The development is located 115 miles from Los Angeles; 40 homes have been completed. Parks, schools, churches have not been provided for. Land has been dedicated for such use. Water and paved streets are not already in this tract. They are guaranteed as provided by California law. The lake illustration should not have been used since we have been informed the only mapped lake in California named "Isabella Lake" is not "near California City."
>
> We regret these errors and pledge they will not occur again.

If the Constitution guarantees to everyone in this country freedom of speech and of the press, why should this development company feel compelled to print a retraction? Were they doing anything illegal? Are there any laws governing the truthfulness of content in print? Must a book of philosophy or economics "tell the truth" as an advertisement should?

III. Examine the following passages and distinguish between those that are essentially "intensional" (based on words rather than facts to which words should guide us) and those that are essentially "extensional" (based upon the things for which words stand). Explain how you reached your conclusions.

1. The rebellion in Detroit, during the "violent summer" of 1967 (by August there had been riots in over 30 cities, climaxed by Detroit in which 1300 buildings were razed and 2700 businesses looted), showed how hard it was—by sensible economic and political reasoning—to explain entirely the reasons for revolt in terms of injustice, or to explain the course it took. Some of the curious features of the Detroit rebellion were that it was not a "race" riot but an aggressive outburst in which whites and Negroes joined in "integrated" looting, that it expressed the alienated spirit of a mass of have-nots sharing a subculture of poverty; that there was an emotional satisfaction in burning and destruction for its own sake (mood of nihilism, carnival spirit, "burn, baby, burn!") which made it clear that psychological rather than mere economic explanations were needed; and, finally, that this peak outburst had occurred in a city where progress in racial reconciliation had been perhaps greatest in the nation.

   ORRIN E. KLAPP, *The Collective Search for Identity*

2. I asked professors who teach the meaning of life to tell me what is
 happiness.
 And I went to famous executives who boss the work of thousands
 of men.
 They all shook their heads and gave me a smile as though I was
 trying to fool with them.
 And then one Sunday afternoon I wandered out along the Desplaines
 River
 And I saw a crowd of Hungarians under the trees with their women
 and children and a keg of beer and an accordion.

CARL SANDBURG

3. Many years ago, the word *square* was one of the most honored words in our vocabulary. The square deal was an honest deal. A square meal was a full and good meal. It was the square shooter rather than the sharp shooter who was admired. What is a square today? He's the fellow who never learned to get away with it, who gets choked up when the flag unfurls. There has been too much glorification of the angle players, the corner cutters, and the goof offs. One of America's greatest needs is for more people who are square.

SEN. MARGARET CHASE SMITH, *Time*

Reactors that produce, say, five million kilowatts of electricity are too large to be accepted by our present economic and political units. The scale of the new energy source determined by the logic of economics and of the inherent nature of the technology is larger than the scale determined by our traditionally fragmented political and economic structures. But it is not only nuclear energy in its peaceful aspects that makes our divided world obsolete. As John von Neumann pointed out some ten years ago, the H-bomb and the ICBM also make geographic boundaries obsolete. The imperative toward unification resulting from the intrinsic massiveness of modern technology is not confined to nuclear energy. Our communications systems, our transportation systems, the possibility of using superconducting cable for transmission of electricity, all these and many other new technologies point strongly to the mismatch between the size of our political or economic units and the size of our technologies. I think all of us who are involved in these new technologies can only hope that before they destroy us, our political instruments will accommodate to the logic of massiveness, and that the major fruit of the new technologies will be a unified and peaceful world.

Alvin M. Weinberg

rats and men

"Insoluble" Problems

Professor N. R. F. Maier of the University of Michigan performed a series of interesting experiments in which "neurosis" is induced in rats. The rats are first trained to jump off the edge of a platform at one of two doors. If the rat jumps to the right, the door holds fast, and it bumps its nose and falls into a net; if it jumps to the left, the door opens, and the rat finds a dish of food. When the rats are well trained to this reaction, the situation is changed. The food is put behind the other door, so that in order to get their reward they now have to jump to the right instead of to the left. (Other changes, such as marking the two doors in different ways, may also be introduced by the experimenter.) If the rat fails to figure out the new system, so that each time it jumps it never knows whether it is going to get food or bump its nose, it finally gives up and refuses to jump at all. At this stage, Dr. Maier says, "Many rats prefer to starve rather than make a choice."

Next, the rats are forced to make a choice, being driven to it by blasts of air or an electric shock. "Animals which are induced to respond in the insoluble problem situation," says Dr. Maier, "settle down to a specific reaction (such as jumping *solely* at the left-hand door) which they continue to execute regardless of consequences. . . . The response chosen under these conditions becomes fixated. . . . Once the fixation appears, the animal is incapable of learning an adaptive response in this situation." When a reaction to the left-hand door is thus fixated, *the right-hand door may be left open so that the food is plainly visible.* Yet the rat, when pushed, *continues to jump to the left,* becoming more panicky each time. When the experimenter persists in forcing the rat to make choices, it may go into convulsions, racing around wildly, injuring its claws, bumping into chairs and tables, then going into a state of violent trembling, until it falls into a coma. In this passive state, it refuses to eat, refuses to take any interest in anything: it can be rolled up into a ball or suspended in the air by its legs—the rat has ceased to care what happens to it. It has had a "nervous breakdown."[1]

It is the "insolubility" of the rat's problem that leads to its nervous breakdown, and, as Dr. Maier shows in his studies of disturbed children and adults, rats and human beings seem to go through pretty much the same stages. First, they are trained to make habitually a given choice when confronted by a given problem; secondly, they get a terrible shock when they find that the conditions have changed and that the choice doesn't produce the expected results; third, whether through shock, anxiety, or frustration, they may fixate on the original choice and continue to make that choice regardless of consequences; fourth, they sullenly refuse to act at all; fifth, when by external compulsion they are forced to make a choice, they again make the one they were originally trained to make—and again get a bump on the nose; finally, even *with the goal visible in front of them,* to be attained simply by making a different choice, they go crazy out of frustration. They tear around wildly; they sulk in corners and refuse to eat; bitter, cynical, disillusioned, they cease to care what happens to them.

[1]Norman R. F. Maier, *Frustration: The Study of Behavior Without a Goal* (1949). See especially Chapter 2, "Experimental Evidence of Abnormal Behavior Reactions," and Chapter 6, "Comparison of Motivational and Frustration-Induced Behavior Problems in Children."

Is this an exaggerated picture? It hardly seems so. The pattern recurs throughout human life, from the small tragedies of the home to the world-shaking tragedies among nations. In order to cure her husband's faults, a wife may nag him. His faults get worse, so she nags him some more. Naturally his faults get worse still—and she nags him even more. Governed, like the rat, by a fixated reaction to the problem of her husband's faults, she can meet it only in one way. The longer she continues, the worse it gets, until they are both nervous wrecks.

Again, white people in a northern city, deploring the illiteracy and high crime rate among Negroes, segregate them, persecute them (it is well known that the police are almost always tougher on Negro suspects than on whites), and deny them opportunities for employment and advancement. The denial of opportunity perpetuates the illiteracy and the high crime rate, which in turn perpetuate the segregation, persecution, and denial of opportunity. The search for a way to break up this vicious circle taxes the best minds among those interested in orderly social change: city councilmen, educators, urban planners, Negro organizations, as well as state governments and federal authorities.

To cite another example, students trying to express themselves in writing may write poorly. In order to improve their writing, says the English teacher, I must teach them the fundamentals of grammar, spelling, and punctuation. By thus placing excessive emphasis on grammar and mechanics while ignoring the students' ideas, the teacher quickly destroys student interest in writing. That interest destroyed, the students write even more poorly. Thereupon the teacher redoubles his dose of grammar and mechanics. The students become increasingly bored and rebellious. Such students fill the ranks of "remedial English" classes in high school and college.

Again, a nation, believing that the only way to secure peace and dignity is through armed strength, may embark on a huge armaments program. The program arouses the fears of neighboring nations, so that they too increase their armaments to match those of the first nation. Anxiety and tension increase. It is clear, the first nation declares, that we shall continue to feel anxious about our national security so long as we are not adequately prepared for all emergencies; we must therefore *double* our armaments. This naturally makes the neighboring nations even more anxious, so that they too double their armaments. Anxiety and tension increase even more. It is clear, the first nation declares, that our mistake has been to underestimate our defense needs. This time we must be *sure* to be sufficiently armed to preserve peace. We must *triple* our armaments. . . .[2]

[2] "Let us represent the explosive power of a World War II blockbuster by a one-foot ruler. On this scale the bomb that demolished Hiroshima would be represented by the height of the Empire State Building, and a 20-megaton weapon by the height of the orbit of Sputnik 1." Since Harrison Brown and James Real wrote these words in their pamphlet, *Community*

Of course these instances are oversimplified, but it is often because of vicious circles of this kind that we are unable to get at or do anything about the conditions that lead to disaster. The pattern is frequently recognizable; the goal may be in sight, attainable by a mere change in methods. Nevertheless, governed by fixated reactions, the rat "cannot" get food, the wife "cannot" cure her husband's faults, Negroes will have to wait two or three generations "until the time is ripe" for social change, and we "cannot afford" to stop devising and manufacturing weapons so deadly that they cannot be used without destroying civilization itself.

There is, however, an important difference between the insolubility of the rat's problems and the insolubility of human problems. Dr. Maier's rats were driven to their nervous breakdowns by problems more complicated than would naturally occur in a rat's environment. But human breakdowns are ordinarily caused by problems that human beings themselves have created: problems of religious and ethical belief; problems of money and credit and mortgages and trust funds and stock-market fluctuations; problems of man-made custom and etiquette and social organization and law.

Rats can hardly be blamed for not being able to solve problems set for them by Dr. Maier; there are limits to a rat's powers of abstraction. But there are no known limits to the human capacity to abstract and organize and make use of abstractions. Hence, if human beings find problems insoluble because of fixated reactions—if they are frustrated because they can respond in only one way, regardless of context or circumstances, to certain symbolically defined situations—they are functioning at less than full human capacity. They can be said, in Korzybski's suggestive phrase, to be "copying animals" in their reactions. Wendell Johnson summarized this idea aptly when he said, "To a mouse, cheese is cheese; that's why mousetraps work." How do these fixations occur in human beings?

Cultural Lag

A basic reason for such "insoluble" problems in society is what might be called "institutional inertia." An "institution," as the word is used in sociology, is "an organized pattern of group behavior, well-established and accepted as a fundamental part of a culture" *(American College*

---

of Fear (1960), the Russian government has claimed a 100-megaton bomb! At the meeting of the American Association for the Advancement of Science in December 1960, Dr. Ralph E. Lapp estimated that the United States had then a bomb stockpile equal to 50,000 bombs of the Hiroshima type, and that in another three years would add the equivalent of another 30,000 Hiroshima-type bombs. All this means, of course, that the U.S.S.R. is also stockpiling atomic and thermonuclear weapons at as nearly as possible the same rate.

Dictionary). Human beings are so constituted that they inevitably organize their energies and activities into patterns of behavior more or less uniform throughout a social group. People who are identified with institutions therefore have their own way of looking at things: people in a communist (or capitalist) society accept and perpetuate communist (or capitalist) habits of economic behavior; the soldier looks at the world through a soldier's eyes and abstracts from it what a soldier has been trained to abstract; the banker and the union official and the stockbroker similarly abstract in accordance with their special training. And through long habituation to a professional or institutional way of looking at the world, each tends to believe that his abstractions of reality—his maps of the territory—*are* reality: defense *is* defense; deficit *is* deficit; a scab *is* a scab; a blue-chip *is* a blue-chip.

Hence we have the peculiar fact that, once people become accustomed to institutions, they eventually get to feeling that their particular institutions represent the *only right and proper* way of doing things. The institution of human slavery, like the caste system in India, was claimed by its defenders to be "divinely ordained," and attacks upon the institution were regarded as attacks upon natural law, reason, and the will of God. Those who had contrary institutions, on the other hand, regarded their system of free labor as "divinely ordained," and slavery as contrary to natural law, reason, and the will of God. In a similar way today, those who believe in corporate capitalist enterprise regard their way of organizing the distribution of goods as the *only proper way;* while communists adhere to their way with the same passionate conviction. This loyalty to one's own institutions is understandable: almost everyone in any culture feels that his institutions are the very foundations of reasonable living. A challenge to those institutions is almost inevitably felt to be a threat to *all* orderly existence.

Consequently, social institutions tend to change slowly, and—most importantly—they tend to continue to exist long after the necessity for their existence has disappeared, and sometimes even when their continued existence becomes a nuisance and a danger. This is not to say, of course, that *all* contemporary institutions are obsolete. Many institutions are changing rapidly enough to keep up with changes in conditions. Many, however, are not. The continued existence of obsolete institutional habits and forms (like the systems of county government in many states of the Union, geographically arranged to suit the needs of a horse-drawn population) is called by sociologists "cultural lag." In everyday language, "cultural lag" is summed up in a peculiarly appropriate expression, "horse-and-buggy" ways.

The Fear of Change

The pressing problems of our world are then problems of cultural lag—problems arising from trying to organize a jet-propelled, supersonic, electronic, and atomic world with horse-and-buggy institutions. The rate of technological advancement for almost two hundred years now has been greater than the rate of the change of our social institutions and their accompanying loyalties and ideologies; and the disparity between the two rates is increasing rather than decreasing. Consequently, in every contemporary culture which has felt the impact of technology, people are questioning the appropriateness of nineteenth-century (eighteenth-century, medieval, or Stone Age) institutions to twentieth-century conditions. They are progressively more alarmed at the dangers arising from old-fashioned nationalism in a world that has become, technologically, one world; they are increasingly anxious over the possibility of attaining a sane world economic order with the instruments of nineteenth-century capitalism (or of nineteenth-century socialism). Wherever technologies are producing changes not adequately matched by changes in social institutions, there are people under strain and tension.

Some, of course, meet these strains and tensions in the only sensible way possible: they strive to change or abandon outmoded institutions and to bring into being new institutions or newer forms of old institutions. Changes in educational practice, in governmental organization, in the responsibilities of trades unions, in the structure of corporations, in the techniques of librarianship, in the marketing of agricultural commodities, and so on, go on all the time because extensional people are constantly striving to bring institutions into closer relationship with reality. An especially successful example of institutional adaptation is the Federal Deposit Insurance Corporation. Prior to 1934, bank failures resulted in the partial or total loss of the savings of depositors; panics, once started, were almost impossible to control. Since the setting up of FDIC, however, panics have disappeared. Bank failures are extremely rare, and even when they occur, depositors do not lose their money. American people now take the stability of their banks for granted, with a serenity that could hardly have been imagined before 1934. A more recent example of successful institutional adaptation in response to new problems is the Peace Corps—an ingenious combination of elements drawn from the military, the Civilian Conservation Corps of Depression days, the Salvation Army, and the missionary organizations of Christian churches. The Common Market is a triumphant example in Europe of what can be done by extensionally minded people when they are really determined to modify ancient social institutions and practices in favor of a more workable economic order.

Some people, however, seeing the need for changes, agitate for cures which, on examination, appear to be no better than the ailment; still others agitate for changes that cannot possibly be brought about. In some of the most important areas of human life—especially in our ideas about international relations and in the closely related problem of an equitable world economic order—areas in which our failure to find solutions threatens the future of civilization itself—we are, all over the world, in a state of cultural lag.

What causes this cultural lag? In the case of many groups, the cause is obviously ignorance. Some people manifestly don't know the score, so far as the realities of the modern world are concerned. Their "maps" represent "territories" that have long since passed out of existence. In other cases, the lag is due to fixed economic or political interests. Many individuals enjoy power and prestige within the framework of outmoded institutions—and with institutional inertia to support them, it is not hard for them to believe that their familiar institutions are beautiful and wonderful things. Indeed, there is little doubt that the desire of the wealthy and powerful to keep their wealth and power is a major reason for cultural lag in any society. Threatened with social change, they often act in such narrowly short-sighted and selfish ways that, like the Bourbons, they seem willing to destroy both the civilization they live in and themselves in grim, pigheaded attempts to hang on to their prerogatives.

But wealth and power are not in themselves guarantees either of social irresponsibility or of stupidity, and the existence of a powerful wealthy class in a culture is not in itself a guarantee that there will be cultural lag. At least some of the rich and powerful have known how to yield gracefully to institutional adjustments—sometimes they have even helped to introduce them—and by so doing they have maintained their favored position and have saved both society and themselves from the disasters that attend complete social disruption. When this happens, cultural lag is kept small enough to be manageable. In some Latin American countries today, there is a touch-and-go race going on between social reform and revolution, the outcome depending largely on the willingness of the privileged class to accept and adjust to change.

But even when the rich and powerful are shortsighted and irresponsible, they must have support among those who are neither rich nor powerful in order to be able to hold back necessary institutional adjustments. To comprehend cultural lag, then, we must account not only for the shortsightedness of the powerful but also for the shortsightedness of the ordinary citizen who supports policies that are contrary to his own interests. In addition to institutional inertia (which is a tremendous force for keeping people busy doing things they should have stopped doing long ago), it appears that fear is another major force influencing both rulers and the ruled in the direction of institutional rigidity. Perhaps the ultimate strength of cultural lag comes from those persons in all walks of life whom change has made afraid.

The Revision of Group Habits

Whether the cultural lag arises from inertia, from shortsighted selfishness, from fear of change, or from a combination of these and other reasons, it is clear that the solution of social problems is basically a matter of adapting institutional habits to new conditions.

Perhaps the most dramatic thing about human behavior is how many problems which are "insoluble" for institutional reasons are promptly solved the moment a war breaks out. War is an institution the demands of which, at least in modern culture, take precedence over almost all other demands. Before World War II, it would have been "impossible" to send the slum children of London to the country for the sake of their health. But when the air raids on London began, the evacuation of all the children took place over a weekend. Institutionally minded men, before the war, demonstrated time and again that it was "impossible" for either Germany or Japan to fight without an adequate gold supply. Nevertheless, Germany and Japan did manage to put up quite a fight in spite of the predictions of extremely reputable editorialists and economists. At Sydenham, England, and at Biarritz, France, the American government put together, almost overnight after the war closed, two great universities for GI's in Europe. Textbooks and equipment were flown over, luxurious quarters were provided for the thousands of students, and distinguished professors from the leading universities of America were hired at handsome salaries in order to provide, for a very short time, an educational Utopia for war-wearied American soldiers. In ordinary times, is there any conceivable way in which a similar university could be set up, say, in Mississippi, the state which, since it has the least per capita to spend on education, would be in greatest need of such a school? One of the lessons of war is that institutions, while powerful and long-lasting, are often not insuperably rigid *if the emergency is great enough.*

The problem, then, the world over, is to learn that the emergency is serious enough—in international affairs, in race relations, in the world population explosion, and in many other areas—to require modifying or abandoning some of our institutions. And the problem for us as citizens, once we understand the emergency, is how we can contrive ways of adjusting our thinking and acting so that institutional adjustments may be made both realistically and rapidly, with a minimum of human suffering and a maximum of general benefit.

The Extensional Approach

Every widely debated public issue—proposed changes in labor laws, proposed changes in the methods of distributing medical care, proposals for unifying the armed services under a single command, proposals to set up new ways of settling disputes between nations—is, then, a discussion of institutional adaptation. If we persist in discussing our social problems in terms of "justice" *versus* "injustice," "natural law, reason, and the will of God" *versus* "the forces of anarchy and chaos," reactions of fear and anger become general on both sides—and fear and anger paralyze the mind and make intelligent decision impossible. The escape from this two-valued debate lies in thinking about social problems as problems of institutional adaptation. Once we begin to do so, our questions with respect to hotly debated social issues begin automatically to become more extensional. We cease to ask whether a proposed institutional change is "right" or "wrong," "progressive" or "reactionary." We begin to ask instead, "What will be the results? Who would benefit, and by how much? Who would be harmed, and to what degree? What safeguards does the proposal contain to prevent further harm? Are people actually ready for such a measure? What will be the effect on prices, on the labor supply, on public health, or whatever? And who says so, on the basis of what kind of research and what kind of expert knowledge?" From extensional answers to such extensionally directed questions, decisions begin to flow. The decisions that flow from extensional information are neither "left-wing" nor "right-wing." They are simply the sensible things to do under the circumstances.

Here, let us say, is a proposed municipal ordinance to permit trucks to pass over Oak Street bridge. Backing the measure are the trucklines, which will save much time and money if the measure is passed. If our discussion of the proposal is reasonably extensional, our questions about it will be of the following kind: "Will the bridge structure stand the additional load? What will be the effect on traffic flow on Oak Street and streets approaching it? Is there danger of an increase in street accidents? Will the beauty of the city be adversely affected? What will be the effect on residences or businesses on and near Oak Street?" When such questions have been answered by persons of known ability in making accurate predictions in their several fields of knowledge, every voter has the materials with which to decide the question for himself according to his own interests and values, whether he is concerned with the safety of his children walking to school, with the beauty of the city, with trucking profits, with the effect on the tax rate, or whatever. Each voter's decision, made against a background of responsibly made predictions, will have some kind of reasonable relationship to his real desires.

Let us further suppose, however, that the measure is advantageous to practically no one in town *except* the trucklines. Then, if the trucklines want the measure passed, they may try to *prevent* the public from discussing the issue extensionally. The technique (familiar in the discussion of legislation affecting railroads, insurance, housing, medical care, and so on) is immediately to move the discussion to higher levels of abstraction and to talk about "unreasonable restraints on business," and the need to protect "free enterprise" and "the American way" against harassment by "politicians," "officeholders," and "petty bureaucrats." By systematic confusion of levels of abstraction, the "freedom" of trucklines to operate over Oak Street bridge is made to appear one with the freedom fought and bled for at Valley Forge.

The tragedy is not only that many of us are innocent enough to be deceived by this sort of talk; a deeper tragedy is that in many communities the newspapers provide us with almost no extensional materials for discussion. Partly because many newspapers have largely given up their news function in favor of entertainment, and partly because the sensational, two-valued utterances of extreme partisans make livelier stories than the testimony of extensionally minded experts, newspapers in some communities are scanty sources of information on important public issues.[3] And television, often governed by the whims of sponsors who are quick to cancel a news commentator's contract at the first hint of controversy, is often as empty of extensional content as the newspapers are.

Then, under present circumstances, the tenor of discussion (and therefore of public opinion) being what it is, what are the chances for institutional adaptation with respect to some of our most pressing problems? The replacement of maladjustments by new maladjustments and the continuation of old maladjustments under new names are about as near as we can get to correcting cultural lag.

The End of the Road

When, as the result of protracted debate of a futile kind, years pass without the successful accomplishment of institutional adjustments, cultural lag widens. As social dislocations grow more serious, fear and confusion spread. As fear and confusion spread, societies, like individuals, grow increasingly disturbed at their failure to solve their problems. Lacking the knowledge or the confidence to try new patterns of behavior and at the same time panicky with the knowledge that their traditional methods no longer work, societies often appear to behave, to a greater or lesser degree, like Dr. Maier's rats, who, "induced to respond in the insoluble problem situation, settle down to a specific reaction which they continue to make regardless of circumstances. . . . The response under these conditions becomes fixated. . . . Once the fixation appears, the animal is incapable of learning an adaptive response in this situation." Thus do societies, as they have so often done in the past and continue to do today, fixate on *one* solution to their most pressing problem: the *only* way to appease the angry gods is to throw *still more* babies to the crocodiles; the *only* way to protect the social order is to detect and hunt down *still more* witches; the *only* way to ensure prosperity is to reduce

[3]See Lester Markel, "The Real Sins of the Press," *Harper's* (December 1962).

federal expenditures; and the *only* way to insure peace is to have *still greater* armaments. (The last two beliefs are, of course, held simultaneously.)

Such are the mental blockages—such are the patterns of repetitious behavior—that prevent us from meeting our "insoluble" problems with the only approach which can ever help us solve them: the extensional approach—for we cannot distribute goods, feed people, or establish cooperation with our neighbors by intensional definitions and high-level abstractions. What is done in the extensional world must be done by extensional means, no matter who does it. If we as citizens of a democracy are going to carry our share in the important decisions about the things that concern us so greatly, such as the problems of peace and a just world economic order, we must prepare ourselves to do so by coming down out of the clouds of high-level abstractions and learning to consider the problems of the world, whether at local, state, national, or international levels, as extensionally as we now consider the problems of getting food, clothing, and shelter.

If, however, we cling to our fixations and our intensional orientations, and the belligerent, two-valued sense of "I am right and you are wrong" which they produce, we have little before us but a fate similar to that of Dr. Maier's rat. We shall remain pathologically incapable of changing our ways of behavior, and there will be nothing for us to do but, like the rat, to try the same wrong solutions over and over again. After prolonged repetition of such futile conduct, would it be remarkable if we found ourselves finally in a condition of political "nervous breakdown" —sick of trying, disillusioned with the processes of democracy, and willing to permit dictators to dangle us upside down by our tails?

The Scientific Attitude

The most striking characteristic of science has been its continued success in the solving of "insoluble" problems. It was once considered "impossible" to devise means of traveling over twenty miles an hour, but now we have attained speeds of over 18,000 miles an hour. It was "impossible" for man to fly—people "proved" it again and again—but now we fly across oceans as a matter of everyday routine. I was told repeatedly during the course of my education that the release of atomic energy was merely a *theoretical* possibility—of course, they would never actually *do* it. The scientist may almost be called the professional accomplisher of the "impossible." He does this because, as a scientist, he is extensionally oriented. He may be, and often is, intensionally oriented toward what he calls "nonscientific" subjects; therefore, the physical scientist talking about social or political problems or about love and marriage is often no more sensible than the rest of us.

As we have seen, scientists have special ways of talking about the phenomena they deal with, special "maps" to describe the "territories" with which they are concerned. On the basis of these maps, they make predictions; when things turn out as predicted, they regard their maps as "true." If, however, things do not turn out as predicted, they *discard* their maps and make new ones; that is, they act on *new sets of hypotheses* that suggest *new courses of action.*[4] Again they check their map with the territory. If the new one does not check, they cheerfully discard it and make still more hypotheses, until they find some that *work.* These they regard as "true," but "true" *only for the time being.* When, later on, they find new situations in which the "working" hypotheses no longer work, they are again ready to discard them, to reexamine the extensional world, and to make still more new maps that again suggest new courses of action.

When scientists work with a minimum of interference from financial or political influences—when, that is, they are free to pool their knowledge with their co-workers all over the world and to check the accuracy of one another's maps by observations independently made and freely exchanged—they make rapid progress. Highly multi-valued and extensional in their orientations, they are troubled less than other men by fixed dogmas and non-sense questions. In a way that is paradoxical in terms of traditional orientations but quite understandable in terms of the new, the conversations and writings of scientific people are full of admissions of ignorance and declarations of partial knowledge. Expressions like the following appear with impressive frequency in the conversation of nuclear physicists with whom the writer has been acquainted: "According to Henderson's last paper—although there may be still later findings not yet published. . . ." "No one knows exactly what happens, but our guess is that it's something like this. . . ." "What I tell you is probably wrong, but it's the only plausible theory we've been able to construct. . . ." It has been said that knowledge is power, but *effective knowledge is that which includes knowledge of the limitations of one's knowledge.*

The last thing a scientist would do is cling to a map because he inherited it from his grandfather or because it was used by George Washington or Abraham Lincoln. By intensional orientation, "If it was good enough for Washington and Lincoln, it's good enough for me." By extensional orientation, *we don't know until we have checked.*

The Left-Hand Door Again

Notice the differences between the technological, scientific attitudes that we have toward some things and the intensional attitudes we have

[4]Alfred North Whitehead, in *Science and the Modern World,* says that it is not unusual for a scientist to *rejoice* when he is proved wrong; that all human progress has depended on "new questions" rather than on "new answers" to the "old questions."

toward others. When we are having a car repaired, we think in terms of mechanisms. We do not ask: "Is the remedy you suggest consistent with the principles of thermodynamics? What would Faraday or Newton have done under similar circumstances? Are you sure that the remedy you suggest does not represent a degenerative, defeatist tendency in the technological traditions of our nation? What would happen if we did this to *every* car? What has Aristotle to say on this?" These are nonsense questions. We only ask, "What will be the *results?*"

But a different thing happens when we are trying to have society repaired. Few people have a sense of societies as mechanisms—as collections of going institutions. Accustomed to thinking of social problems in terms of simple moral indignation, we denounce the wickedness of labor unions (or of capitalists), we denounce the wickedness of those who clamor for Negro rights (or of those who persecute Negroes), we denounce Russia (or, if we are Russians, we denounce "American imperialism"). In so doing, we miss entirely the basic requirement of "mapping" social problems, namely, the initial task of describing the *established patterns of group behavior* (i.e., the institutions) that constitute a society and create its social problems. Indignant at the wickedness of those with whom we disagree, we do not ask of a proposed institutional change what the results will be. We are usually more interested in "punishing the wicked" than in determining the results. And suggested social remedies are almost always discussed in the light of questions to which verifiable answers cannot be given: "Are your proposals consistent with sound economic policy? Do they accord with the principles of true liberalism (or true conservatism)? What would Alexander Hamilton, Thomas Jefferson, or Abraham Lincoln have said? Would it be a step in the direction of communism or fascism? What would happen if everybody followed your scheme? Why don't you read Aristotle?" And we spend so much time discussing non-sense questions that often we never get around to finding out exactly what the results of proposed actions would be.

During the course of our weary struggles with such non-sense questions, someone or other is sure to come along with a campaign to tell us, "Let's get *back* to normalcy. . . . Let's stick to the good *old-fashioned, tried-and-true* principles. . . . Let's *return* to *sound* economics and *sound* finance. . . . America must get *back* to this. . . . America must get *back* to that. . . ." Most of such appeals are, of course, merely invitations to take another jump at the left-hand door—in other words, INVITATIONS TO CONTINUE DRIVING OURSELVES CRAZY. In our confusion we accept those invitations—with the same old results.

APPLICATIONS

I. List the most serious examples of cultural lag to be found in your community, or in another community with which you are familiar.

How would an extensionally oriented person ask questions that would be useful in helping to solve some of the problems created by cultural lag? Where can you get information and assistance in answering these questions?*

II. Discuss the following passage with reference to this question—What similarities do you find between General Semantics and Pragmatism?

> A conviction that consequences in human welfare are a test of the worth of beliefs and thoughts has some obvious beneficial aspects. It makes for a fusion of the two superlatively important qualities, love of truth and love of neighbor. It discourages dogmatism and its child, intolerance. It arouses and heartens an experimental spirit which wants to know how systems and theories work before giving complete adhesion. It militates against too sweeping and easy generalizations, even against those which would indict a nation. Compelling attention to details, to particulars, it safeguards one from seclusion in universals; one is obliged, as William James was always saying, to get down from noble aloofness into the muddy stream of concrete things. It fosters a sense of the worth of communication of what is known. This takes effect not only in education, but in a belief that we do not fully know the meaning of anything till it has been imparted, shared, made common property.
>
> JOHN DEWEY, *New Republic*

III. Two friends of yours, both strongly opinionated but not at all well informed, one vigorously in favor of and the other vigorously opposed to "socialized medicine" (whatever either of them might mean by the term), are coming to your house tonight to spend the evening in conversation. Prepare some remarks you can throw into the discussion and some questions you can ask that might help make them see the problem of medical-care distribution as a problem of institutional adjustment (of course, you will avoid using such fancy terms) and that might therefore help them keep the discussion at more extensional levels than would otherwise be the case. Warning: Do not start out by making them define "socialized medicine" (see pp. 155–59).

IV. Resistance to and fear of change are, of course, not the only human forces operative in "cultural lag." Sometimes people undergo a good deal of intellectual and spiritual transformation, but for the wrong reasons or goals. Consider, for example, the following passage from Kurt Vonnegut's novel, *God Bless You, Mr. Rosewater*. A psychiatrist is attempting to define the territory of a map describing

*The term "cultural lag" was popularized by William Fielding Ogburn, a sociologist, who wrote "The thesis is that the various parts of modern culture are not changing at the same rate, some parts are changing much more rapidly than others; and that since there is a correlation and interdependence of parts, a rapid change in one part of our culture requires readjustments through other changes in the various correlated parts of culture." *Social Change*, 1922.

what he calls "samaritrophia," which is "a hysterical indifference to the problems of those less fortunate than oneself." Does the psychiatrist's map correspond to the territory? What, for example, is meant by "mental processes"? Do people generally undergo such a revolution of the mind?

> Samaritrophia . . . is the suppression of an overactive conscience by the rest of the mind. "You must all take instructions from me!" the conscience shrieks, in effect, to all the other mental processes. The other processes try it for a while, note that the conscience is unappeased, that it continues to shriek, and they note, too, that the outside world has not been even microscopically improved by the unselfish acts the conscience has demanded.
>
> They rebel at last. They pitch the tyrannous conscience down an oubliette, weld shut the manhole cover of that dark dungeon. They can hear the conscience no more. In the sweet silence, the mental processes look about for a new leader, and the leader most prompt to appear whenever the conscience is stilled, Enlightened Self-interest, *does* appear. Enlightened Self-interest gives them a flag, which they adore on sight. It is essentially the black and white Jolly Roger, with these words written beneath the skull and crossbones, "The hell with you, Jack, I've got mine!"

V. Read, ponder, and digest:

Triolet

TO AN INDOLENT STUDENT
IN A CLASS IN GENERAL SEMANTICS

To a mouse, cheese is cheese; that's why mousetraps work.

Wendell Johnson, *People in Quandaries*

To a rodent, cheese is cheese;
  That's why mousetraps work.
No date or index, if you please,
To a rodent, cheese *is* cheese
Without semantic subtleties
  (Listen, you mouse-brained jerk!).
To a rodent, cheese is cheese;
  That's why mousetraps. (Work!)

S. I. HAYAKAWA

VI. Comment on the following passage by Norbert Wiener, himself a brilliant scientist, in the light of what you have read in this chapter concerning scientists and the scientific attitude:

> The scientist is thus disposed to regard his opponent [nature] as an honorable enemy. This attitude is necessary for his effectiveness as a scientist, but tends to make him the dupe of unprincipled people in war and in politics. It also has the effect of making it hard for the general public to understand him, for the general public is much more concerned with personal antagonists than with nature as an antagonist.
>
> NORBERT WIENER, *The Human Use of Human Beings*

VII. Discuss the following passage in relation to the ideas about fear of change. Do the Durants' ideas conflict with or supplement the belief in cooperation expressed in Chapter 1 of this book?

> So the conservative who resists change is as valuable as the radical who proposes it—perhaps as much more valuable as roots are more vital than grafts. It is good that new ideas should be heard, for the sake of the few that can be used; but it is also good that new ideas should be compelled to go through the mill of objection, opposition, and contumely; this is the trial heat which innovations must survive before being allowed to enter the human race. It is good that the old should resist the young, and that the young should prod the old.
>
> WILL and ARIEL DURANT, *The Lessons of History*

> *But I say unto you, That every idle word that men shall speak, they shall give account thereof in the day of judgment. For by thy words thou shalt be justified, and by thy words thou shalt be condemned.*
>
> Matthew 12:36–37

toward order within and without

Rules for Extensional Orientation

Just as a mechanic carries around a pair of pliers and a screw driver for use in an emergency—just as we all carry around in our heads tables of multiplication for daily use—so can we all carry in our heads convenient rules for extensional orientation. These rules need not be complicated; a short, rough-and-ready set of formulas will do. Their principal function will be to prevent us from going round in circles of intensional thinking, to prevent automatic reactions, to prevent us from trying to answer unanswerable questions, to prevent us from repeating old mistakes endlessly. They will *not* magically show us what better solutions are possible, but they will *start us looking* for courses of action that are better than the old ones. The following rules, then, are a brief summary of the parts of the book that directly apply to problems of evaluation. These rules should be memorized.

1. A map is NOT the territory it stands for; words are NOT things.

   A map does not represent ALL of a territory; words never say ALL about anything.

   Maps of maps, maps of maps of maps, and so on, can be made indefinitely, with or without relationship to a territory. (Chapters 2 and 10.)

2. The meanings of words are NOT in the words; they are in US. (Chapters 2 and 11.)

3. Contexts determine meaning (Chapter 4):

I like fish. (Cooked, edible fish.)
He caught a fish. (Live fish.)
You poor fish! (Not fish at all.)
To fish for compliments. (To seek.)

4. Beware of the word "is," which, when not used simply as an auxiliary verb ("he is coming"), can crystallize misevaluations:

The grass *is* green. (But what about the part our nervous system plays? Chapters 10 and 11.)
Mr. Miller *is* a Jew. (Beware of confusing levels of abstraction. Chapters 11 and 12.)
Business *is* business. (This is a directive, not to be mistaken for a statement of fact. Chapter 7.)
A thing *is* what it *is*. (Unless this is understood as a rule of language, there is danger of ignoring alternative ways of classifying, as well as of ignoring the fact that everything is in a process of change. Chapters 10, 12, 13, and 17.)

5. Don't try to cross bridges that aren't built yet. Distinguish between directive and informative statements. (Chapter 7.)

6. Distinguish at least four senses of the word "true":

Some mushrooms are poisonous. (If we call this "true," we mean that it is a *report that can be and has been verified*. Chapter 3.)
Sally is the sweetest girl in the world. (If we call this "true," we mean that *we feel the same way* toward Sally. Chapters 5 and 8.)
All men are created equal. (If we call this "true," we mean that this is a *directive which we believe should be obeyed*. Chapter 7.)
$(x + y)^2 = x^2 + 2xy + y^2$. (If we call this "true," we mean that this statement is *consistent with the system of statements possible to be made in the language called algebra*. Chapter 14.)

7. When tempted to "fight fire with fire," remember that the fire department usually uses water. (Chapter 14.)

8. The two-valued orientation is the *starter, not the steering apparatus*. (Chapter 14.)

9. Beware of definitions, which are words about words. Think with examples rather than definitions wherever possible. (Chapter 10.)

10. Use *index numbers* and *dates* as reminders that *no word ever has exactly the same meaning twice*.

Cow_1 *is not* cow_2, cow_2 *is not* cow_3, . . .
Smith_{1963} is *not* Smith_{1964}, Smith_{1965} is *not* Smith_{1972}, . . .

If these rules are too much to remember, the reader is asked to memorize *at least* this much:

Cow_1 is not cow_2, cow_2 is not cow_3, . . .

This is the simplest and most general of the rules for extensional orientation. The word "cow" gives us the intensional meanings, informative and affective; it calls up in our minds the features that this "cow" has *in common* with other "cows." The index number, however, reminds us that this one is *different;* it reminds us that "cow" does *not* tell us "all about" the event; it reminds us of the *characteristics left out* in the process of abstracting; it prevents us from equating the word with the thing, that is, from confusing the abstraction "cow" with the extensional cow.

Symptoms of Disorder

Not to observe, consciously or unconsciously, such principles of interpretation is to think and react in primitive and infantile ways. There are a number of ways in which we can detect unhealthy reactions in ourselves. One of the most obvious symptoms is sudden displays of temper. When blood pressure rises, when quarrels become excited and feverish, and when arguments end up in snarling and name-calling, there is a misevaluation somewhere in the background.

Another obvious symptom is worry—when we keep going round and round in circles. "I love her. . . . I love her. . . . If I could only forget that she is a *waitress!*" But waitress$_1$ is not waitress$_2$. "Gosh, what a terrible governor we've got! . . . We thought he was a businessman, but he proves to be only a *politician.*" But politician$_1$ is not politician$_2$. As soon as we break these circles and think about *facts* instead of *words,* new light is thrown on our problems.

Still another symptom of unhealthy reactions is a tendency to be oversensitive, easily hurt, and quick to resent insults. The immature mind, equating words with things, regards unkind words as unkind acts. Attributing to harmless sets of noises a power of injuring, such a person is "insulted" when those noises are uttered at him. So-called "gentlemen" in semisavage and infantile societies used to dignify reactions of this kind into "codes of honor." By "honor," they meant extreme readiness to pull out swords or pistols whenever they imagined that they had been "insulted." Naturally, they killed each other off much faster than was necessary, illustrating again a principle often implied in this book: the lower the boiling point, the higher the mortality rate.

It has already been pointed out that the tendency to talk too much and too readily is an unhealthy sign. We should also be wary of "thinking too much." It is a mistake to believe that productive thinkers necessarily "think harder" than people who never get anywhere. They only think more efficiently. "Thinking too much" often means that somewhere in the back of our minds there is a "certainty"—an "incontrovertible fact," an "unalterable law," an "eternal principle"—some statement which we believe "says all" about something. Life, however, is constantly throwing into the face of our "incontrovertible certainties" facts that do not fit our preconceptions: "politicians" who *aren't* corrupt, "friends" who *aren't* faithful, "benevolent societies" that *aren't* benevolent. Refusing to give up our sense of "certainty" and yet unable to deny the facts that do not fit, we are forced to "think and think and think." And, as we have seen before, there are only two ways out of such dilemmas: first, to deny the facts altogether, and secondly, to reverse the principle altogether, so that we go from "*All* insurance companies are reliable" to "*No* insurance companies are reliable." Hence such infantile reactions as, "I'll *never* trust another woman!" "Don't *ever* say politics to me again!" "I'm through with lawyers for good!" "Men are *all* alike, the heels!"

The mature mind, on the other hand, knows that words never say all about anything, and such a mind is therefore *adjusted to uncertainty.* In driving a car, for example, we never know what is going to happen next; no matter how often we have gone over the same road, we never find *exactly* the same traffic conditions. Nevertheless, a competent driver travels over all kinds of roads, even at high speeds, without either fear or nervousness. As driver, he is *adjusted to uncertainty*—the unexpected blowout or the sudden hazard—and *he does not feel insecure.*

Similarly, the intellectually mature person does not "know all about" anything. And this does not make him insecure, because he knows that the only kind of security life offers is the *dynamic security that comes from within: the security derived from infinite flexibility of mind—from an infinite-valued orientation.*

"Knowing all" about this, "knowing all" about that, we have only ourselves to blame when we find certain problems "insoluble." With some working knowledge of how language acts, in ourselves and others, we save both time and effort; we prevent ourselves from running around in verbal squirrel cages. With an extensional orientation, we are adjusted to the inevitable uncertainties of all our science and wisdom. And whatever other problems the world thrusts upon us, we at least escape those of our own making.

The Lost Children

Then there are the unhappy people who *don't* know "all about this" or "all about that," and *wish they did.* Being in a more or less chronic state of anxiety about not knowing all the answers, they are always looking for "the answer" that will forever still their anxieties. They drift from one church, political party, or "new thought" movement to another; they may drift from one psychiatrist to another if they are educated, or from one fortuneteller to another if they are not. Occasionally such people happen upon fortunetellers, political leaders, or systems of thought that hit them just right. Thereupon they are suddenly overwhelmed with relief and joy. Feeling that they have found *the* answer to all their problems, they become passionately devoted to spreading the news to everyone they know.

A major source both of the excessive anxiety which such people feel and of their excessive enthusiasm when they do find their problems "solved" has been described by psychiatrists. An adult—an emotionally mature person—is independent, able to work out his own answers to problems, and able to realize that there is no one answer to everything. If, however, we have not been brought up to be independent—if, for example, we were deprived of love and care at an age when we needed love and care, or if we had parents who did too much for us through excessive and misdirected love—we grow up physically mature but emotionally immature. No matter what our age, we continue to need a *parent-symbol:* some figure of comforting authority to whom we can turn for "all the answers." If we are so troubled, we will successively seek one parent-symbol after another, when we can no longer depend on our own parents—sometimes a kindly teacher, sometimes an authoritative and impressive clergyman, sometimes a fatherly employer, sometimes a political leader.

From our point of view as students of human linguistic behavior, the verbal aspects of this search for a parent-symbol deserve attention. Those who, for one reason or another, are unable to accept a priest, teacher, or political leader as a parent-symbol, may find a parent-symbol in a *big, systematic collection of words*—for example, a huge and difficult-to-understand philosophical work, a politico-economic philosophy, a system of "new thought," or the Hundred Great Books. "Here, here," they cry, "are all the answers in one place!" Finding "all the answers" in such collections of words is a sophisticated and, in our culture, a respectable form of both emotional immaturity and what we have earlier called naiveté regarding the symbolic process. It is emotional immaturity because it involves the giving up of independent thought in favor of dependence on a (verbal) parent-symbol. It is nevertheless respectable, because those who manifest their immaturity in this way acquire, in doing so, an impressively complicated and abstract vocabulary which they exhibit on all possible occasions—and our culture respects the fluent talker, especially one who talks at high levels of abstraction. This dependence on verbal parent-symbols is also naive because it assumes what we have already seen to be an impossible assumption, namely, that a verbal "map" can "say all" about the "territory" of experience.

This is not to say, of course, that an enthusiasm for a "great book," or for a hundred of them, is necessarily a symptom of immaturity. However, there is a world of difference between the enthusiasm of the emotionally immature and that of the mature. An immature person, discovering a new intellectual system or philosophy that somehow meets his needs, tends to adopt it uncritically, to repeat endlessly the verbal formulas with which he has been provided, and *to resent any imputation that anything more needs to be discovered.* The mature reader, on the other hand, pleased and excited as he may be by the "great book" he has found, is *eager to test it.* Are these new and exciting principles or human insights as general as they appear to be? Are they true in many different cultural or historical contexts? Do they need correction or revision or refinement? How do the principles or attitudes apply in specific cases and under different conditions? As he asks himself these and other questions, he may find that his newly discovered system is quite as important as he originally thought it to be, but, along with his increased sense of power, he also gets a deep sense of *how much more there is to be learned.*

Indeed, the better and more widely useful a new philosophical or scientific synthesis is, the greater will be the number of fresh problems raised. The answers given to perplexing questions by Darwin in his *Origin of Species* did not stop biological inquiry; they gave biology the greatest spurt to fresh inquiry in modern times. The answers given by Freud to psychological questions did not stop psychology; they opened up whole new areas of investigation.[1] "Great books" are those which open great new questions. Great books are misread if their effect is to stop investigation.

In other words, the wiser people become, whether in science, religion, politics, or art, the less dogmatic they become. Apparently, the better we know the territory of human experience, the more aware we are of the limitations of the verbal maps we can make of it. We have earlier (Chapter 11) called this awareness of the limitations of maps "consciousness of abstracting." The mature person retains "consciousness of abstracting" even with respect to philosophies or systems of thought about which he feels the greatest enthusiasm.

"Know Thyself"

Another area in which "consciousness of abstracting" is necessary is in *what we say to ourselves about ourselves.* We are all a great deal more complex than Bessie the Cow, and even more than Bessie, we are constantly undergoing change. Furthermore, we all describe ourselves to ourselves in some kind of language (or other abstractions, like "mental pictures," "idealizations," or "images"). These descriptions of ourselves are more or less clearly formulated: "I am the home-loving type," "I am beautiful," "I am hopelessly unattractive," "I believe in efficiency," "I am kind-hearted," "I can't understand mathematics," "I have a natural talent for music," "I'm not that kind of a girl," "I am not a snob," "I am a friend of the downtrodden," and so on. All such statements are *more or*

[1]The communist use of the writings of Marx appears to me to be a misreading of books which were in their time important contributions to social science. The communists have treated all deviations from Marx (or at least deviations from their interpretations of Marx) as attacks upon "Truth," and they seem thereby to have rendered the process of social science in the Soviet Union almost impossible. See Anatol Rapoport, "Dialectical Materialism and General Semantics," *ETC.*, V (1948), pp. 81–104.

less accurate "maps" of that "territory" which is ourselves. Some people make better maps of themselves than others. If a person makes a reasonably good map of himself, we say that he "knows himself"—that he accurately assesses his strengths and his limitations, his emotional powers and his emotional needs. The psychologist Carl R. Rogers refers to this "map" we make of ourselves as the "self-concept," which, according to his terminology, may be "realistic" or "unrealistic." What we do, how we dress, what manners or mannerisms we affect, what tasks we undertake and what tasks we decline, what kind of society we seek, and so on, are determined not so much by our *actual* powers and limitations as by what we *believe to be* our powers and limitations—i.e., by our "self-concepts."[2]

All that has previously been said in this book about maps and territories applies with special relevance to our "self-concepts." A map *is not* the territory: one's self-concept *is not* one's self. A map represents *not all* of the territory: one's self-concept *omits* an enormous amount of one's actual self—we never know ourselves *completely*. We can make maps of maps of maps, and so on: we can describe ourselves to ourselves, and then make about ourselves *any number of inferences and generalizations at higher levels of abstraction.*

The pitfalls of map-territory relationships therefore threaten the adequacy of our evaluations of ourselves just as much as they threaten the adequacy of our evaluations of other people and of external events. Indeed, as is suggested in the famous Socratic injunction, "Know thyself," it is more than probable that our wisdom in evaluating other people and external events rests largely upon our wisdom in evaluating ourselves. What kinds of "maps," then, do we make of ourselves?

Some people obviously have extremely unrealistic self-concepts. The person who says, "I have the ability to act as general manager" and accepts such a job, and then turns out not to have the ability, seriously disappoints himself and others. If another person says, "I'm not any good" and takes himself seriously when he says this, he may dissipate his talents, his opportunities, his entire life. The not uncommon sight of the middle-aged woman who dresses and acts like an eighteen-year-old is another instance of a person who lives in terms of an extremely *unrealistic* self-concept.

Students in school often defeat themselves by saying, "I'm not good at mathematics," or "I just *can't* learn to spell." They will be poor at mathematics or spelling not because of lack of ability, but because their self-concepts prevent them from tackling mathematics and spelling with any hope of victory.

Furthermore, there are those who do not seem to realize that their

[2]See Carl R. Rogers, *Client-Centered Therapy* (1951) and *On Becoming a Person* (1961); also Prescott Lecky, *Self-Consistency: A Theory of Personality* (1945); Gardner Murphy, *Personality: A Biosocial Approach to Origins and Structure* (1947); Donald Snugg and Arthur Combs, *Individual Behavior* (1949).

self-concepts do *not* include *all* the relevant facts about themselves. As psychiatrists have shown us time and again, we all have a way of concealing from others and from ourselves our deeper reasons for doing things; instead, we offer, in justification of our acts, more or less elaborate rationalizations. Let us suppose, for example, that a critic has given as his reason for attacking a book its "shoddy argument and bad prose style." Let us suppose, furthermore, that his deeper reasons are entirely different, reasons such as professional jealousy, fear of the book's upsetting ideas, or a personal quarrel with the author ten years earlier. If the reviewer believes that his self-concept "says all" about himself, his picture of himself as "one who believes in rigorous logic and high standards of prose style" becomes to him a complete and adequate account of why he dislikes the book. In other words, the most common effect of not knowing that one's self-concept does not "say all" about one's self is *the tendency on the part of many people to believe their own rationalizations.* Some persons, indeed, believe their "self-concepts" so completely and sincerely—that is, they surround themselves with such airtight rationalizations—that they become incapable of any genuine self-knowledge.

Self-knowledge, of course, is often disturbing: statements of the kind "My real reason for not liking this book is that I'm jealous of the author," "The reason I am not getting ahead is that I am less intelligent than my colleagues," and so on, are extremely difficult to face if we are emotionally insecure. Therefore, we often *need* to believe our rationalizations: "The book is shoddy in its arguments," "The reason I am not getting ahead is that my colleagues are conspiring against me." If the need to believe in these inaccurate maps is strong enough, we can shut our eyes to any amount of evidence that contradicts them.

How do we prevent ourselves from getting into this emotional predicament? Those who are already in it can probably be helped only by a professionally trained counselor or a psychiatrist. But for the rest of us, there remain the day-to-day problems of action and decision; the more realistic our self-concepts are, the more likelihood there is of fruitful action and sane decision. Can we do anything to achieve a greater realism about ourselves? It is important that we do, because those who cannot be realistic about themselves are as a rule also incapable of being realistic about their relations with other people.

Reports and Judgments

In at least one respect, people who are capable of some degree of self-insight can do for themselves what psychological counselors and many psychiatrists do. As we have seen, we manufacture false self-concepts because truer statements are unbearable. The reason they are unbearable is often that they involve the uncritical acceptance from our environment (from what our friends and neighbors say, or what we think they are saying) of *other people's judgments.* Using the word "judgment" here as we have used it in Chapter 3, notice the difference between "I am a service-station attendant" (which is a report) and "I am *only* a service-station attendant" (which involves a judgment, implying that I ought to be something different and that it is disgraceful that I am what I am).

One of the most important aspects of a psychiatrist's or counselor's assistance is the fact that he *does not pass any judgments on us.* When the patient admits that he is "only" a service-station attendant, or that ten years ago he lost his grocery store through bankruptcy, the counselor indicates by word or by manner that, while he understands the patient's feelings of shame or guilt or embarrassment, he does not condemn him for being what he is or for having done what he has done. In other words, he helps the patient change the *judgment,* "I am *only* a service-station attendant and *therefore not much good,*" into the *report,* "I am a service-station attendant."[3] The judgment, "I am a *bankrupt* and a *failure,*" is changed into "Ten years ago I lost my grocery store through bankruptcy." As a result of the accepting attitude of the psychiatrist or counselor, the patient is better able to accept himself.

The fact that we permit other people's judgments (and what we believe to be their judgments) to influence us unduly is one of the commonest reasons for feelings of inferiority and guilt and insecurity. If a man, saying to himself, "I am a Negro," simultaneously accepts the judgment of certain white people on Negroes, he will find it very hard to be a Negro, and may spend the rest of his life being jumpy and defensive and miserable. If a man makes a hundred dollars a week and accepts the real or imagined judgment of others that if he were any good he would be making two hundred, he will find it difficult to face the fact of making a hundred. The training suggested in Chapter 3 of *writing reports from which judgments are excluded* may be applied to writing *about ourselves.* Such self-descriptions are an especially helpful technique in arriving at more realistic self-concepts.

We should, in performing this exercise, put down facts about ourselves—especially the facts about which we feel some shame or embarrassment—and then ask with respect to each fact such questions as these: "Is it necessary to pass judgment at all on this fact?" "Who passes judgment on this fact, anyway, and should I also do so?" "Are no other judgments possible?" "What does an unfavorable judgment on one of my actions *in the past* prove about what I am *today?*" Reports of the following kind may lead to such reevaluations as are indicated in the parentheses:

> I am a service-station attendant. (Some people think it is somehow inferior to be a service-station attendant. Do *I* have to think so, too?)

[3] I once had a fireman as a student in a graduate class. Several weeks elapsed before he could say in class, "I am a fireman," and contribute to the discussion from his own unique experiences.

> I went through bankruptcy. (But that was ten years ago! I've had a lot more business experience since then. Who knows what will happen if I start again—in a different line of business? in a different location?)
>
> I cracked up on the battlefield. (Who says I shouldn't have cracked up? Were they in South Vietnam? Did they have to go through what I did? I was psychologically wounded in battle; others were physically wounded. Why don't they give Purple Hearts to psychiatric casualties?)
>
> I am a housewife. (Well?)

Naturally, if one's rationalizations are deeply rooted, this technique is difficult to practice. For example:

> My real reason for disliking this book is professional jealousy. (Oh, no! The author's arguments *are* shoddy and his style *is* awful!)

But as we grow increasingly extensional about our own feelings—as we grow in our ability to accept ourselves, so that we are able to confront *without judgments of good or bad* such reports as, "I am below average in height," "I am not athletic," "I am the child of divorced parents," "My sister gets better grades than I do," "I never went to college," and so on—we progressively have less and less need to deceive ourselves. *In self-knowledge as in science, the conquest of little areas leads progressively to the conquest of larger and more difficult areas.* As our self-concepts grow more realistic, our actions and decisions become progressively wiser, since they are based on a more accurate "mapping" of that complex territory of our own personalities.

Institutionalized Attitudes

Another way in which we can increase our extensional awareness of ourselves is by distinguishing between attitudes *institutionally* arrived at and attitudes *extensionally* arrived at. As we have seen in Chapter 17, we are all members of institutions, and as members of institutions we incorporate into ourselves certain institutionally demanded attitudes. If we are Democrats, we are expected to support all Democratic candidates. If we belong to an employers' association, our fellow members may expect us to be hostile to all labor unions. If we are Montagues, we are expected to be hostile to the Capulets.

A source of widespread misevaluation implicit in such institutionalized attitudes is that each of them involves a generalization at a high level of abstraction, while actual Democratic candidates, labor unions, and Capulets exist at the level of extensional fact. Many persons are, through emotional insecurity as well as through lack of an extensional orientation, unable to depart from institutionally expected attitudes. Seeking security by adopting the "official" point of view prevalent in the institutions of which they are members, they become excessively conventional and excessively given to commonplace ideas and emotions.

They feel what they are expected to feel by their political party, their church, their social group, or their family; they think what they are expected to think. They find it both easier and safer not to examine too extensionally any *specific* Democratic candidate, any *specific* labor union, any *specific* Capulet, because extensional examination of any one of these *might* lead to an evaluation different from the institutionally accepted point of view.

But to have nothing but institutionalized attitudes is eventually to have no personality of one's own, and therefore to have nothing original or creative to contribute to the institutions of which one is a member. Furthermore, there is the danger to one's personal adjustment implicit in continually living by high-level generalizations and repressing (or avoiding) extensional evaluations.

The rule already suggested for the avoidance of excessively intensional attitudes is helpful for the avoidance of excessively conventional, institutionalized attitudes, because intensional attitudes are often the result of the uncritical acceptance of institutional dogmas. With the application of the cow_1 is not cow_2 rule, we begin to *look* in order to find out if $Democrat_1$ differs in any important respects from $Democrat_2$, if labor $union_1$ differs from labor $union_2$, if $Capulet_1$ differs from $Capulet_2$. As the result of such extensional examination we may find that the original institutional attitudes were the correct ones after all; or we may find it necessary, as Romeo and Juliet did, to depart from them.[4] But whatever conclusions we may arrive at, the important thing is that they will be our own—the result of *our own* extensional examination of the events or objects to be evaluated.

People who are not accustomed to distinguishing between attitudes institutionally arrived at and those extensionally arrived at are capable of real self-deception. In a real sense, they don't know which of their opinions are simply parrot-like repetitions of institutional opinions, and which are the result of their own experience and their own thinking. Lacking that self-insight, they are unable to arrive at realistic self-concepts; they are unable to map accurately the territory of their own feelings and attitudes.

Reading Toward Sanity

A few words, finally, need to be said on the subject of reading as an aid to extensional orientation. Studying books sometimes has the effect of producing excessive intensional orientation; this is especially true in literary study, for example, when the study of words—novels, plays,

[4]Of course Romeo and Juliet were not always as extensional as they might have been. Had they not been prone to confusing inferences with facts, they might both have lived a little longer.

poems, essays—becomes an end in itself. When the study of literature is undertaken, however, not as an end in itself, but as a guide to life, its effect is extensional in the best sense.

Literature works by intensional means; that is, by the manipulation of the informative and affective connotations of words. By these means, it not only calls our attention to facts not previously noticed, but it also is capable of arousing feelings not previously experienced. These new feelings in turn call our attention to still more facts not previously noticed. Both the new feelings and the new facts, therefore, upset our intensional orientations, so that our blindness is little by little removed.

The extensionally oriented person, as has been repeatedly said, is governed not by words only, but by the facts to which the words have guided him. But supposing there were no words to guide us? Should we be able to guide ourselves to those facts? The answer is, in the vast majority of cases, no. To begin with, our nervous systems are extremely imperfect, and we see things only in terms of our training and interests. If our interests are limited, we see extremely little; a man looking for cigarette butts in the street sees little else of the world passing by. Furthermore, as everyone knows, when we travel, meet interesting people, or have adventures before we are old enough to appreciate such experiences, we often feel that we might just as well not have had them. Experience itself is an extremely imperfect teacher. Experience does not tell us what it is we are experiencing. Things simply happen. And if we do not know *what to look for* in our experience, the happenings often have no significance to us whatever.

Many people put a great deal of stock in experience as such; they tend automatically to respect the person who has "done things." "I don't want to sit around reading books," they say; "I want to get out and do things! I want to travel! I want to have experiences!" But often the experiences they go out and get do them no good whatever. They go to London, and all they remember is their hotel and the American Express Company office; they go to Mexico and remember only their gastro-intestinal difficulties. The result is that some people who have never traveled know more about the world than some people who have. We all tend to go around the world with our eyes shut unless someone opens them for us.

And this eye-opening, then, is the tremendous function that language, in both its scientific and its affective uses, performs. In the light of abstract scientific generalizations, "trivial" facts lose their triviality. When we have studied, for example, surface tension, the alighting of a dragonfly on a pool of water is a subject for thought and explanation. Those who have never read Wordsworth have missed something of the English lake country, even if they have lived there all their lives; to those who have read Faulkner, a trip through Mississippi is a doubly meaningful experience. In the light of the subtleties of feeling aroused in us by literature and poetry and drama, every human experience is filled with rich relationships and significances.

The communications we receive from others, insofar as they do not simply retrace our old patterns of feeling and tell us things we already know, increase the efficiency of our nervous systems. Poets, as well as scientists, have aptly been called "the window washers of the mind"; without their communications to widen our interests and increase the sensitivity of our perceptions, we could very well remain as blind as puppies.

Language, as has been repeatedly emphasized in these pages, is social. Reading or listening, writing or talking, we are constantly involved in the processes of social interaction made possible by language. Sometimes, as we have seen, the result of that social interaction is the sharing of knowledge, the enrichment of sympathies and insight, and the establishing of human cooperation. But at other times, the social interaction does not come out so well: every exchange of remarks, as between two drunks at a bar or between two hostile delegates at the United Nations Security Council, leads progressively to the conviction on the part of each that it is impossible to cooperate with the other.

We come back, then, to the judgments explicitly announced at the beginning of this book—the ethical judgments on which the argument has been based throughout—that widespread intraspecific cooperation through the use of language is the fundamental mechanism of human survival, and that, when the use of language results, as it so often does, in the creation or aggravation of disagreements and conflicts, there is something wrong with the speaker, the listener, or both. Sometimes, as we have seen, this "something wrong" is the result of ignorance of the territory which leads to the making of inaccurate maps; sometimes it is the result, through faulty evaluative habits, of refusing to look at the territory but insisting on talking anyway; sometimes it is the result of imperfections in language itself, imperfections which neither speaker nor listener have taken the trouble to examine; often it is the result of using language not as an instrument of social cohesion, but as a weapon. The purpose of this book has been to lay before the reader some of the ways in which, whether as speakers or listeners, we may use or be used by the mechanisms of linguistic communication. What the reader may wish to do with these mechanisms is up to him.

postscript

Although the principles which have been explained throughout this book have as their purpose the establishment of agreement and the avoidance of conflict, some people may be tempted to use them as weapons with which to stir up arguments, as clubs with which to beat people over the head: "The trouble with you, Joe, is that you've got a bad case of two-valued orientation," "For God's sake, Mabel, stop being so intensional!" Those who use the formulations of this book in this way may be said to have understood the book but dimly.

bibliography and index

selected bibliography

*Arnold, Thurman W. *The Symbols of Government.* New Haven, Conn.: Yale University Press, 1935.

* ———. *The Folklore of Capitalism.* New Haven, Conn.: Yale University Press, 1937.

*Ayer, A. J. *Language, Truth and Logic.* New York: Oxford University Press, 1936.

Barnlund, Dean C., and Franklyn S. Haiman. *The Dynamics of Discussion.* Boston: Houghton Mifflin, 1960.

Bell, Eric Temple. *The Search for Truth.* New York: Reynal and Hitchcock. 1934.

*Benedict, Ruth. *Patterns of Culture.* Boston: Houghton Mifflin, 1934.

Bentley, Arthur F. *Linguistic Analysis of Mathematics.* Bloomington, Ind.: The Principia Press, 1932.

*Berne, Eric. *Games People Play: The Psychology of Human Relationships.* New York: Grove Press, 1964.

Berrien, F. K., and Wendell H. Bash. *Human Relations: Comments and Cases.* New York: Harper, 1957.

Bloomfield, Leonard. *Language.* New York: Henry Holt, 1933.

Bois, J. Samuel. *Explorations in Awareness.* New York: Harper, 1957.

———. *The Art of Awareness.* Dubuque, Iowa: William C. Brown, 1966.

*Breal, Michael. *Semantics: Studies in the Science of Meaning.* New York: Henry Holt, 1900. Republished New York: Dover Publications, 1964.

*Bridgman, P. W. *The Logic of Modern Physics.* New York: Macmillan, 1927.

Bruner, Jerome, Jacqueline J. Goodnow and George A. Austin. *A Study of Thinking.* New York: John Wiley and Sons, 1956.

*Burke, Kenneth. *The Philosophy of Literary Form.* Baton Rouge: Louisiana State University Press, 1941.

* ———. *A Grammar of Motives.* Englewood Cliffs, N.J.: Prentice-Hall, 1945.

Burrow, Trigant. *The Social Basis of Consciousness.* New York: Harcourt Brace Jovanovich, 1927.

*Carnap, Rudolf. *Philosophy and Logical Syntax.* London: Psyche Miniatures, 1935.

*Carpenter, Edmund and Marshall McLuhan (eds.), *Exploration in Communication.* Boston: Beacon Press, 1960.

*Cassirer, Ernst. *An Essay on Man.* New Haven, Conn.: Yale University Press, 1944.

Chase, Stuart. *Roads to Agreement.* New York: Harper, 1951.

———. *Power of Words.* New York: Harcourt Brace Jovanovich, 1954.

———. *Guides to Straight Thinking.* New York: Harper, 1956.

*Cherry, Colin. *On Human Communication.* New York: Science Editions, 1957.

Chisholm, Francis P. *Introductory Lectures on General Semantics.* Lakeville, Conn.: Institute of General Semantics, 1945.

*Dantzig, Tobias. *Number: The Language of Science.* New York: Macmillan, 1933.

*Deutsch, Karl W. *Nationalism and Social Communication.* New York: John Wiley, 1953.

Doob, Leonard W. *Public Opinion and Propaganda.* New York: Henry Holt, 1948.

Embler, Weller. *Metaphor and Meaning.* DeLand, Fla.: Everett/Edwards, 1966.

Asterisk indicates titles obtainable in paperback editions.

*Empson, William. *Seven Types of Ambiguity*. London: Chatto and Windus, 1930.

ETC.: A Review of General Semantics (quarterly); published since 1943 by the International Society for General Semantics, San Francisco, California.

*Frank, Jerome. *Law and the Modern Mind*. New York: Brentano, 1930.

*Fromm, Erich. *Escape from Freedom*. New York: Rinehart, 1941.

Garey, Doris. *Putting Words in Their Places*. Chicago: Scott, Foresman, 1957.

*Gorman, Margaret. *General Semantics and Contemporary Thomism*. Lincoln, Nebr.: University of Nebraska Press, 1962.

Haney, William V. *Communication and Organizational Behavior: Text and Cases*. Homewood, Ill.: Richard D. Irwin, 1967 revised edition.

Hayakawa, S. I. (ed.). *Language, Meaning and Maturity: Selections from ETC., 1943–1953*. New York: Harper, 1954.

——— (ed.). *Our Language and Our World: Selections from ETC., 1953–1958*. New York: Harper, 1959.

*——— (ed.). *The Use and Misuse of Language*. New York: Fawcett, 1962. Selections from *Language, Meaning and Maturity* and *Our Language and Our World*.

Hockett, C. F. *A Course in Modern Linguistics*. New York: Macmillan, 1958.

*Horney, Karen. *The Neurotic Personality of Our Time*. New York: W. W. Norton, 1937.

Huse, H. R. *The Illiteracy of the Literate*. New York: D. Appleton-Century, 1933.

Huxley, Aldous. *Words and Their Meanings*. Los Angeles: Jake Zeitlin, 1940.

Huxley, Julian. *Evolution: The Modern Synthesis*. New York: Harper, 1942.

*Isaacs, Harold R. *Scratches on Our Minds: American Images of China and India*. New York: John Day, 1958.

Jacobs, Noah Jonathan. *Naming-Day in Eden*. New York: Macmillan, 1958.

*Johnson, Alexander Bryan. *A Treatise on Language* (1836); edited by David Rynin. Berkeley: University of California Press, 1947.

———. *The Meaning of Words* (1854); with introduction by Irving J. Lee. Milwaukee, Wisc.: John W. Chamberlin, 1948.

Johnson, Wendell. *People in Quandaries: The Semantics of Personal Adjustment*. New York: Harper, 1946.

———. *Your Most Enchanted Listener*. New York: Harper, 1956.

Kelley, Earl C. *Education for What Is Real*. New York: Harper, 1947.

Kepes, Gyorgy. *Language of Vision*; with introductory essays by Siegfried Giedion and S. I. Hayakawa. Chicago: Paul Theobald, 1944.

*Keyes, Kenneth S., Jr. *How To Develop Your Thinking Ability*. New York: McGraw-Hill, 1950.

Korzybski, Alfred. *The Manhood of Humanity*. New York: E. P. Dutton, 1921.

———. *Science and Sanity: An Introduction to Non-Aristotelian Systems and General Semantics*. Lancaster, Pa.: Science Press Printing Company, 1933.

*Kropotkin, Petr. *Mutual Aid, A Factor of Evolution*; with foreword by Ashley Montagu. Boston: Extending Horizons Books, 1955.

*La Barre, Weston. *The Human Animal*. Chicago: University of Chicago Press, 1954.

*Langer, Susanne K. *Philosophy in a New Key*. Cambridge, Mass.: Harvard University Press, 1942.

*Lasswell, Harold D. *Psychopathology and Politics*. Chicago: University of Chicago Press, 1930.

*Lecky, Prestcott. *Self-Consistency: A Theory of Personality*. New York: Island Press, 1945.

Lee, Irving J. *Language Habits in Human Affairs*. New York: Harper, 1941.

*———. *The Language of Wisdom and Folly*. New York: Harper, 1949.

———. *How to Talk with People*. New York: Harper, 1952.

*———. *Handling Barriers to Communication*. New York: Harper, 1957.

Lieber, Lillian R. *The Einstein Theory of Relativity*. New York: Farrar & Rinehart, 1945.

———. *The Education of T. C. Mits*. New York: W. W. Norton, 1944.

*Maier, Norman R. F. *Frustration: The Study of Behavior Without a Goal*. New York: McGraw-Hill, 1949.

Malinowski, Bronislaw. "The Problem of Meaning in Primitive Languages"; Supplement I in Ogden and Richards, *The Meaning of Meaning*.

Maslow, A. H. *Motivation and Personality*. New York: Harper, 1954.

Masserman, Jules. *Behavior and Neurosis*. Chicago: University of Chicago Press, 1943.

*Mayer, Martin. *Madison Avenue, U.S.A.* New York: Harper, 1958.

*McLuhan, Marshall. *The Mechanical Bride: Folklore of Industrial Man*. New York: Vanguard, 1951.

*———. *The Gutenberg Galaxy*. Toronto: University of Toronto Press, 1962.

*———. *Understanding Media: The Extensions of Man*. New York: McGraw-Hill, 1964.

———. *Culture is Our Business*. New York: McGraw-Hill, 1970.

*Mead, Margaret (ed.). *Cooperation and Competition Among Primitive People*. New York: McGraw-Hill, 1936.

*Meerloo, Joost A. M. *Unobtrusive Communication: Essays in Psycholinguistics*. Assen, Netherlands: Van Gorcum, 1964.

*Menninger, Karl. *Love Against Hate*. New York: Harcourt Brace Jovanovich, 1942.

*Miller, George A. *Language and Communication*. New York: McGraw-Hill, 1951.

Minteer, Catherine. *Words and What They Do to You*. Evanston, Ill.: Row, Peterson, 1952.

———. Irene Kahn, J. Talbot Winchell. *Teacher's Guide to General Semantics*. San Francisco: International Society for General Semantics, revised edition, 1968.

*Morain, Mary (ed.). *Teaching General Semantics*. San Francisco: International Society for General Semantics, 1969.

Morris, Charles. *Signs, Language and Behavior*. Englewood Cliffs, N.J.: Prentice-Hall, 1946.

Newton, Norman. *An Approach to Design*. Reading, Mass.: Addison-Wesley, 1951.

*Ogden, C. K., and I. A. Richards. *The Meaning of Meaning*, 3rd ed., rev. New York: Harcourt Brace Jovanovich, 1930.

*Osgood, Charles E., G. J. Suci, and P. H. Tannenbaum. *The Measurement of Meaning*. Urbana, Ill.: University of Illinois Press, 1957.

*Packard, Vance. *The Hidden Persuaders*. New York: David McKay, 1957.

*Piaget, Jean. *The Language and Thought of the Child*. New York: Harcourt Brace Jovanovich, 1926.

*———. *The Child's Conception of the World*. New York: Harcourt Brace Jovanovich, 1929.

*Popper, Karl R. *The Open Society and Its Enemies*. London: Hutchinson, 1950.

Postman, Neil. *Language and Reality*. New York: Holt, Rinehart and Winston, 1966.

Rapoport, Anatol. *Science and the Goals of Man*. New York: Harper, 1950.

*———. *Operational Philosophy*. New York: Harper, 1953.

———. *Fights, Games, and Debates*. New York: Harper, 1960.

Richards, I. A. *Science and Poetry*. New York: W. W. Norton, 1926.

*———. *Practical Criticism, A Study of Literary Judgment*. New York: Harcourt Brace Jovanovich, 1929.

———. *The Philosophy of Rhetoric*. New York: Oxford University Press, 1936.

———. *Interpretation in Teaching*. New York: Harcourt Brace Jovanovich, 1938.

Rogers, Carl R. *Counseling and Psychotherapy*. Boston: Houghton Mifflin, 1942.

*———. *Client-Centered Therapy*. Boston: Houghton Mifflin, 1951.

*———. *On Becoming a Person*. Boston: Houghton Mifflin, 1961.

*Rokeach, Milton. *The Open and Closed Mind*. New York: Basic Books, 1960.

Ruesch, Jurgen. *Disturbed Communication*. New York: W. W. Norton, 1957.

———. *Therapeutic Communication*. New York: W. W. Norton, 1961.

*———, and Gregory Bateson. *Communication: The Social Matrix of Psychiatry*. New York: W. W. Norton, 1951.

———, and Weldon Kees. *Nonverbal Communication*. Berkeley: University of California Press, 1956.

*Salomon, Louis B. *Semantics and Common Sense*. New York: Holt, Rinehart and Winston, 1966.

*Sapir, Edward. *Language: An Introduction to the Study of Speech*. New York: Harcourt Brace Jovanovich, 1921.

Schaff, Adam. *Introduction to Semantics*. New York: Pergamon Press, 1962.

Skinner, B. F. *Verbal Behavior*. New York: Appleton-Century-Crofts, 1957.

Smith, Bruce L., Harold D. Lasswell, and Ralph D. Casey. *Propaganda, Communication, and Public Opinion: A Comprehensive Reference Guide*. Princeton, N.J.: Princeton University Press, 1946.

Snygg, Donald, and Arthur Combs. *Individual Behavior*. New York: Harper, 1949.

Stefansson, Vilhjalmur. *The Standardization of Error*. New York: W. W. Norton, 1927.

*Szasz, Thomas S. *The Myth of Mental Illness*. New York: Harper, 1961.

Taylor, Edmond. *The Strategy of Terror*. Boston: Houghton Mifflin, 1940.

*Thurman, Kelly. *Semantics*. Boston: Houghton Mifflin, 1960.

Ullmann, Stephen. *Semantics: An Introduction to the Science of Meaning*. Oxford: Basil Blackwell & Mott, Ltd., 1962.

Upward, Allen. *The New Word: An Open Letter Addressed to the Swedish Academy in Stockholm on the Meaning of the Word IDEALIST*. New York: Mitchell Kennerley, 1910.

Vaihinger, Hans. *The Philosophy of "As If."* New York: Harcourt Brace Jovanovich, 1924.

*Veblen, Thorstein. *The Theory of the Leisure Class*. New York: Modern Library, 1934.

*Vygotsky, L. S. *Thought and Language*. New York: John Wiley, 1962.

Wagner, Geoffrey. *On The Wisdom of Words*. Princeton, N.J.: Van Nostrand, 1968.

Walpole, Hugh R. *Semantics*. New York: W. W. Norton, 1941.

Weinberg, Harry L. *Levels of Knowing and Existence*. New York: Harper, 1959.

Weiss, Thomas S. and Kenneth H. Hoover, *Scientific Foundations of Education*. Dubuque, Iowa: Wm. C. Brown, 1964.

Welby, V. *What Is Meaning?* New York: Macmillan, 1903.

*Whorf, Benjamin Lee. *Language, Thought and Reality: Selected Writings of B. L. Whorf*; edited by John B. Carroll. New York: John Wiley, 1956.

*Wiener, Norbert. *Human Use of Human Beings: Cybernetics and Society*. Boston: Houghton Mifflin, 1950.

*Wilson, John. *Language and the Pursuit of Truth*. New York: Cambridge University Press, 1956.

*Windes, Russel R. and Arthur Hastings. *Argumentation and Advocacy*. New York: Random House, 1965.

Yerkes, Robert M. *Chimpanzees: A Laboratory Colony*. New Haven, Conn.: Yale University Press, 1943.

*Young, J. Z. *Doubt and Certainty in Science: A Biologist's Reflections on the Brain*. New York: Oxford University Press, 1951.

index

2
C 3
D 4
E 5
F 6
G 7
H 8
I 9
J 0

NOTES

NOTES

NOTES

NOTES

NOTES

NOTES

NOTES

NOTES